# Quilting
## Patchwork and Appliqué

## DK

**LONDON, NEW YORK, MUNICH,
MELBOURNE, DELHI**

**DK UK**
**Project Editor** Kathryn Meeker
**Senior Art Editor** Glenda Fisher
**Editor** Hilary Mandleberg
**US Editor** Margaret Parrish
**Managing Editor** Penny Smith
**Managing Art Editor** Marianne Markham
**Senior Jacket Designer** Nicola Powling
**Producer, Pre-Production** Andy Hilliard
**Senior Producer** Ché Creasey
**Creative Technical Support** Sonia Charbonnier
**Photography** Ruth Jenkinson
**Art Director/Stylist for Photography** Isabel de Cordova
**Art Director** Jane Bull
**Publisher** Mary Ling

**DK INDIA**
**Senior Editor** Dorothy Kikon
**Senior Art Editor** Ivy Roy
**Editor** Arani Sinha
**Art Editors** Neha Wahi, Swati Katyal, and Tanya Mehrotra
**Managing Editor** Alicia Ingty
**Managing Art Editor** Navidita Thapa
**Pre-Production Manager** Sunil Sharma
**DTP Designers** Satish Gaur, Anurag Trivedi, and
Manish Upreti

First American Edition, 2014
Published in the United States by DK Publishing
4th floor, 345 Hudson Street
New York, New York 10014

14 15 16 17 18   10 9 8 7 6 5 4 3 2 1
001—256499—Oct/2014

A catalog record for this book is available from
the Library of Congress.
ISBN 978-1-4654-2290-3

DK books are available at special discounts when purchased in bulk
for sales promotions, premiums, fund-raising, or educational use. For
details, contact: DK Publishing Special Markets, 345 Hudson Street,
New York, New York 10014 or SpecialSales@dk.com.

Printed and bound in China by Hung Hing.

Discover more at
**www.dk.com/crafts**

# Contents

# Introduction

Making a quilt is an absorbing and rewarding activity and, with a little bit of know how, it is something anyone can achieve. With the help of this book you will learn dozens of techniques so you succeed with your very first quilting project. Or, if you are a seasoned quilter, you may be inspired to learn or try a technique you never knew before.

By learning the skills needed for each project you will feel comfortable with the different aspects of quilting. Becoming confident with your sewing machine and starting with some of the simple projects first will lead you through to completing more advanced patterns in no time at all.

In some cases you will find several different options for completing parts of a project, such as attaching a binding. Try these out and see what suits your style and comfort level best. There is no right or wrong answer in quilting—just remember to adjust your fabric requirements if needed. If something doesn't look right, simply take it apart and try again.

Some people find choosing their fabrics to be a challenging part of the process, but with an understanding of the color wheel you will soon be on your way to designing your own visually appealing quilts. A good starting point is to pick one fabric you like and build the design from there.

Quilting should be fun and relaxing and if something doesn't work right away, simply take a break and try again. Soon you will see how rewarding completing your first quilt is and you will want to continue making more beautiful projects to give as gifts or to keep for yourself and pass down through your family.

Flying Geese

Chisholm Trail

Courthouse Steps

# History of quilting

The word "quilt" comes from the Latin *culcita*, meaning a stuffed sack or pillow. There are several different meanings of the word in use today. For some, it refers to the process of piecing fabric together; for others, it means the sewing used to finish a quilt. Its different meanings reflect the long and varied history of quilting.

## Quilting around the world

Quilting has its origins as far back as ancient Egypt and has appeared in different forms in different cultures throughout history. Like today, early quilts were sewn for both warmth and as a decorative art form. The oldest known surviving example of a quilt comes from the Noin-Ula region in Mongolia and dates from approximately the first or second century BCE.

In India, the tradition of making quilts dates back to the 4th century BCE. Today, quilts called *ralli* are still made from bright, hand-dyed fabrics. Rallis are used as blankets, floor coverings, and in some villages are a symbol of wealth.

In Japan, the art of Sashiko quilting dates back to the early 18th century, when stitching technique were used to decorate, reinforce, and repair clothing. The term Sashiko means *little stabs* and uses a traditional running stitch with white thread on an indigo-colored cloth.

In Europe, the quilt is thought to have evolved from a type of padded jacket called a *gambeson* worn during the Crusades in the 12th century. The oldest known surviving European quilt, the Tristan Quilt, is thought to have been made in Sicily around 1360. Today its two sections are on display in London and Florence.

In the United Kingdom, whole cloth quilts, known as *North Country* or *Durham* quilts, date back to the Industrial Revolution, when readily available, cheap, cotton fabric and sometimes a sateen-type fabric were used for the top of the quilt. The layers were joined together with running stitch worked in intricate patterns.

## The American quilt

It wasn't until the late 18th century that quilting as we now know it today became commonplace in the United States. Born out of necessity, quilts were originally constructed to provide warmth, used both on beds and as coverings for windows. Since they were strictly for comfort, the look of early American quilts was very simple, reusing old and worn clothing and blankets to construct them.

Perhaps some of the best-known American quilts are those made by the Amish. After settling in Pennsylvania from Europe in the early 1700s, most Amish colonists used traditional featherbeds as they had in the past. But over the years and from contact with other settlers, Amish women began creating beautiful, artistic quilts, which have today become a hallmark of the Amish community. While creating art for admiration was frowned upon, creating art in a quilt-form became a simple way of expression and was considered acceptable, since a quilt served a necessary purpose.

What we know today as a *quilting bee* started in the 1800s when members of outlying rural communities gathered and joined with others to help finish large projects. What would take one person several weeks or months could be finished in just a single day with the help of the local community.

## Quilting in the 20th century

With the introduction of the sewing machine in the mid 1800s, the speed at which quilting progressed increased ten-fold. As living conditions improved, so did the fabrics being used in patchwork. Quilts were being made of new, finer fabrics and what was once a craft born out of necessity was quickly becoming a creative art. More and more upper class women with both time and resources took to quilting during the early 1900s.

As America entered the First World War in 1917, the US government urged citizens to "Make Quilts—Save the Blankets for our Boys over There" and quilting became a household word. Its popularity grew further during World War II, when quilts were made to raise money for charities such as the Red Cross. The popularity of quilting was lowest in the 1960s, but the craft was kept alive by older quilters. During the American Bicentennial in 1976, the quilt became an expression of national pride and a reminder of where the country had come from and its popularity increased once again.

## Quilting today

Now, the popularity of quilting has grown again, welcoming new, young quilters into the craft. Modern generations have adapted the traditional techniques and put a new twist on what was once seen as an outdated hobby. You will find small groups of dedicated quilters meeting in local communities, working in the spirit of the 1800s quilting bees. With the addition of new technology, such as the internet, quilters of today can share quilting advice, patterns, and finished projects with others all over the world.

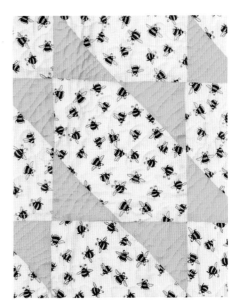

Pinwheel

Elongated Hexagon

Modern Zigzag

# Getting started

# Tools and materials

Quilting does not require a lot of equipment. If you are a beginner, you probably won't need more than needles and threads or a sewing machine, scissors, pins, a ruler or measuring tape, a pencil, and a thimble. There is, however, an enormous selection of specialized tools that have been designed to make quilting easier.

## General sewing equipment

To make a quilt you will need a set of hand-sewing needles—both "sharps" and "betweens." Both types come in several lengths, thicknesses, and eye size. Needles are sized by number: the higher the number, the finer the needle. Pins are essential for pinning the layers of a quilt together while you work. Always press seams as you go, with an iron or by finger pressing.

### Sharps
"Sharps" are standard hand-sewing needles and are usually used for processes such as basting, hand piecing, and finishing the edge of binding.

### Betweens or quilting needles
Shorter than sharps, these allow quick, even sewing for hand quilting and appliqué.

### Quilter's pins
Long quilter's pins are useful for holding the layers of a quilt together as you work. Flower-headed pins are easy to pick up.

### Glass quilter's pins
Glass-headed pins are easy to handle and are not affected by a hot iron. These are extra long for quilting, too.

### Glass-headed straight pins
Ordinary dressmaking pins are used to hold pieces together during hand piecing.

### Iron
It is essential to press seams as you work, so have an iron and ironing board set up in your work area.

### Safety pins
If the layers of the quilt are not too thick, you can use ordinary safety pins to hold them together.

### Hera
This is a plastic, bladelike device for creasing a temporary line on the fabric. A small wooden "iron" or chisel can also be used.

### Thimble
Made from metal, leather or suede, plastic, or a combination, a thimble protects the middle finger when pushing the needle through the fabric.

### Curved safety pins
These are most commonly used for pin-basting the layers of a quilt. The curve helps prevent the layers from shifting.

### Pin cushion
Pin cushions range from traditional emery-powder-filled shapes to magnetic pin-catchers. Magnetic types can interfere with the smooth operation of computerized sewing machines.

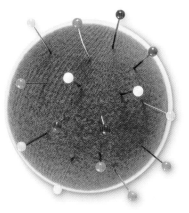

# Sewing machine

You can use any modern sewing machine for quilting as long as you can adjust the stitch length and the machine has a zigzag function. Other useful features to look for are feed dogs—the toothed bars in the needle plate that feed the fabric through—that can be dropped, and a large throat area—the area between the needle plate and the machine's horizontal arm. This is useful when working on bulky items. Needle sizes are in universal/American (e.g., 10) and metric (e.g., 70). For quilting you will need a range of needles in sizes from 10/70 to 14/90, depending on your project.

# Feet

All sewing machines come with a standard presser foot as well as a selection of specialized feet for different purposes. You should have a ¼in seam foot for piecing patchwork. Among the most useful for quilting are:

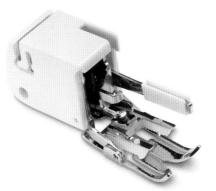

**Walking foot**
This strange-looking foot "walks" across the fabric, so that the upper layer of fabric is not pushed forward. When used for quilting, it also guides the layers of fabric and batting through the feed dogs at an even speed. It is also commonly known as an even feed foot.

**Zipper foot**
This foot fits to either the right- or left-hand side of the needle and is normally used for sewing close to the teeth of a zipper. If you are finishing the edges of a quilt with piping, it enables you to sew close to the piping cord.

**Darning foot**
Also known as a free-motion quilting foot, this foot "floats" on a spring mechanism for free-motion quilting of fancy patterns. The clear acrylic foot gives you a good view of your sewing area.

# Measuring tools

Many of the basic measuring tools that a quilter needs are standard items in a home office or workshop. Others can be found in a general sewing kit.

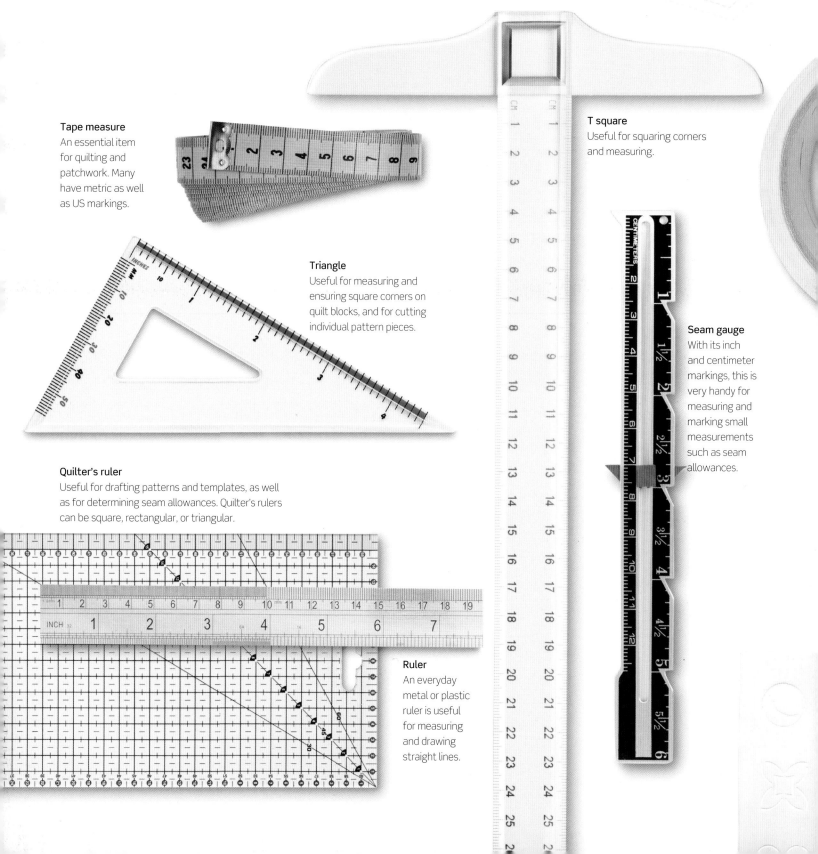

### Tape measure
An essential item for quilting and patchwork. Many have metric as well as US markings.

### Triangle
Useful for measuring and ensuring square corners on quilt blocks, and for cutting individual pattern pieces.

### T square
Useful for squaring corners and measuring.

### Seam gauge
With its inch and centimeter markings, this is very handy for measuring and marking small measurements such as seam allowances.

### Quilter's ruler
Useful for drafting patterns and templates, as well as for determining seam allowances. Quilter's rulers can be square, rectangular, or triangular.

### Ruler
An everyday metal or plastic ruler is useful for measuring and drawing straight lines.

# Marking tools

Various pencils and pens are used to draw designs and mark seam allowances on both paper and fabric. Some, such as tailor's chalk and removable markers, are not permanent.

### Soft pencils
Have a selection of these. Light-colored pencils show up well on darker fabrics or paper when tracing or transferring patterns or designs.

### Water-soluble pen
Marks made by a water-soluble pen are removed with a dab of water or by washing.

### Hard pencil
Use a hard pencil with a fine point for drawing around templates.

### Low-tack masking tape
Ideal as a guide for straight lines on large pieces of fabric, it should be removed promptly after use.

### Tailor's chalk
This is available in a range of colors and the marks it makes are easily brushed away.

# Templates and stencils

The most durable templates and stencils are cut from translucent template plastic, rather than cardboard. Cut using a sharp scalpel to ensure accuracy. Freezer paper can also be used to create templates and is especially useful in some appliqué work.

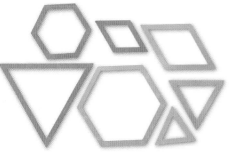

### Ready-made window template
Made from sturdy template plastic or metal, a window template is used to mark both the outline and the seam line without the need for two templates.

### Ready-made quilting stencil
A quilting stencil can be used to transfer a pattern onto the fabric. Trace the stencil design with a nonpermanent marker.

### Freezer paper
The shiny side sticks to fabric when ironed and can be reapplied several times. It is handy for appliqué.

### Tracing paper
This is essential for tracing motifs or pattern pieces onto template plastic or cardboard before cutting out.

### Cardboard
Stiff cardboard can be used to make templates but will not last as long as plastic.

# Miscellaneous items

Other useful items for quilting include graph paper, dressmaker's carbon paper, slivers of soap, flexible curves, drawing compasses, protractors, and erasers, which can all help with designing and transferring pattern pieces or motifs.

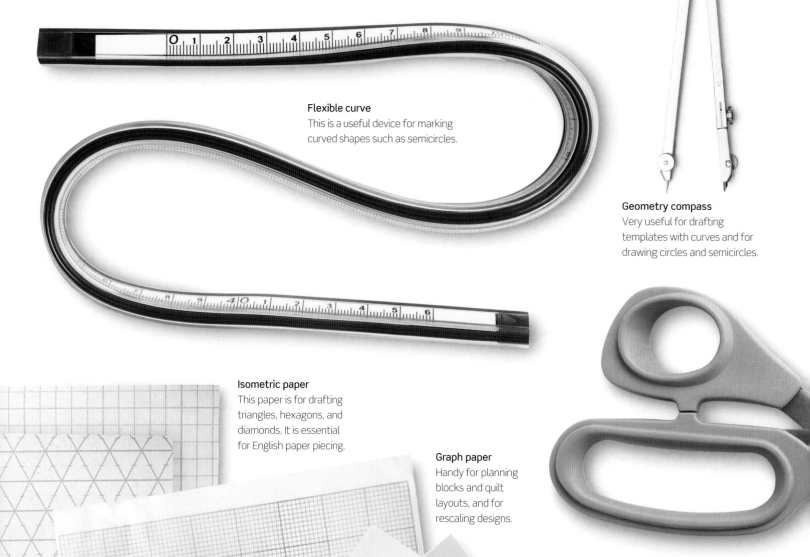

**Flexible curve**
This is a useful device for marking curved shapes such as semicircles.

**Geometry compass**
Very useful for drafting templates with curves and for drawing circles and semicircles.

**Isometric paper**
This paper is for drafting triangles, hexagons, and diamonds. It is essential for English paper piecing.

**Graph paper**
Handy for planning blocks and quilt layouts, and for rescaling designs.

**Eraser**
Have this item on hand when drawing or tracing designs.

**Dressmaker's carbon paper**
This is a permanent method of transferring designs to the wrong side of the fabric, using a marking wheel or pencil.

# Cutting equipment

Scissors are absolutely essential in quilting and you should have at least three pairs: one dedicated to cutting fabric; one for paper or cardboard and batting; and a small, sharp pair for snipping threads. A rotary cutter speeds up fabric cutting.

**Small sharp scissors**
Use for snipping thread ends, clipping seams, and trimming seam allowances. A specialized version of small scissors called appliqué scissors can be helpful in appliqué work. The blades are curved to protect fabric that is not being trimmed from being damaged by sharp points, but appliqué scissors should not be seen as a replacement for ordinary small scissors.

**Pinking shears**
Handy when cutting fabric that tends to fray.

**Seam ripper**
Used for removing stitches that have gone awry. It incorporates a small cutting blade.

**Cutting shears**
These come with blades of varying lengths. Buy good-quality shears, ideally ones that can be resharpened.

**Rotary cutter**
Used with a quilter's ruler and self-healing mat, this makes light work of cutting fabric, and especially of cutting through many layers at the same time. Handle with caution.

**Craft knife**
This is invaluable for cutting stencils from template plastic. Never use it on fabric.

**Self-healing mat**
Marked with a grid in 1in (2.5cm) increments, the surface "heals" itself after cutting with a rotary cutter, leaving it smooth and without any notches or grooves that might catch the cutter next time you cut. Do not use with a craft knife.

# Threads

There are so many threads available and knowing which ones to choose can be confusing. Threads are designed for certain tasks, such as machine embroidery or quilting. Threads also vary in fiber content, from pure cotton to rayon to polyester. Some threads are very fine while others are thick and coarse. Failure to choose the correct thread can spoil your project and lead to problems with the stitch quality of the sewing machine. For piecing, it is important to match the thread to the fabric, such as cotton with cotton, to ensure they both shrink at the same rate. Match the color to the lighter fabric or use a neutral shade. For appliqué, match the thread color to the piece being sewn. Specialty threads include silk, metallics, and rayon.

## Cotton thread

A 100 percent cotton thread. Smooth and firm, this is designed to be used with cotton fabrics and is much favored by quilters.

## Sewing thread

Threads come in a dazzling choice of colors, types, and weights. Sewing thread is used for sewing by hand and machine.

## Quilting thread

Quilting thread is heavier than sewing thread and is waxed to prevent breaks.

## Polyester all-purpose thread

A good-quality polyester thread that has a very slight "give," making it suitable to sew all types of fabric. It is the most popular type of thread.

## Silk thread

A sewing thread made from 100 percent silk. Used for machine sewing delicate fabrics. It is also used for basting or temporary sewing in areas that are to be pressed, because it can be removed without leaving an imprint.

## Topstitching thread

A thicker polyester thread used for decorative topstitching and buttonholes. Also for hand sewing buttons on thicker fabrics and some soft furnishings.

# Metallic thread

A rayon and metal thread for decorative machine sewing and machine embroidery. This thread usually requires a specialized sewing-machine needle.

# Machine embroidery thread

Often made from a rayon yarn for shine. This is a finer thread designed for machine embroidery. Available on much larger spools for economy.

# Hand embroidery threads

Hand embroidery threads can be thick or thin. They can be made from cotton, silk, and linen as well as synthetic fibers. Some threads are single ply, while others are spun in multiple and can be divided into single strands: the fewer the filaments, the finer the embroidery line.

**Pearl cotton**
This is a strong, glossy thread with a twisted construction. It comes in three weights: No. 3 (the thickest), No. 5 (which comes in the greatest range of colors), and No. 8 (the finest).

**Stranded cotton floss**
This versatile thread consists of six fine strands of lustrous, mercerized cotton, which can easily be separated if desired.

# Types of fabric

The fabrics you choose to use for your project can make a world of difference to the final outcome. A single pattern can look completely different across many quilts depending on the fabric patterns and types used and how they are put together.

**Quilting cotton**

The usual fabric of choice when making a quilt is a good-quality cotton. Quilting cotton has a higher thread count than many other cottons, which means that it is both strong and wears well. Available in solid colors as well as numerous prints, there are thousands of options to choose from. It's a good idea to prewash quilting cotton and to buy more than your pattern requires, since it can shrink up to five percent.

**Denim**

Denim is a versatile choice, especially for projects that will receive a lot of use. Because of its weight, it can result in bulky seams, and it is not suitable for hand quilting. When sewing denim by machine, use a special denim needle with a walking foot. New denim should always be prewashed to remove any excess dye.

**Organza**

A sheer fabric that can be used to add an artistic touch when layered over other fabrics.

**Wool**

Available in a variety of weights and colors, wool is a warm, durable, natural fabric. Heavyweight wool can be difficult to use in patchwork but can make interesting appliqué. Any unfelted wools must be dry cleaned.

**Velvet**

The nap of velvet can make it difficult to work with and attention must be paid to the direction of the nap when cutting and joining pieces. Velvet usually requires dry cleaning. Iron carefully so as not to destroy the pile. Always sew in the direction of the nap and use a fine needle.

### Linen

Made from the flax plant, linen is a cool, breathable fabric that is perfect for quilting. It is available in many different weights and can sometimes be found blended with cotton (cotton-blend). It can be expensive and difficult to work with. Always prewash and zigzag stitch the raw edges to minimize fraying.

### Calico

The term calico generally refers to the print on the fabric rather than to the fabric itself; meaning an all-over, small print, often of a floral pattern. Calico can at times be used to describe a heavy, white cotton cloth that is sturdier than muslin.

### Muslin

This soft, loosely woven cotton fabric is generally white or natural in color and comes in a variety of different weights. It is typically used as a foundation fabric when foundation piecing. Good-quality muslin also makes a pretty backing fabric.

### Hand-dyed and batik

With one-of-a-kind patterns, hand-dyed fabrics are becoming very popular among quilters thanks to their uniqueness. A variety of different fabrics are available hand-dyed, but cotton is best for quilting. Variations in color and pattern can occur across a cut of hand-dyed fabric. Always prewash hand-dyed fabrics using a dye magnet—a product that picks up the loose dye—and a color fixer.

### Corduroy

Corduroy is soft and durable, but due to the nap and ribs, it can be difficult to work with. Narrow-rib and pinwale corduroy are the best choices for quilting. Always use a walking foot and prewash the fabric. Iron carefully so as not to destroy the nap.

### Blends

Many fabrics are available as a blend between two different fibers. A fabric blend can often offer the best of both in one. For example, a silk-blend will be less expensive than a pure silk fabric.

# Precut and recycled fabric

Precut fabrics are a package of coordinating fabrics from a manufacturer that have all been cut to the same size. This makes them very handy for patchwork projects in which you'd like a large variety of fabrics, but without buying fabric from the bolt. The popularity of precut fabrics has grown dramatically in the last few years. Manufacturers have increased their ranges available in precuts as well as the available shapes they produce. Many manufacturers have patterns made specifically from precuts. Today you can easily find Charm Squares™, Layer Cakes™, Jelly Rolls™, and even precut triangles and hexagons in craft stores and online. Using these precuts is a quick and easy way to lay out and sew together a quilt in hours, rather than days.

### Fat quarters

Fat quarters are the most common type of precut and refer to a quarter-yard cut of fabric. A normal quarter-yard cut off the bolt would give you 9 x 44in (23 x 112cm), but a fat quarter is an 18in (46cm) cut from the bolt, which is folded selvage to selvage and trimmed in half down the middle to give you an 18 x 22in (46 x 56cm) piece of fabric, although sizes can vary slightly from manufacturer to manufacturer. Fat quarters are sometimes more useful than a 9in (23cm) cut from the bolt, since they allow for a larger pattern repeat.

### Fat eighths

Fat eighths are half of a fat quarter ($\frac{1}{8}$ yard), measuring approximately 9 x 22in (23 x 56cm), rather than a typical $\frac{1}{8}$ yard cut off the bolt, which would give you $4\frac{1}{2}$ x 44in (12 x 112cm) of fabric.

### Recycled fabric

The very first quilts were often made from whatever worn-out fabrics were available, giving them a second life and saving money. Recycled fabric can be salvaged from almost anything. A slightly stained shirt, old table linen, or denim from jeans can be used to create a personal project. Very often the fabric is already broken-in, giving it a soft feel and an heirloom appearance. It also usually will not shrink any more or leach dye, since it has most likely been laundered on many previous occasions. Be aware that when adding recycled fabrics to any project the weight of the fabrics may be different from that of the other fabrics you are using.

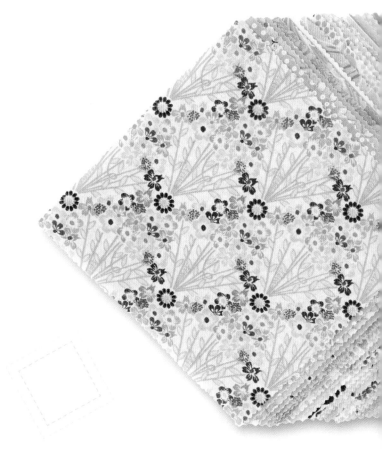

### Diecut

Diecuts are specific shapes cut by the manufacturer. Hearts and hexagons are popular shapes, but they can be almost any other shape and come in a variety of sizes. Diecuts are often useful for appliqué projects.

### Jelly Roll™

Jelly Rolls™ are precut collections of 2½in x 44in (6.5 x 112cm) fabric strips. The strips are cut selvage to selvage across a piece of fabric. A Jelly Roll™ typically contains 40 strips of fabric, but this can vary from manufacturer to manufacturer.

### Layer Cakes™

Layer Cakes™ are precut 10in (25.5cm) squares from a designer's range of fabric. They contain one print of each pattern and colorway in the line. Depending on the range, they typically have 36–42 squares in a pack.

### Charm Packs™ and Mini Charm Packs™

Charm Packs™ and Mini Charm Packs™ are the same as Layer Cakes™, but smaller in size. Charm Packs™ measure 5in (12.5cm) squares and Mini Charm Packs™ measure 2½in (6.5cm) square.

# Battings and fillings

Batting is the soft middle layer between the quilt top and the backing that gives a quilt its plushness and warmth. It is available in a variety of different materials and thicknesses, depending on your preferences and needs. Knowing a little about what options are available will help you choose the right batting or filling for your project. Always follow the manufacturer's instructions for washing and quilting the batting of your choice.

### Cotton

Batting that is 100 percent cotton is a natural, warm, and breathable choice. Cotton batting can shrink significantly during washing (about 5 percent), which gives the quilt some texture and a more traditional look.

### Poly/cotton blend

A synthetic/natural blend gives you the best of both worlds. These battings are machine washable and will not shrink as much as 100 percent cotton battings. The cotton part may shrink during washing though, so it may be wise to prewash it.

### Polyester

Polyester battings are light in weight, available in many thicknesses, and usually inexpensive. But, being synthetic, they do not breathe well and are more flammable than a natural batting; therefore, they are not recommended for baby quilts. They do not shrink, so you should not need to prewash.

## Loft

Loft, or weight, refers to the thickness of a batting. The higher the loft, the thicker the batting and the warmer the quilt. A low-loft batting is typically less than ¼in (6mm) thick and is easy to quilt. A medium-loft batting is about ¼-½in (6-12mm) in thickness and can still be machine or hand quilted. A high-loft batting is generally over ½in (12mm) and is difficult to quilt. It should therefore be held together with evenly spaced ties (see p.213).

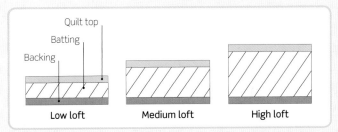

Quilt top
Batting
Backing
Low loft      Medium loft      High loft

## Quilting your batting

The product label on your batting should state the amount of space you can have un-quilted between quilting stitches for that specific type of batting. If you are planning to have limited quilting on your quilt, you should take this into consideration when choosing your batting to make sure it can accommodate the design. The distance can vary significantly, anywhere from approximately 2-10in (5-25cm), depending on what the batting is made of and how it has been formed.

## Buying batting

Batting is available to buy off the bolt in different widths and often in precut standard bed quilt sizes. When buying batting, you need to know the finished size of the quilt you are making first. The batting should be at least 6in (15cm) larger in both width and length than the finished quilt top, to allow it to overhang on all sides when making your quilt sandwich (see p.46).

If you're not able to find a piece of batting that is wide enough to fit your quilt, you will need to buy enough batting so that you can piece together several pieces to meet your requirements. You can piece the batting with either a vertical or horizontal seam, depending on which will result in the least waste.

**Bamboo**
Natural and eco-friendly, bamboo is soft and strong. It generally has a low loft and will not shrink very much. Bamboo blends are also available, often as a 50/50 cotton blend.

**Toy filling**
Some projects in this book use toy filling to stuff a shape (see pp.128-133, the Bird toy, and pp.244-245, the Mouse doorstop). The most commonly used and inexpensive type of toy filling is made from polyester, but cotton (including organic cotton), wool, and even bamboo are also available.

# A quilt explained

The terms patchwork and quilting are very often confused with one another. Patchwork usually refers to piecing, or sewing, pieces of fabric put together to make a larger, more intricate, piece of fabric. The quilting is the stitches that hold the three layers of a quilt together. Read below to find out more about how a quilt comes together and its different elements.

## The five elements of a quilt

There are five main elements needed to complete a quilt. The first element is a finished quilt top, often made of patchwork or appliqué. Your quilt top can be assembled using a repeating block pattern or several different blocks, such as in the diagram. You can also add sashing and borders (see pp.108–113) either to make the quilt fit a specific dimension or enhance the design.

The second element is batting. Most quilters prefer to use 100 percent cotton batting or a 50/50 blend of cotton and silk, or cotton and bamboo. See pages 24–25 for more information on battings.

The third element is the backing, which needs to be larger than both the quilt top and the batting. A quilt back can be made of a single print or pattern, or it can be pieced just like the top. Very often several pieces of fabric will need to be joined to make a large enough backing for a quilt (see p.47).

The fourth element is quilting. Quilting is a very important part of a quilt and has a double duty. The main purpose is to hold all three layers of the quilt (the "quilt sandwich") together securely. The second purpose is to create texture. The more a project is quilted, the more stiff it will become. A loosely stitched pattern will give the quilt more softness. Quilting can either be done by hand or machine (see pp.202–205, 210–213).

The fifth and final part of a quilt is the binding. The binding is a strip of fabric sewn around the perimeter of the quilt to enclose the raw edges (see pp.48–53). A traditional binding should be finished at the back by hand. This method will give the quilt a professional finish.

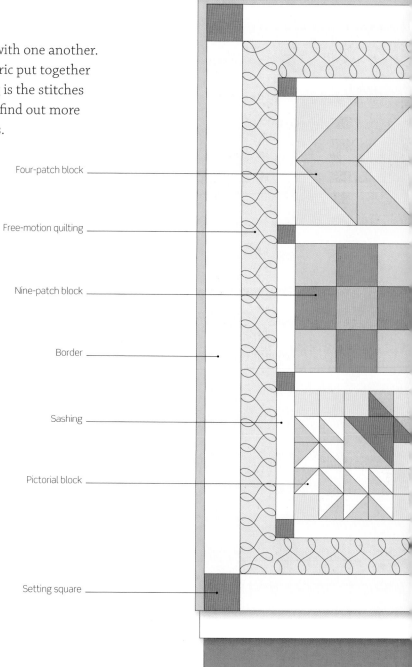

Four-patch block

Free-motion quilting

Nine-patch block

Border

Sashing

Pictorial block

Setting square

## Quilt sandwich

The term "quilt sandwich" refers to the three basic layers in a quilt: the backing, batting, and quilt top. Starting with the backing and quilt top as the bottom and top layers, the batting is then placed between them to complete the sandwich. Once all of the layers have been sewn together, or quilted, the sandwich is squared up and the raw edges are enclosed with a binding.

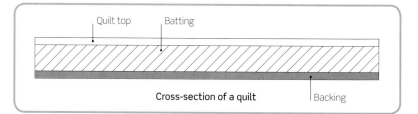

Quilt top          Batting

**Cross-section of a quilt**          Backing

Log cabin block

Star block

Hand-quilted block

Binding

Quilt top

Quilting

Batting

Backing

Curved block

Strip-pieced block

Appliqué block

Five-patch block

Fan block

Mosaic block

# Quilt sizes and measurements

Standard bed sizes vary around the world, so depending on where you live you may need to adapt a pattern to fit your specific needs. Mattress depth is another factor that can vary significantly and will influence the way your finished quilt looks on a bed. A deep mattress will make a quilt look much smaller than a shallow mattress of the same size. Follow the simple instructions below to measure your bed for the perfect quilt size.

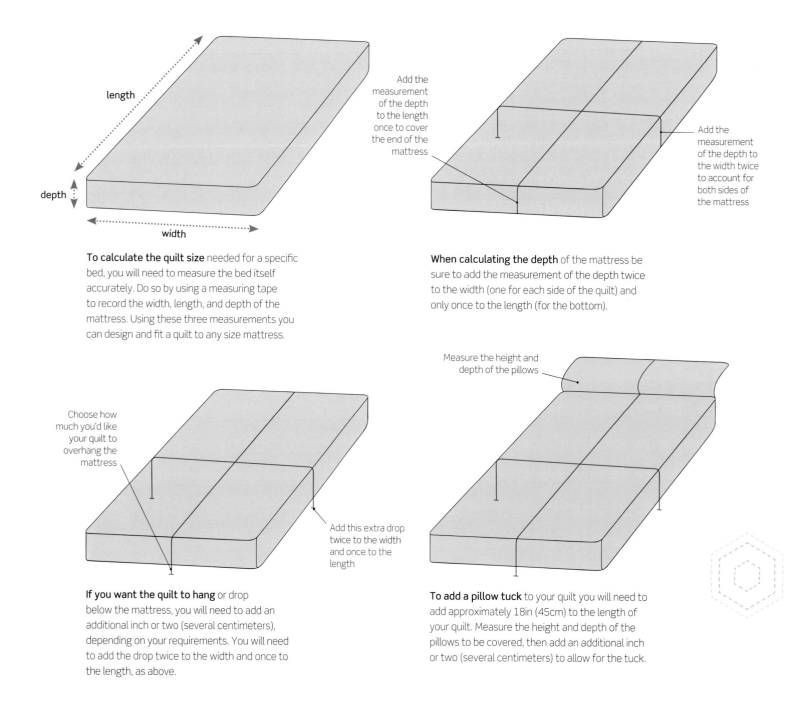

length

depth

width

Add the measurement of the depth to the length once to cover the end of the mattress

Add the measurement of the depth to the width twice to account for both sides of the mattress

Choose how much you'd like your quilt to overhang the mattress

Add this extra drop twice to the width and once to the length

Measure the height and depth of the pillows

**To calculate the quilt size** needed for a specific bed, you will need to measure the bed itself accurately. Do so by using a measuring tape to record the width, length, and depth of the mattress. Using these three measurements you can design and fit a quilt to any size mattress.

**When calculating the depth** of the mattress be sure to add the measurement of the depth twice to the width (one for each side of the quilt) and only once to the length (for the bottom).

**If you want the quilt to hang** or drop below the mattress, you will need to add an additional inch or two (several centimeters), depending on your requirements. You will need to add the drop twice to the width and once to the length, as above.

**To add a pillow tuck** to your quilt you will need to add approximately 18in (45cm) to the length of your quilt. Measure the height and depth of the pillows to be covered, then add an additional inch or two (several centimeters) to allow for the tuck.

# Adapting a pattern

Once you have determined the dimensions of the quilt you'd like to make, you may need to make some adjustments to the pattern. If you are making a quilt without a pattern you may also find the following information helpful.

## Number of blocks

Most quilts are made from blocks of one size. Once you have determined the size of the finished block (the size minus seam allowances), divide the total width of the quilt by that block size to find out how many blocks you will need per row. Then, divide the total length of the quilt by the block size to determine how many rows you will need. Chances are these numbers will not come out evenly, so round both numbers down. Multiply the two numbers together to determine the total number of blocks you will need for your quilt top.

## Making up the difference

If the measurements for the number of blocks needed did not come out evenly there are several ways to remedy this. Adding borders around the quilt top (see pp.110–113) to make up the difference is the easiest way. Adding sashings between the blocks, or making them wider if they are already part of the design, can also make up the difference (see pp.108–109), but this will alter the look of the quilt top. The third, and most difficult, option is to change the size of the blocks until they meet your requirements.

## Fabric requirements

If altering a pattern, it is important to take these changes into consideration when purchasing your fabrics for the quilt. It is usually a good idea to purchase more fabric than you need anyway, to allow for shrinkage during prewashing and also for any mistakes when cutting or sewing. Don't forget to add any extra fabric you might need for the backing and binding, too.

**Most quilts hang** a bit below the depth of the mattress. The type of bed should also be taken into consideration when planning your quilt. Daybeds will only need extra to hang down on one side, for example.

**Determine how you'd like the quilt to sit** on the bed, as well as how it will be used. For example, baby quilts are very often too small for a standard size bed, but still add a personal touch when on display.

**A large quilt** that falls all the way to the floor can look very plush and impressive. Don't make it too much longer though, or it will look as if it were meant for a larger bed.

# Design principles

Most patchwork and many appliqué quilts are based on patterns comprised of blocks—that is, squares made following the same pattern, which are then assembled to make the quilt top. This means that they can be broken down into working units that are easier to cope with than a large overall design. There are literally hundreds of existing block designs that you can make in fabrics and colors of your own choice (see pp.56–59) but, once you understand the basic principles, it's fun to come up with patterns of your own.

## Using templates

Some elements require templates, which are copies of the pieces of the pattern. Ready-made templates are available from craft stores and online. Find out if the seam allowances have been added. Elements to be machine pieced must include the exact seam allowances, while appliqué patterns and those for hand piecing do not need a precise allowance, but are generally cut larger than the finished shape. Many templates are cut with a "window" that shows the area of fabric you will finish up with; this also enables you to mark the seam line and the cutting line without moving the template. Alternatively, you can make your own long-lasting or limited-use templates following these instructions.

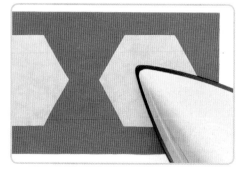

**Limited-use templates using freezer paper:**
Trace the pattern pieces onto freezer paper and cut them out. Iron the waxy side onto the wrong side of the fabric and then cut out around the shape.

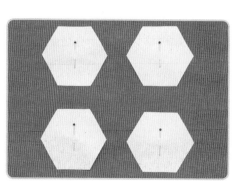

**Limited-use templates using tracing paper:** Pin the template in place and cut out the shape, again adding the seam allowances by eye.

**Durable templates using cardboard:**
Draw the shapes on paper or tracing paper. Cut them out, draw around them again on cardboard, and cut them out, or glue the shapes to the cardboard and cut out.

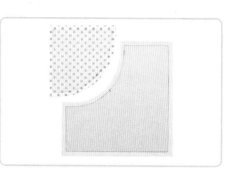

**Durable templates using template plastic:**
Trace the shapes directly onto the template plastic, or cut the desired shapes from paper and glue them to template plastic. Cut them out with paper scissors.

## Planning your own blocks

**The main patchwork block categories** are four-patch (see p.56), nine-patch (see p.56), five-patch, and seven-patch (see p.57). Each one lends itself to certain finished block sizes. Four-patch patterns can always be divided by even numbers, while nine-patch blocks are easiest to work with if the finished size is divisible by three. Five-patch and seven-patch patterns are more limited; they are multiples of 5 x 5 and 7 x 7 units (or patches) per block respectively.

**If you want to design your own block pattern,** start by deciding what size you want your finished block to be and draw it on paper, subdividing it into the relevant number of patches. Further subdivide each patch into strips, triangles, smaller squares, or rectangles to create your design. When you are satisfied, transfer each element to another piece of paper and add a seam allowance to each side of each separate element.

**With appliqué patterns,** enlarge or reduce the pattern if necessary (see p.36) and copy it onto tracing paper. Decide which elements should be cut as separate pieces and trace them individually onto another piece of tracing paper so they can be cut out and used as patterns.

**Many blocks can be supersized** by dramatically increasing the dimensions of a single block, making quilts of an ideal size for baby quilts. Combining several of these bigger blocks allows the quick creation of a full-sized quilt.

# Understanding color

Understanding the basic principles of color theory is crucial to designing a successful quilt. Even a simple design gains impact from good color choices. The three primary colors (red, yellow, and blue) can be placed side by side to create a color wheel. When two primary colors are combined, they create "secondaries." Red and yellow make orange, yellow and blue make green, and blue and red make purple. Intermediate colors called tertiaries occur when a secondary is mixed with the nearest primary.

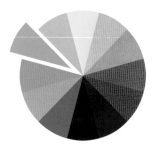

**Monochromatic designs:**
These use different versions of the same color. So a quilt based on greens will not stray into the other sections of the color wheel, but will only use green fabrics.

**Complementary colors:**
Colors that lie opposite one another on the wheel, such as yellow and violet, or red and green, are called complementaries. They provide contrasts that accent design elements and make both colors stand out. Don't forget black and white, the ultimate opposites.

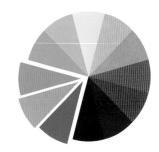

**Analogous colors (side by side):**
Starting with a primary or dominant color, expand in each direction on the color wheel by one color. Similar to a monochromatic color scheme, but with a bit more variation.

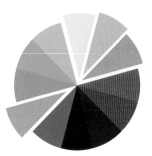

**Analogous with complementary:**
Similar to an analogous color scheme, but with the addition of a complementary primary color. The addition of a complementary color provides a nice contrast to the analogous color grouping.

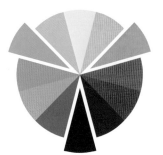

**Triad:**
A triad or triangle uses three colors that are evenly spaced out around the color wheel. This offers a strong contrast while retaining a harmony among the colors. On the color wheel above, every fourth color is grouped.

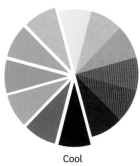

Cool            Warm

**Temperature:**
The temperature of a color can usually be described as cool or warm. You can split the color wheel in half between the green, blue, and blue-violet—cool—side and the yellow, red, and red-violet—warm—side. Cool colors will tend to recede and do well in the background while warm colors will advance and give the feeling of closeness.

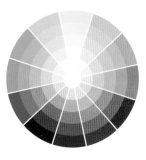

**Tint, shade, and tone:**
When you add white to a color it is called a tint of the color and when you add black to a color it is called a shade of a color. Adding both black and white to a color is called a tone of the color and will leave the color with a gray quality.

# Scale, prints, and design

There are so many quilt designs and fabrics to choose from that getting started on designing your quilt can be a bewildering experience. Most quilts are a mixture of printed and solid-colored fabrics. When using prints, first consider whether the pattern lends itself to being a primary or secondary pattern. The solid areas will act as a foil. Using a design wall can help with planning.

## The scale

The size of the image—its scale—is an important factor when working with print fabrics. A large-scale pattern is generally more difficult to work with, but it can be used successfully, especially in bigger blocks.

Try combining large prints, especially conversation prints—prints that have themed motifs—with solid fabrics. Large prints are useful for making quick-and-easy baby and children's quilts. Medium-scale prints can be fussy cut (see p.40) quite effectively, and small-scale patterns are usually simple to use, since they can be cut into small units that have a consistent look.

There are also hand-dyed and batik fabrics (or fabrics printed to look as if they are hand-dyed) and tone-on-tone fabrics that have tiny motifs printed on a background of the same color that look almost like solid colors from a distance. These give more visual texture than a plain solid color and can really help to bring a design to life.

## Geometric-patterned fabrics

Fabrics such as stripes, checks, and plaids can make fascinating secondary patterns when they are cut and reassembled. Widely used in country-style quilts, they require careful handling to be most effective. Stripes, in particular, can be set in different directions to create visual movement within a block, while checks and plaids can be combined with each other or with solid-colored fabrics to great effect. Be careful to align stripes and checks when cutting and sewing.

## Borders and sashing

A solid color can act as a foil to a busy print, giving the eye somewhere to rest and providing the avid quilter with a place to show off skills. Solid sashing (see p.108) can direct a viewer to the block pattern within, and, while borders can be patterned and pieced, solid borders frame and contain a quilt in a special way. Balance—between prints and solids, lights and darks, warmth and coolness—is key to any successful design, and the more quilts you see, and make, the better your judgment will become. One way to work is to choose a main print first and then coordinate the solids and other prints around it.

## Creating a design wall

Using a design wall is a good way to test how fabrics will look, since it allows you to step back and view different options from a distance. Hang a solid white sheet over a door to make a temporary design wall, or fashion a moveable one from foam board covered with white flannel over a layer of batting. If you have room for a permanent design wall, mount cork or foam board on a wall in your sewing area and pin fabrics to it.

**Stripes**
Stripes add interest that varies depending on the way the fabric is cut. Striped fabrics can be cut with the stripe, across the stripe, or at an angle to the stripe.

**Solids**
Solid-colored fabrics are often used as the basis of a quilt design, as borders, and for the quilt backing.

### Checked fabric

Checks work well combined with solids for simple patchwork or quilting designs.

### Small-scale prints

Many small-scale prints almost give the effect of solid-colored fabrics, but with added interest. You may need to align the pattern where two pieces with the same pattern meet.

### Large-scale prints

Large-scale prints work best in large blocks. Individual motifs can be cut out and used in appliqué, or can be fussy cut for patchwork.

### Medium-scale prints

Ideal for patchwork, medium-scale prints can be successfully combined with solid fabric and small-scale prints for texture and interest.

# General techniques

Quilting involves different techniques at different stages, but many techniques are the same, whether the quilt is pieced, appliquéd, or wholecloth. The techniques outlined in this section are key, whichever type of quilt you choose to make. You will use them over and over again.

## Prewashing and preparing fabrics

While many people are divided on whether to prewash fabric or not, if you plan to wash a finished project in the future it is usually a good idea to prewash the fabrics before you cut or sew them together. Different fabrics shrink at different rates, so prewashing will help prevent uneven shrinkage, and therefore puckering, when the finished item is first washed. Prewashing fabrics can also help to remove any excess dye, which can leech out and discolor the other fabrics. Small precuts do not need to be washed before use since the washing process may ruin them. Check before prewashing any precut fabrics.

### Prewashing fabrics

There are many things to consider when deciding whether to prewash your fabrics or not:

**Shrinkage** The quality and type of fabric will yield different percentages of shrinkage. You can expect the shrinkage of cotton to be anywhere from ⅛in (3mm) to ½in (1.2cm). If you choose not to prewash your fabric, but do wash them in the future, the fabrics may pucker or distort as they each shrink at different rates and in different directions from one another. Therefore, a quilt made from prewashed fabrics will stay flatter and look more even after washing. However, many people prefer this crinkly look and feel it gives a quilt a vintage feel. Most manufacturers' washing instructions are given on the bolt, so note these down when purchasing the fabric.

**Bleeding** While it is not a guarantee, prewashing a fabric may help to remove any excess dye from it. Certain colors—such as reds, blues, and purples—are more prone to bleeding than others. You can test a small piece of the fabric for colorfastness by submerging it in a clear bowl of warm, soapy water and leaving it to sit. After about 30 minutes to an hour, place the bowl on a white surface and check to see if the water has changed color. If the water has,

you know that the item is not colorfast and will bleed when washed. If the water has not changed color, leave the wet piece of fabric to sit on a scrap of white fabric. If the color transfers to the white fabric after a short period of time then the fabric is not colorfast. If it does not, the fabric is colorfast.

If the fabric is not colorfast, you should prewash it several times using a dye magnet or color catcher. After each wash cycle, perform the colorfastness tests to check if any dye still remains. Continue to prewash the fabric until it no longer bleeds. You can also buy color fastener to treat a fabric. Follow the manufacturer's instructions.

**Handling and chemicals** Fabric right off the bolt usually contains sizing and other chemicals to help protect it. These make the fabric easier to cut and machine sew, but may not be suitable for people sensitive to chemicals. If you prewash it to remove the chemical, pressing your washed fabric well will help to set the fibers and allow for more precise cutting and piecing.

**How will the finished item be used?** If you are making an item for display, such as a wall hanging, there may be no need to prewash the fabrics, since they will probably never be washed in the future.

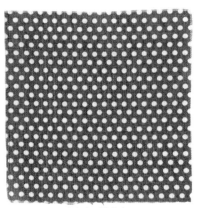

New fabric          Washed fabric

**This swatch shows** what can happen to a piece of cotton fabric during washing. Some of the dye bled out and the fabric shrunk.

## Tips for prewashing

- **You should prewash fabric** in the same manner you intend to launder the finished item in the future. For example, if you plan to wash the finished quilt on a cold wash cycle and dry it on a medium dryer setting, you should prewash the fabric in the same way.

- **You can serge or zigzag stitch** along the cut edges of some looser weave fabrics before washing to help prevent them from unraveling during prewashing.

- **Always prewash large pieces** of fabric when you first buy them, so you don't forget to do it when you work with them at a later stage.

- **When prewashing fabric**, snip off a small triangle at each corner to prevent fraying. Washing small pieces of fabric in a lingerie bag will also help prevent fraying.

- **Hand-dyed or Batik fabric** should always be washed and dried to set the dyes and keep them from running and fading. Use a dye catcher to help prevent the excess dye from spoiling the colors around them.

## Preparing fabrics

After it has been washed there is not much that needs to be done to fabric before you use it, but there are a few things to keep in mind:

**Drying** If using a tumble dryer, dry your prewashed fabrics on a medium heat setting and remove them from the dryer before they are completely dry. Drying a fabric completely can set the wrinkles firmly into the fabric and make them difficult to remove.

**Ironing** Iron the fabric straight out of the dryer while it is still damp. Starching the fabric can make the ironing easier and more effective.

**Cutting** Before you cut, check the straight of grain is true by checking it against the selvage of the fabric.

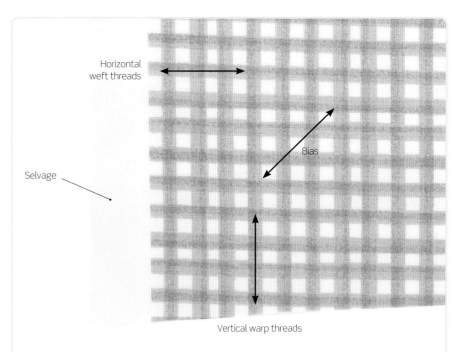

Horizontal weft threads

Bias

Selvage

Vertical warp threads

## Tips for preparing

- **Cut quilt borders on the lengthwise grain** to minimize stretching.

- **To find the lengthwise grain**, pull the fabric gently along both straight grains. The stretch will be greater along the weft, or widthwise, grain.

- **Try to position any bias edges** away from the edges of a block to minimize stretching and to keep the size of the block accurate.

**Each fabric has three grains:** the lengthwise grain (warp), which runs parallel to the selvages; the horizontal grain (weft), which runs perpendicular to the selvages; and the diagonal grain (bias). The rigid edge on each side is called the selvage. The bias should be handled carefully since it stretches easily, which can lead to distortions in the patchwork.

# Altering the size of a motif

The easiest way to alter the size of a motif is to use a photocopier. Whether enlarging or reducing, divide your desired size by the actual size of the template. Multiply that figure by 100 to give the percentage of the enlargement or reduction you will need. You can also use gridded paper to alter the size of a motif, as below.

**1** For non-geometric motifs, trace the outline onto gridded paper. To make a pattern twice the size of the original, draw a grid double the size on another piece of paper. If you start with ½in (1.2cm) squares, for example, increase the size of each square in your new grid to 1in (2.5cm).

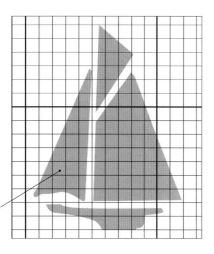

The original motif traced onto paper gridded into ½in (1.2cm) squares.

**2** Transfer the lines within each square of the grid so they correspond to the lines of the original motif. When you have finished, trace the motif onto a new piece of paper to smooth out any distortions. You are now ready to transfer the newly sized motif to a template.

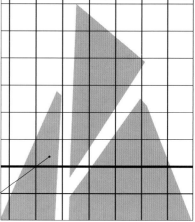

The motif enlarged onto a 1in (2.5cm) grid.

# Rotary cutting

Many of the most popular patterns can be rotary cut. You will need a rotary cutter, a quilter's ruler, and a self-healing mat. When cutting a square into other shapes, such as half-square triangles that will be reassembled into a square, you must start with a square that is larger than your finished square will be, to allow for the seam allowances. Always keep your fingers away from the cutting edge.

## Cutting a strip

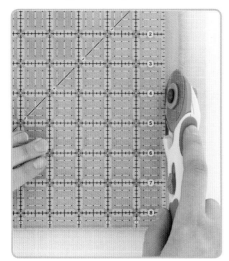

**1** First, you must straighten the edge of the fabric. Fold the washed and pressed fabric so the selvages are together. Place it on the mat, with the folded edge aligned with the top of the ruler. Lay the ruler on top and cut along the edge of the ruler, away from your body, to remove the selvages. Keep the hand holding the ruler steady.

Align the folded edge of the fabric with a horizontal mark on the ruler

**2** Turn the mat so as not to disturb the newly cut edge and reposition the ruler over the area of fabric that is to be your strip. Align the ruler carefully along the cut edge to give the desired width and line up the folded edge with a horizontal mark. Cut the fabric strip along the grain.

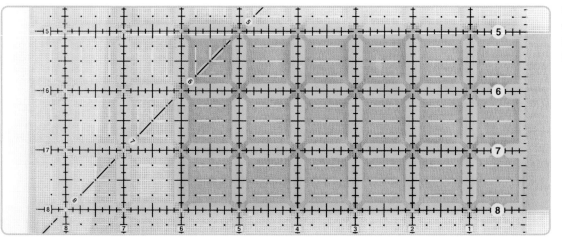

3 To cut the strip into smaller units, position it horizontally on the mat and measure using the ruler grid. Cut as before.

## Cutting squares and rectangles

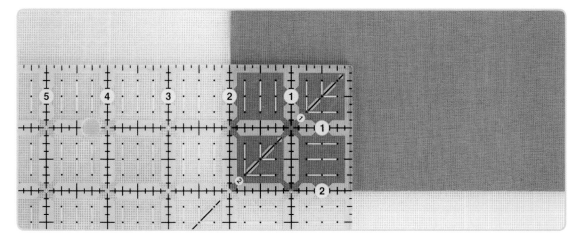

**Squares and rectangles** can also be cut using a quilter's ruler, which has a guideline marked across the diagonal from corner to corner. Add a $7\frac{}{8}$in (2.2cm) seam allowance when cutting a right-angled triangle and a $1\frac{3}{8}$in (2.75cm) seam allowance when cutting a quarter-square triangle.

## Cutting a pieced strip into smaller strips

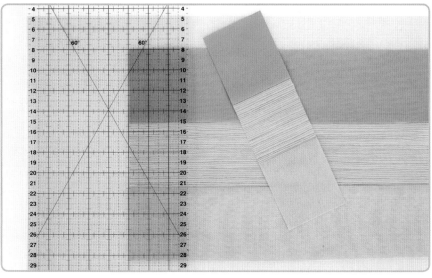

**Press your pieced strip** and position it right-side up horizontally on the mat. If necessary, straighten the pieced strip at one end, as in Step 1 of Cutting a strip (see opposite). Turn the strip and reposition the ruler over the area that you want to use. Cut pieced strips of the desired width.

# Cutting a pieced strip on the bias

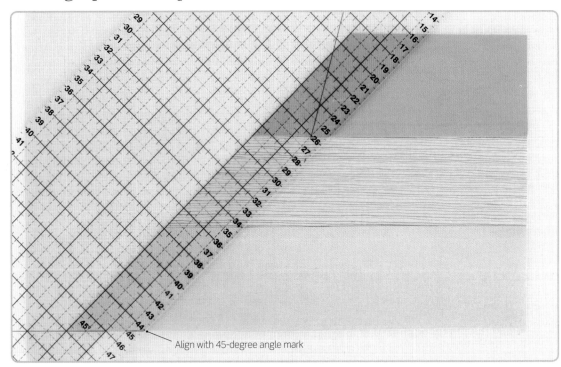

Align with 45-degree angle mark

**Trim one end** of the pieced strip at a 45-degree angle, using the line marked on the quilter's ruler. Cut strips of the desired width at the same angle by measuring along the straight edge of the ruler.

# Cutting true bias strips

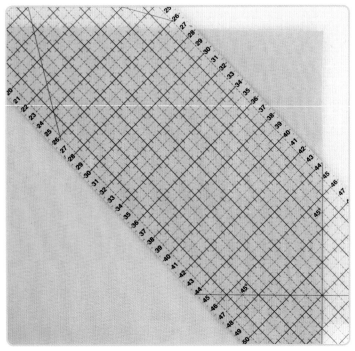

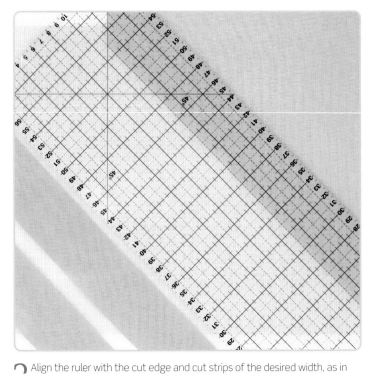

1 Straighten the edge of the fabric as in Step 1 of Cutting a strip (see p.36). Align the 45-degree mark on the ruler with the straightened edge and cut away the top corner of the fabric along the ruler.

2 Align the ruler with the cut edge and cut strips of the desired width, as in Cutting a pieced strip on the bias, above. Be careful when using bias strips, since the 45-degree cut brings stretch to the fabric.

# Cutting half-square triangles

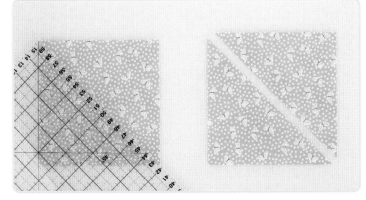

**Cut half-square triangles** across the diagonal of a square. Remember to cut the square large enough so that it includes a seam allowance.

# Cutting quarter-square triangles

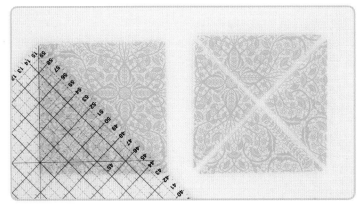

**Cut a square diagonally** from both corners to create four quarter-square triangles. Again, include a seam allowance when cutting the square.

# Cutting irregular triangles

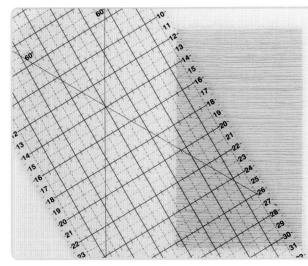

**Cut a rectangle** across the diagonal to create two irregular long triangles. To make a matching pair of irregular triangles, cut another rectangle across the diagonal, starting at the opposite corner.

# Cutting 45-degree diamonds

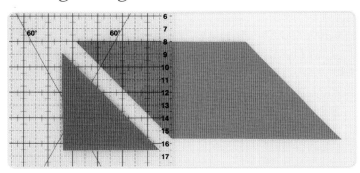

**Cut a strip the desired width** of the diamond, plus the seam allowances. Cut a 45-degree angle at one end. For the second cut, align the quilter's ruler along the cut edge according to the width of diamond required.

# Cutting curves

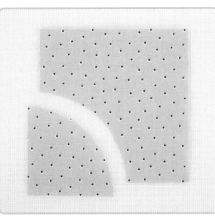

**Gentle curves** can be cut with a rotary cutter, but it is advisable to use a small blade. Blades are available in standard 1, 1¾, and 3½in (25, 45, and 90mm) sizes.

# Cutting by hand

Quilters generally cut with scissors if the pieces are small or intricate, or if they have unusual angles or shapes. Appliqué motifs are almost always best cut by hand. You should keep at least one pair of good-quality, sharp dressmaker's scissors just for cutting cloth. Do not cut paper, template plastic, batting, and the like with the same pair. Most quilters have several pairs of scissors in different sizes.

## Cutting without a pattern

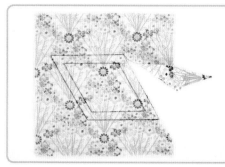

**1** Mark the outline of the shape to be cut on the wrong side of the fabric and add the seam allowance, if you wish.

**2** Cut out the shape along the marked cutting line—or cut a short distance away, if you have only marked the sewing line.

## Cutting with a pattern

**Patterns made from paper** are familiar to dressmakers and can provide an easy way for quilters to cut the same shape several times over. Pin the pattern to the fabric and cut around it, adding the seam allowance if necessary.

## Fussy cutting

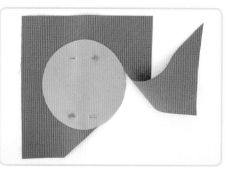

**This is a method** of isolating particular motifs in printed fabric and cutting them so they show as a feature in a block of patchwork or appliqué. It can seem like a waste of fabric, but the results are usually worth it. It is easier to delineate the area you want if you cut a window template to the desired size and shape.

# Unpicking a seam

Everyone makes the occasional mistake and sometimes seams must be unpicked; moreover, some patterns depend on taking out seams during construction. It is vital that the unpicking process does not stretch the edges of the fabric. Unpicking works best on seams that haven't been pressed. Never use scissors to unpick a seam.

## Method 1

**1** Working from the right side, insert the point of the seam ripper into the stitches to cut the thread.

**2** Pull the layers of fabric apart gently as you work to the end of the seam.

## Method 2

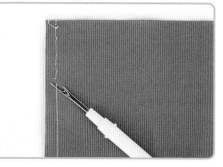

**1** Working from the wrong side, hold the seam taut and insert the seam ripper into every third or fourth stitch to cut the thread. Work your way along the seam.

**2** Hold the lower piece of fabric flat and pull gently on the top piece to separate the two. Do not use this method on bias seams.

# Starting and finishing

Securing the thread at the beginning and end of any sewing is, of course, essential. Traditional hand sewing begins and ends with a knot at the end of the thread, but knots can interfere with quilting and sometimes show on the top of the quilt. There are several knots that are useful for quilting. Backstitched loops lie almost flat and are a secure way of finishing off a seam.

## Threading a needle

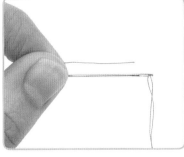

1 Trim the end of the thread. Insert the end of the thread through the eye of the needle, then cut to the desired length from the spool. Because of the way thread is twisted as it is made, threading the needle with the end that comes off the spool first will help prevent tangles.

2 After threading, run the thread between your thumb and forefinger in the direction that the thread came off the spool to smooth it.

### Tips

● **Thread weight:** Use a thread weight that is appropriate for the size of the needle and a needle size that is suited to the weight of the fabric.

● **Thread length:** Keep the thread length to no more than 20in (50cm) long; it will be less likely to kink and fray.

● **Needle threader:** Use a needle threader if you have difficulty getting the thread through the eye.

● **Cutting direction:** Always cut away from your body when possible.

● **Knot size:** Knots make lumps wherever they occur, so make sure that knots are as small as possible so that they can be easily hidden.

## Wrapped knot

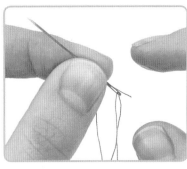

1 Thread the needle, then hold one free end of the thread parallel with the needle, as shown.

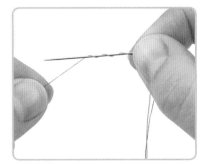

2 Take hold of the free end of the thread securely and wrap it around the needle a few times.

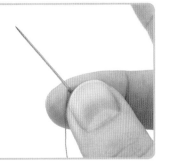

3 Slide the wraps toward the eye of the needle and hold them with your thumb and forefinger.

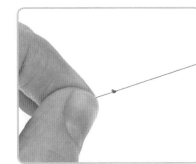

4 Grab the wraps between your index finger and thumb of the opposite hand.

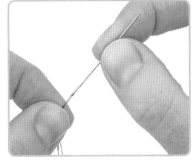

5 Slide the wraps down the end of the needle, over the eye, and down the thread.

6 Keep pulling the knot down the thread until it reaches near the bottom of the length of thread.

# Backstitched loop

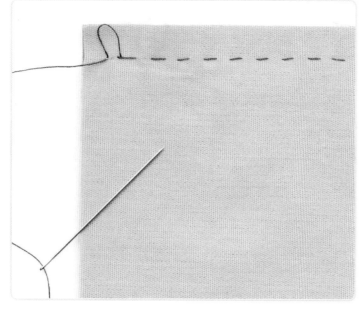

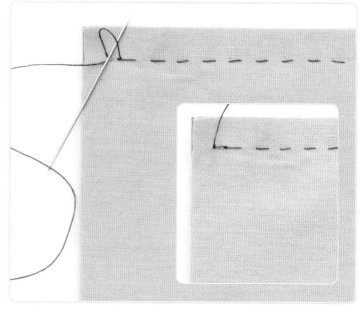

1 This method doesn't have the bulk of a knot but is a secure way to finish a line of stitches. Backstitch once at the end of the sewing and pull the needle through; do not pull the thread taut, but leave a small loop of thread.

2 Take the needle through the loop, then pull the thread tight.

# Double backstitched loop

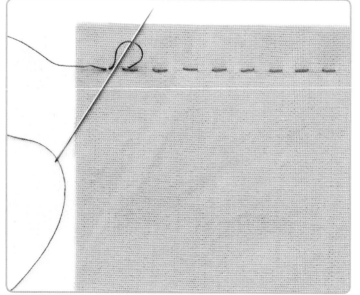

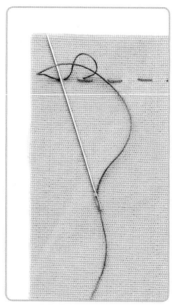

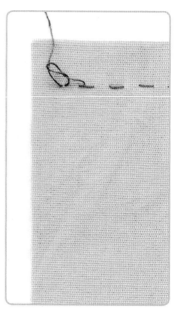

1 This method is even more secure. Backstitch once at the end of the line of stitches, leaving a small loop of thread as in Step 1 of the backstitched loop (see above). Insert the tip of the needle through the loop and pull it through to form a second loop, creating a figure eight.

2 Insert the tip of the needle through the second loop.

3 Pull the thread taut to form a knot.

# Hand stitches for quilting

Although most quilts today are made by machine, there are a number of techniques that require hand sewing; it is important to choose the correct stitch for the best result.

## Running stitch

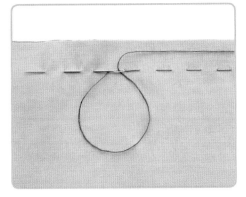

**This is the most common stitch** for hand piecing. Take the needle in and out of the fabric several times, making small, evenly spaced stitches. Pull the needle through gently until the thread is taut, but not tense. Repeat to the end of the seam.

## Stab stitch

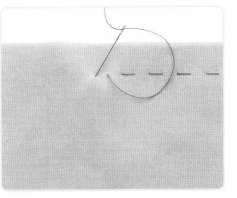

**This popular quilter's stitch** is useful for sewing through several layers or into thick fabric. Take the needle vertically through the fabric layers from the top and pull until the thread is taut but not tense. For the next stitch, bring the needle through vertically from below. Continue sewing to the end of the seam.

## Backstitch

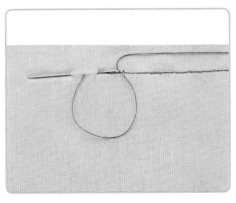

**Backstitch can be worked in a row** as an alternative to running stitch to join units together. Bring the needle through all the layers to the right side, then insert it a short distance behind the point where it emerged. Bring it back up to the right side again, the same distance in front of the point where it first emerged. Repeat to the end of the seam.

## Whipstitching

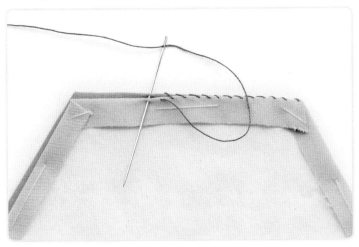

**Also known as oversewing** or overcasting, whipstitching is used to join two edges with an almost invisible seam. Bring the needle through the back edge to the front edge, picking up a few threads from each edge as you go. Pull gently on the thread until it is taut but not tense, and repeat.

## Slip stitch

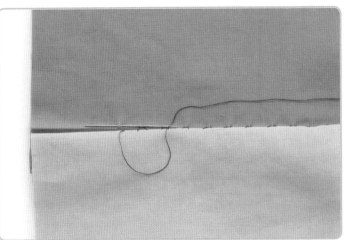

**Used mainly in appliqué,** slip stitch joins two pieces of fabric with an invisible line of stitches. Knot the thread and bring the needle to the front, hiding the knot in the folded edge of the top piece. Now pick up a thread or two on the back piece, then take the needle into the top piece right next to this stitch and slide it a short distance inside the fold. Bring the needle to the front again, then repeat, catching a few threads on the back piece with each stitch.

# Pressing

Pressing is essential when making accurate patchwork. It is different from ironing, which can cause fabric and seams to distort. When pressing, press down in one place, then lift the iron and move it before pressing down on another area. Set pieces aside to cool after each pressing and always press the seam toward the darker fabric to prevent darker colors from showing through lighter fabrics. The temperature of the iron should be appropriate for the fabric.

## Pressing straight seams

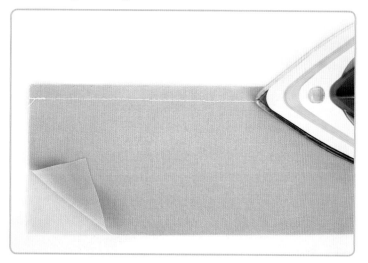

1 Place the unit or sewn strips with right sides together on the ironing board with the darker fabric on top. Press the iron along the seam, lifting the iron at regular intervals. This is called "setting the seam." It helps ensure accuracy by locking the threads in place and smoothing the fibers of the fabric.

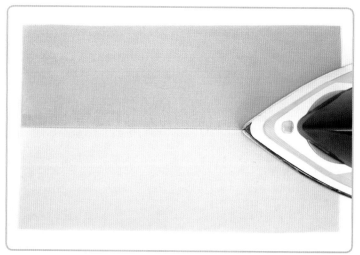

2 Open the unit to the right side and press from one end to the other along the seam. If you keep the lighter piece nearest you and press with the tip of the iron, you can press the seam to the darker side at the same time as you open the unit.

## Pressing bias seams

Work along the straight grain to prevent the seam from being pulled out of shape. Lift the iron and replace it rather than dragging it along the seam.

## Working in rows

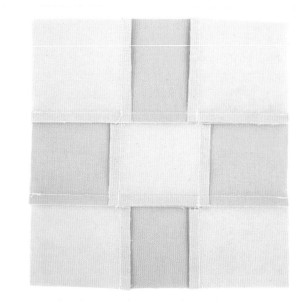

Press the seams in adjoining rows in opposite directions from one another to minimize bulkiness where the seams join.

## Pressing a pieced block

Place the block wrong-side up on the ironing board. Do not press hard, but make sure the seams lie as flat as possible.

## Pressing seams open

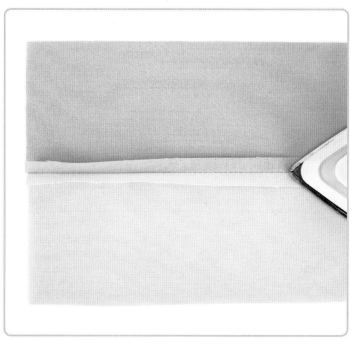

Where several seams meet, you may need to press seams open to reduce bulk. After setting the seam as in Step 1 of Pressing straight seams (opposite), turn the piece to the wrong side, open the seam, and press along the length with the tip of the iron.

## Thumbnail

Work on a hard surface. Open the unit out and press first on the wrong side, then on the right side, running your thumbnail gently but firmly along the seam line and pressing the lighter fabric toward the darker fabric.

## Small wooden iron

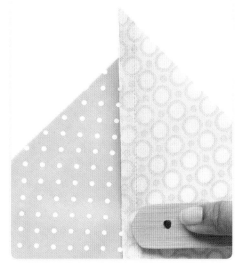

Working on the wrong side, place the flat, chisel-shaped edge of the tool on the seam line and run it gently along the seam.

## Hera

A hera is a plastic, bladelike device. It is used in certain embroidery techniques but is also useful for creasing a temporary line on the fabric.

# Assembling the quilt layers

Once you have marked the quilting pattern on the quilt top, it is time to assemble the quilt "sandwich," which is the layers of top, batting, and backing that make up the quilt. If the batting has been folded, open it out flat and leave it for several hours to relax the wrinkles.

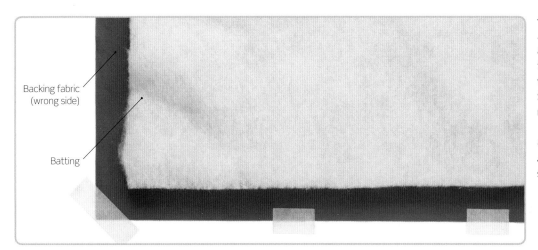

Backing fabric
(wrong side)

Batting

1 Trim the batting and backing 3-6in (7.5-16cm) larger all around than the finished top. Lay the backing wrong-side up on the work surface and smooth it flat. Secure it to the surface with masking tape.

2 Center the batting on the backing and smooth it out.

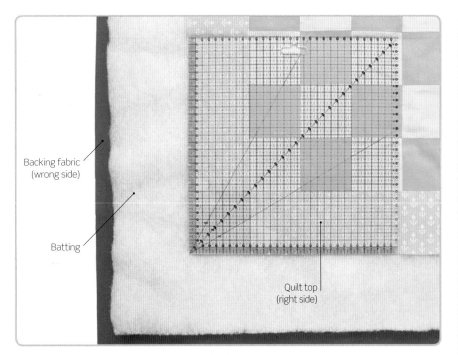

Backing fabric
(wrong side)

Batting

Quilt top
(right side)

3 Position the quilt top right-side up, centering it on the batting. Use a ruler to check that the top is squared up. Using large quilter's straight pins, temporarily pin along each squared edge as you work.

4 Working from the center out diagonally, horizontally, and vertically, baste or pin the layers together. Remove the pins along the edge as you reach them. Keep smoothing the layers. Make basting stitches 2in (5cm) long—first vertically and horizontally, then diagonally. If pinning using safety pins, follow the same pattern and insert the pins at 3-4in (7.5-10cm) intervals.

# Making a bigger backing

Most bed quilts are wider than most fabrics, so it is often necessary to piece the backing. There are several ways to do this, but you should avoid having a seam down the vertical center of the quilt.

**1** Cut two full widths of fabric of the required length. Set one aside, and cut the other in half lengthwise. Trim off all selvages.

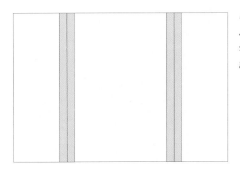

**2** Add one half-width to each vertical side of the full width to get the required width.

# Turning

Sometimes you may want to finish the edges of the quilt before you quilt it. The technique works well on smaller projects, such as baby quilts. Cut the batting and backing slightly larger than the quilt top.

**1** Center the quilt top right-side up on the batting. Center the backing on the quilt top, right-side down. Pin or baste the layers together around the edge.

**2** Start machine sewing at the bottom edge, about an inch (several centimeters) from the corner, taking a ¼in (6mm) seam. Secure with backstitching.

**3** At the corners, stop ¼in (6mm) from the edge with the needle down. Raise the presser foot. Pivot the fabric, lower the presser foot, and continue sewing. On the fourth side leave an opening of 5-10in (12-25cm). Secure with backstitching.

**4** Clip the corners to reduce bulk. If necessary, trim and grade the seams, then turn right-side out through the opening.

**5** Level the edges on the inside. Pin or press lightly. Blind stitch the opening closed.

# Bindings

Premade bias binding is available in various colors and widths, or you can make your own. Bindings should be applied as a continuous strip. If possible, cut straight binding strips along the lengthwise grain of the fabric or join pieces before applying. Bias binding has more stretch than straight binding, making it suitable for binding work with curved edges.

## Making a straight binding strip

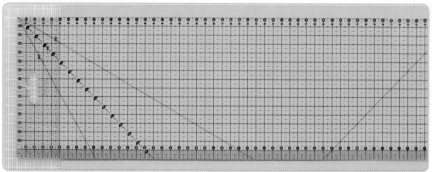

1 Measure the edges of the piece being bound and decide on the width of the finished binding. Cut strips six times this width plus an additional ½in (1.2cm), allowing extra length for mitering corners and joining pieces.

2 Ensure your edges are square and cut along the straight grain of the fabric. Add about 16in (40cm) extra to the length for full quilts, 12in (30cm) for baby quilts, wall hangings, and large embroideries, and 8in (20cm) for small works.

## Making a bias strip

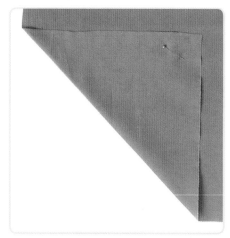

1 Buy at least 60in (1.5m) of fabric so you can cut very long strips. Cut off selvages and smooth the fabric flat. Straighten the right-hand edge of the fabric, then fold this edge back so that it aligns with the top edge and forms an exact 45-degree angle. Cut along this bias fold.

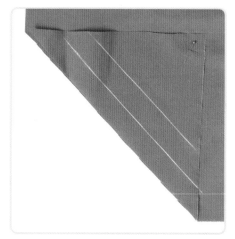

2 Using a metal ruler and a sharp piece of tailor's chalk, mark lines on the fabric parallel to the bias edge and 1½in (4cm) apart. Cut out the strips along the chalked lines. Cut as many strips as you need for your project plus a few extra.

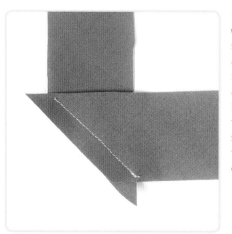

3 Join strips together to make a continuous strip. Pin the strips together at a 90-degree angle with right sides facing and sew a ¼in (6mm) seam on the bias. The seam should run from edge to edge of each strip, with a triangle of fabric left at either end of the seam.

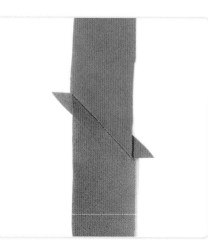

4 Press the seam open and trim off the seam allowances and the extending little triangles (dog ears). You can also make bias binding with these prepared strips. To do this, press under the edges or run the strip through a bias binding maker.

# Making a continuous bias strip

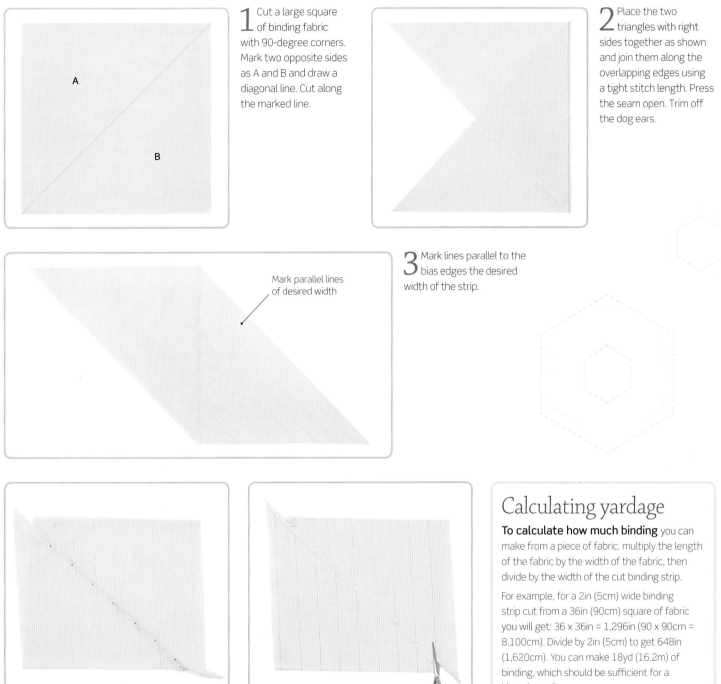

**1** Cut a large square of binding fabric with 90-degree corners. Mark two opposite sides as A and B and draw a diagonal line. Cut along the marked line.

**2** Place the two triangles with right sides together as shown and join them along the overlapping edges using a tight stitch length. Press the seam open. Trim off the dog ears.

Mark parallel lines of desired width

**3** Mark lines parallel to the bias edges the desired width of the strip.

**4** Bring the remaining two straight-grain edges together and offset the marked lines by aligning one tip of the fabric to the first marked line on the other side. Pin carefully to match the marked lines and sew together, right-sides facing, to make a tube.

**5** Start cutting at one end along the marked lines to make a continuous strip.

## Calculating yardage

**To calculate how much binding** you can make from a piece of fabric, multiply the length of the fabric by the width of the fabric, then divide by the width of the cut binding strip.

For example, for a 2in (5cm) wide binding strip cut from a 36in (90cm) square of fabric you will get: 36 x 36in = 1,296in (90 x 90cm = 8,100cm). Divide by 2in (5cm) to get 648in (1,620cm). You can make 18yd (16.2m) of binding, which should be sufficient for a king-size quilt.

Always work in either the US or metric system when doing your calculations.

# Binding with premade bias binding

Every quilt will need some form of binding to finish the raw edges and a premade bias binding, or bias tape, is a quick and easy way to do this. Bias tape can be used on small projects and projects that will not receive a lot of wear, such as wall hangings. Steps 3–8 show how to miter a corner when binding. Mitering should be used when attaching any binding around a corner.

Pin the bias tape along the edge of the quilt

Open up the folded edges of the bias tape

1 After squaring up the quilt, measure all four sides, add them together, then add approximately 16in (40cm) to the total length. Cut the bias tape to this final measurement. Open up the long, folded edges of the bias tape and with right sides together, align the bias tape along one side of the quilt top, starting in the middle of the side, not a corner. Pin in place.

2 Beginning an inch or so (a few centimeters) from the end of the bias tape, with the quilt right-side up, sew along the outside edge of the tape through all the layers. Use a seam allowance that is one-quarter the width of the open bias tape. The stitch should land approximately on the open fold of the binding.

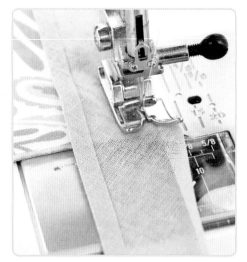

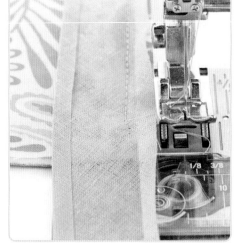

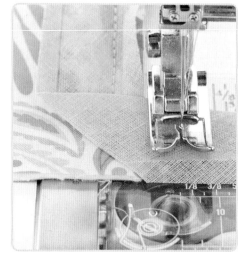

3 Carefully sew along the edge, stopping a seam allowance's distance from the corner. Backstitch a few stitches.

4 Remove the quilt from under the machine foot, but do not cut the threads or pull it out too far.

5 Create a mitered corner by folding the tape 45-degrees to the right of the quilt top. The tape should run parallel with the bottom edge of the quilt.

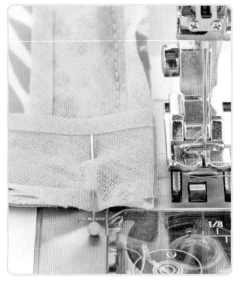

6 Carefully fold the binding back 180-degrees to the left, aligning the edge with the bottom edge of the quilt. Pin as needed.

7 Turn the quilt 90 degrees and place it back under the machine, inserting the needle back into the same place you last finished sewing. Continue sewing down the second side.

8 Repeat the process for the remaining sides until you are approximately 12in ( 30cm) from your starting point. Measure the distance between the finishing point and the beginning end of the binding tape. Trim and connect the two ends of the tape so they fit along the final section, then finish sewing the binding in place along the edge.

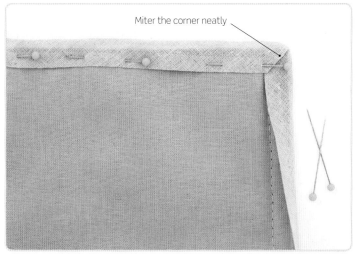

Miter the corner neatly

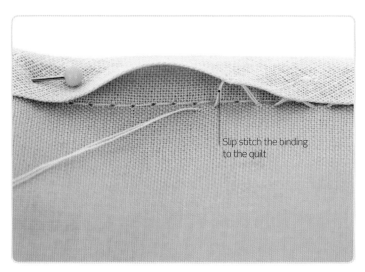

Slip stitch the binding to the quilt

9 Fold the binding to the back of the quilt, making sure to miter each corner neatly as you do. Fold under the long raw edge of the binding tape that had previously been open. Pin the binding in place.

10 With a needle and thread, slip stitch the binding (see p.43) to the back of the quilt, enclosing the raw edges of the quilt sandwich and covering the stitches made from sewing the binding to the front. Secure tightly and finish by embedding the knot inside the quilt.

# Turned-edge binding

Adding a turned-edge binding is a simple way of finishing off the edge of a quilt. The binding is formed by folding the backing of the quilt to the front. It has the appearance of traditional bias binding.

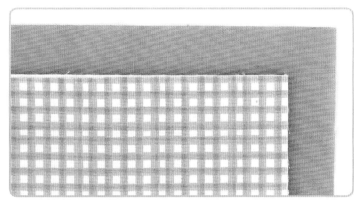

**1** Pin the backing fabric out of the way and trim the batting and quilt top so they are even and square with one another. Unpin the backing fabric and trim it to twice the width you want the finished turned-edge binding to be.

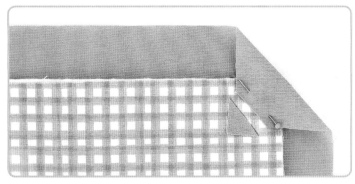

**2** Fold one corner of the backing fabric over the corner of the quilt and pin it in place. Trim off the tip, as shown above.

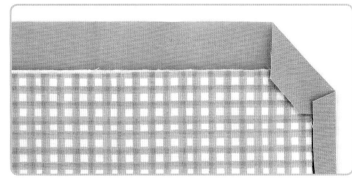

**3** Fold the adjacent edge of the backing fabric over so that it aligns with the cut edges of the batting and the quilt top.

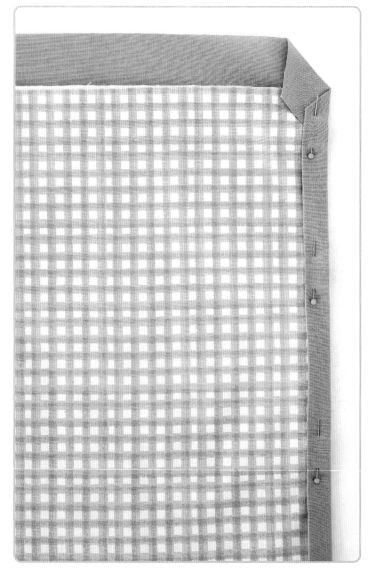

**4** Fold the edge of the backing fabric over a second time so all the raw edges are enclosed. Neatly and evenly pin the folded edge in place along the entire length.

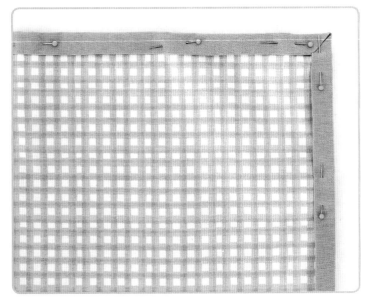

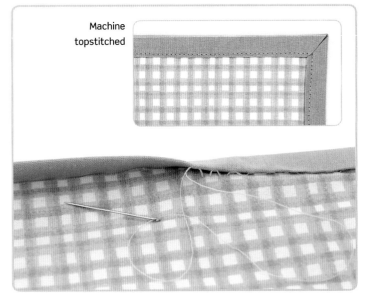

**Machine topstitched**

5 Repeat Steps 2–4 for the other corners and other edges, making sure adjacent edges meet in clean miters at the corners, as shown above. If any trimmed corners from Step 2 are visible, you may need to trim them back some more.

6 Neatly slip stitch (see p.43) the turned-edge binding to the quilt top or, for a much quicker finish, you can machine topstitch along the edge of the binding (see inset).

# Double-fold binding

Double-fold binding is stronger than bias-tape binding (see pp.50–51) and is recommended for binding bed quilts. Quilted wall hangings and other small, layered items that won't get routine wear and tear can be bound with a premade bias tape.

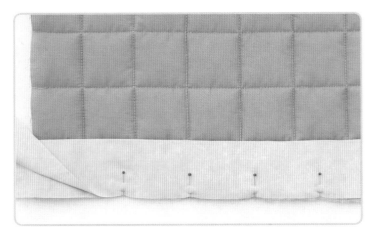

1 Cut strips of binding fabric six times the desired width of your finished binding, plus ¼in (6mm) extra. Cut enough strips to fit around the perimeter of the quilt top, plus approximately 16in (40cm) extra. Join them all together (see pp.48–49). Fold the strip in half lengthwise, wrong sides together, and press.

2 Lay the doubled binding strip on the right side of the quilt, raw edges to raw edges. Pin the binding strip in place along the first side, starting about halfway down the side and checking that none of the binding seams land on a corner. If they do, reposition the binding and pin again.

3 Start machine sewing about 8in (20cm) from the start of the binding using the seam allowance used in the calculation of the binding width. Sew along the raw edges, mitering the binding when you reach a corner, then pin and continue to sew the next side (see pp.50–51) until all sides have the binding attached. Join the ends in your preferred method.

4 Turn the folded edge of the binding to the back of the quilt, making sure to miter the corners on the back too. Neatly slip stitch (see p.43) the binding in place.

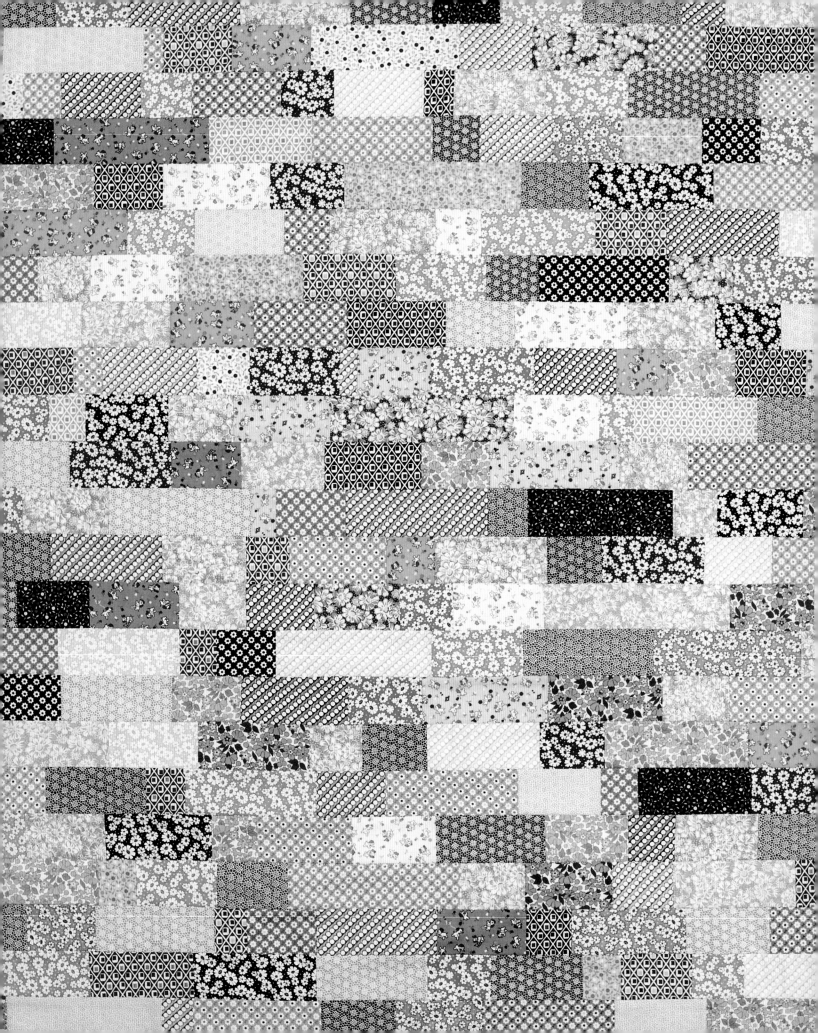

# Patchwork

# Patchwork block gallery

There are hundreds of traditional patchwork patterns and we have space to show only a few—but once you've mastered the basic construction techniques, you will be able to look at a block pattern and work out both the constituent elements and how to piece it together.

## Four-patch blocks

The simplest four-patch blocks are made up of just four squares (patches), but those four squares can also be created by piecing together two half-square triangles, or four quarter-square triangles, or various combinations thereof.

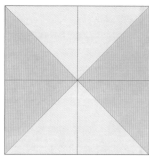
Yankee puzzle

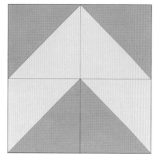
Chevron or Streak of lightning

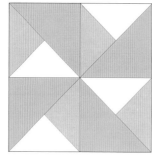
Broken pinwheel

Flyfoot

## Nine-patch blocks

Nine-patch blocks are made of nine units in three rows of three. By adding a third color to a simple nine-patch of two colors, you can create myriad variations.

## Pictorial blocks

Patchwork pictorial blocks tend to be highly stylized, with the individual elements of the design being made up of square and triangle units in varying combinations.

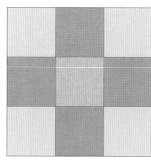
Red cross—Three-color nine-patch

Three-color double nine-patch

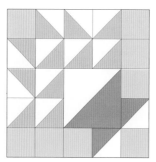
Grape basket

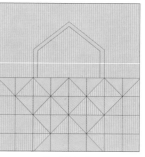
Colonial basket

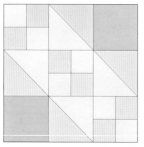
Rocky road to California

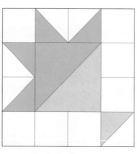
Building blocks

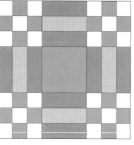
Basket of scraps

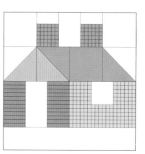
House with fence

# Five- and seven-patch blocks

Five-patch blocks consist of a grid of five units in each direction, or 25 units in total, while seven-patch blocks have no fewer than 49 units (seven in each direction). With so many elements, each one of which can be subdivided in several ways, there is almost infinite scope for creating different patterns.

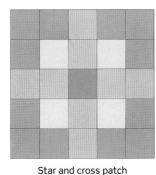

Star and cross patch

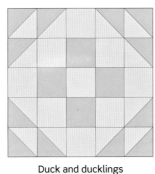

Duck and ducklings

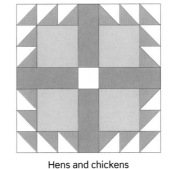

Hens and chickens

Dove in a window

# Strip-pieced blocks

Strip-pieced patterns can be put together in random color and fabric combinations or in repeating patterns. If two fabrics are pieced A–B–A and B–A–B, the resulting squares can be alternated to create a Basketweave block, similar to the one below. Seminole bands can be angled or set square and are wonderful for creating pieced border strips.

Basketweave

String-pieced divided square

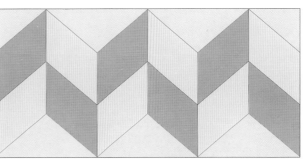

Double chevron seminole

# Log cabin blocks

There are many variations in log cabin blocks and settings. Strips of light and dark fabrics can be alternated, placed on adjacent or opposite sides, made of varying widths, or pieced from a combination of smaller squares and rectangles. The center square can be pieced, turned "on point," or made from a rectangle, triangle, or diamond.

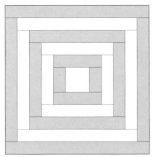

Cabin in the cotton

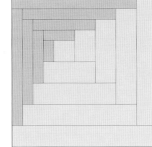

Thick and thin

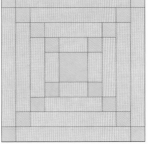

Chimneys and cornerstones

Pineapple

# Star blocks

There are probably more kinds of star blocks than any other patchwork motif; the construction ranges from simple four-patch stars to extremely complex designs created by cutting 60-degree diamonds in half lengthwise or crosswise. The basic eight-point star alone, with its 45-degree angles, is the starting point for numerous variations, including the intricate lone star.

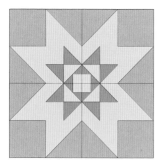

Repeating star

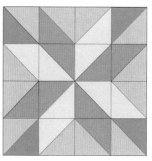

Evening star—Morning star

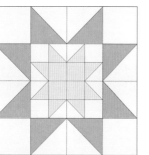

Constellation block

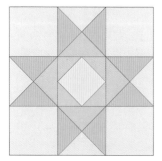

Braced star

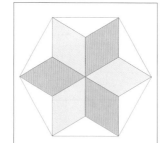

Card basket

Eisenhower star

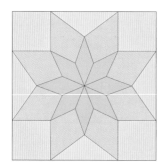

Tennessee star

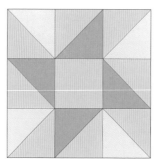

Silver and gold

Nine-patch star

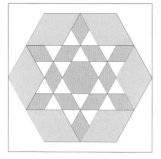

Ozark diamonds

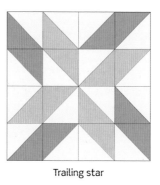

Lone star

Trailing star

## Tips for making blocks

- When marking, make sure the marker has a sharp point. If you mark with dashes, not a continuous line, the fabric is less apt to shift or stretch.

- Remember the rule: measure twice, cut once. And keep in mind that measurements from one brand of ruler or mat are not always exactly the same as another brand. For accuracy, try to use the same ruler and mat, as well as the same machine foot, throughout the piecing process.

- If you make a sample block to begin, you can measure your finished blocks against it to ensure accuracy.

- Whenever possible, sew a bias edge to a straight edge to minimize stretching.

- If you need to trim a block to make it smaller, trim back an equal amount from all sides to keep the design of the block accurate and centered.

# Curved blocks

Probably the most popular of all traditional curved blocks is the Drunkard's path (see pp.120–121). When the orientation or color values of the four units is altered, a number of complex curving patterns result. Changing the size and shape of the curves alters the block considerably.

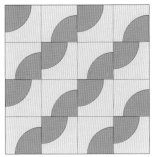
Falling timbers

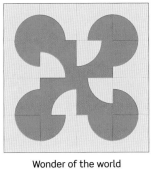
Wonder of the world

Chain links

Drunkard's puzzle

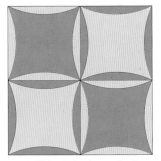
Robbing Peter to pay Paul

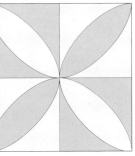
Orange peel

# Fan blocks

Fans are based on quarter-circles and can be arranged in a number of different ways. However they are arranged, a curving pattern results. Variations such as Dresden plate patterns are full circles and are often appliquéd to a background. The segments can be curved or pointed, or both. The center can be open to allow the background to show through or applied separately for contrast.

# Mosaic blocks

Though many of these can be sewn by machine, most are made by piecing together geometric shapes using the English paper-piecing method (see p.134). The most familiar block is Grandmother's flower garden.

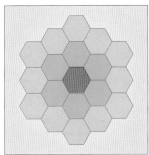
Grandmother's flower garden

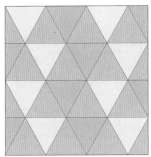
1,000 pyramids

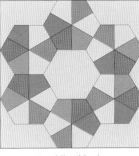
Tumbling blocks

Flower basket

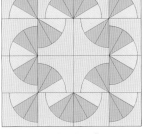
Mohawk trail

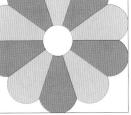
Dresden plate

# Piecing

Piecing, or sewing pieces of fabric (units or patches) together, lies at the heart of patchwork. In fact, piecing is, simply, creating patchwork. First you join smaller pieces, then you join these to make your final design. You can choose between hand and machine piecing. Piecing by machine obviously produces faster results.

## Hand piecing

Mark all seam lines on the wrong side of the fabric to give you an accurate guide of where to sew. Take care when sewing seams on bias-cut edges (for instance, on diamond, triangle, or hexagon shapes) or around curves, since the raw edge is prone to stretching. Secure the seam with a small backstitch each time you bring the needle through and use a double backstitched loop (see p.42) at the end of a bias seam; do not sew into the seam allowance.

### Joining two units with a straight seam

**1** Place the two units to be joined right sides together. You must not sew across the seam allowance of the adjacent seam, so mark that seam allowance with pins at the start and end points of the seam you are about to sew. Add more pins along the seam line you are about to sew, making sure that the seam line aligns on both units.

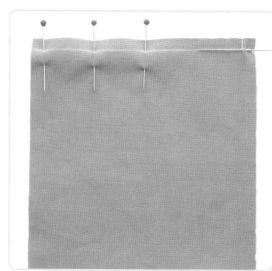

**2** Remove the first pin and take the needle through both the front and the back units at that point. Secure the thread with a knot or take a couple of tiny backstitches into the seam allowance.

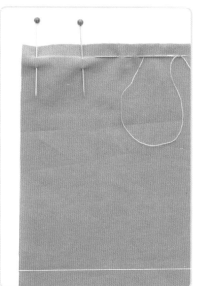

**3** Take several short running stitches along the seam line, then pull the needle through. Repeat along the length of the seam, removing pins as you work.

**4** From time to time, check the back of the fabric to make sure that your stitches are on the seam line on both sides. Stop at the end point marked with a pin in Step 1. Finish with a couple of backstitches to secure the thread.

# Joining hand-pieced rows

When joining rows of hand-pieced units together, you must avoid sewing into the seam allowances, just as you did when hand piecing two units together (see Joining two units with a straight seam, opposite).

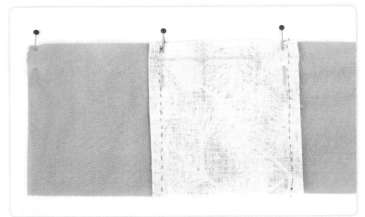

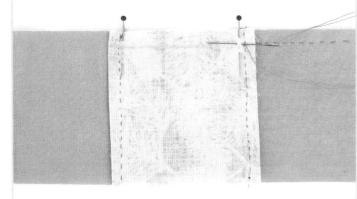

1 Place two rows of hand-pieced units with right sides together. Match the seam lines front and back, and pin through both layers at each corner at the start and end points (see Step 1, opposite). Align the seam lines and pin at intervals to hold the rows in place.

2 Start sewing at one end, working as for straight seams (see opposite), until you reach the first seam intersection. Sew through the start and end points but do not sew across the seam allowance.

3 Make your first stitch in the second pair of units a backstitch right next to the seam allowance.

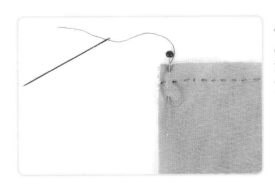

4 Continue in this way to the end of the row. Secure your stitches with a backstitched loop (see p.42).

(see p.42)

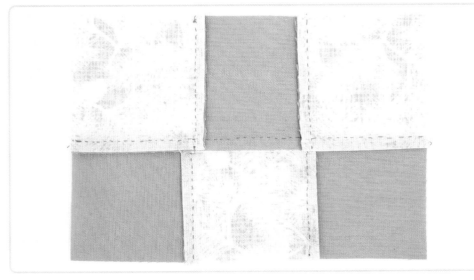

5 Open the joined rows out and press the seams on each row to opposite sides. Press the just-completed seam to one side.

# Machine piecing

Sewing patchwork pieces by machine is a quick way of assembling a piece. As for hand piecing, always make sure that your fabrics are aligned with right sides facing and with raw edges matching. Leave a ¼in (6mm) seam allowance unless otherwise specified, and use a standard straight stitch.

## Joining two or more strips

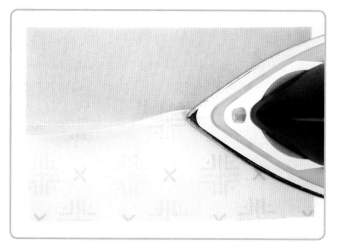

1 Place two strips of fabric right sides together, raw edges aligned. Sew a straight ¼in (6mm) seam along the length of the strip.

2 Press the seam toward the darker fabric.

3 When piecing several strips together, each time you add a strip, reverse the direction of your sewing; this helps to keep the strips straight and prevents the fabric from bowing. The seams should all be pressed in the same direction. The pieced strip can be cut into pieced units, which can then be combined to make a new pattern.

# Checking seam allowances

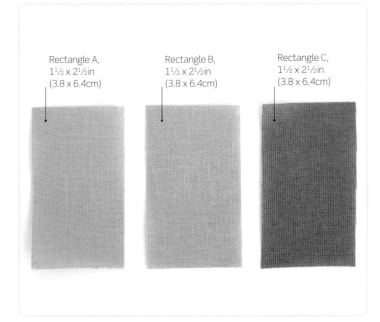

Rectangle A,
1½ x 2½in
(3.8 x 6.4cm)

Rectangle B,
1½ x 2½in
(3.8 x 6.4cm)

Rectangle C,
1½ x 2½in
(3.8 x 6.4cm)

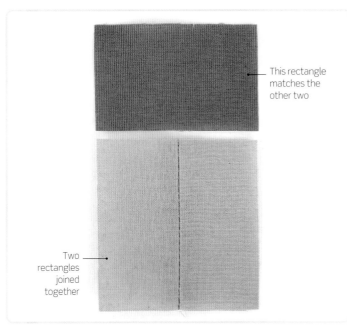

This rectangle matches the other two

Two rectangles joined together

1 When sewing any pattern, for your finished pieces to fit together well, it is important to ensure you sew using the correct seam allowance. One way to check that your machine is sewing a standard ¼in (6mm) seam allowance is to cut three pieces of fabric, A, B, and C, each 1½ x 2½in (3.8 x 6.4cm).

2 Pin and sew rectangles A and B, right sides together, along their long edges. Press the seam to one side. If your seam allowance is accurate, rectangle C should be an exact size match to the joined pieces, as shown. If it is not, adjust the needle position until the seam allowance is accurate.

# Chain piecing

1 Place the pairs of units to be joined right sides together, then feed them through the machine in sequence without lifting the presser foot or breaking the thread. You will have a chain of units with a short length of thread between each.

2 Snip the units in the chain apart using a small pair of sharp scissors.

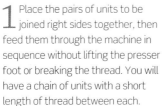

# Patchwork strip pillow

This super simple, visually appealing pillow can be made in less than an hour.
Depending on the fabrics you choose, the design possibilities are endless and can
produce any number of different effects. Try fussy cutting some of the patches.

## Essential Information

**DIFFICULTY** Easy

**SIZE** 16 x 16in (40 x 40cm)

**TOOLS AND MATERIALS**
Rotary cutter
Cutting mat
Quilter's ruler
Sewing machine
Threads to match your fabrics
Pins
Iron and ironing board
Scissors
Pillow cushion 16 x 16in (40 x 40cm)

**FABRICS**
Nine scraps of coordinating fabric to make nine
   squares, 2½ x 2½in (6.5 x 6.5cm) each
35½ x 16½in (90 x 42cm) main fabric

**SKILLS**
Joining two or more strips (see p.62)

**SEAM ALLOWANCE**
¼in (6mm) throughout, unless otherwise stated

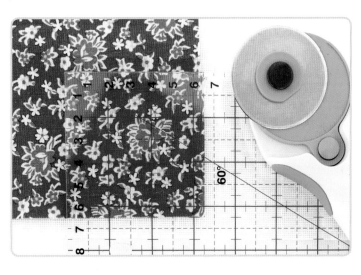

1 Cut nine scraps of coordinating fabric, each 2½in (6.5cm) square. Use the rotary cutter, mat, and quilter's ruler to make sure that each piece is perfectly square. If there is a particular part of a fabric that you'd like to appear in the center of a square, center it as you cut (see p.40, Fussy cutting).

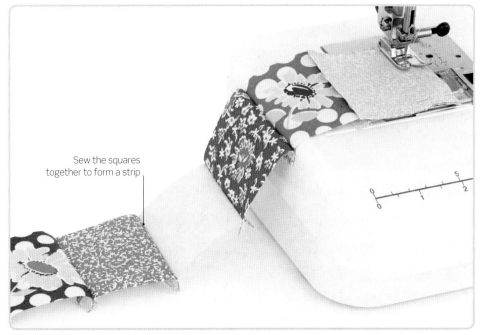

Sew the squares together to form a strip

2 Join the nine fabric squares into a patchwork strip (see p.62) in the order you'd like to see them. Place each square in turn right sides together with the next square, pin along the edges to be joined, and sew them together. Secure each seam at the end with a few backstitches.

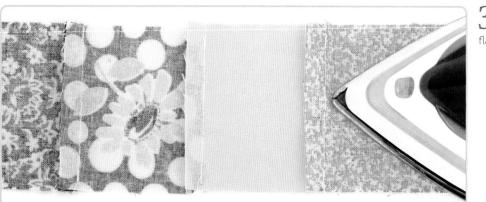

**3** Lay the strip facedown and press the seams flat to one side.

Press the seam toward the main fabric

**4** Cut the two panels for the pillow front from the main fabric, one 9½ x 16½in (24 x 42cm) and another 5½ x 16½in (14 x 42cm). With right sides together, pin the long edge of the patchwork strip to one of the long edges of a front panel. Sew along the edge.

**5** Open up the two pieces and on the wrong side of the fabric, press the seam toward the main fabric. With right sides together, pin the other long edge of the patchwork strip to one of the long edges of the other front panel. Sew along the edge.

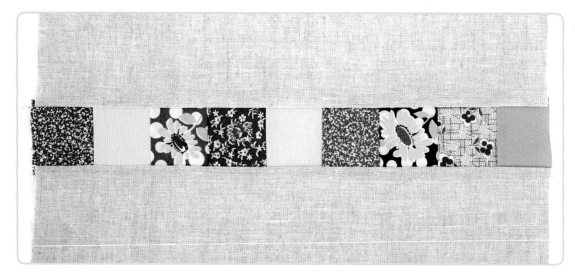

**6** Open up the two pieces and on the wrong side press the seam toward the main fabric. You have now completed the pillow front.

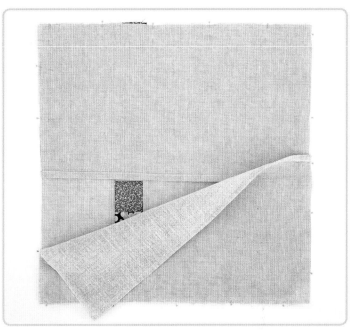

7 To make the pillow back, cut two pieces from the main fabric, each 16½ x 10 in (42 x 26cm). Fold one of the long edges of one piece to the wrong side of the fabric by ³⁄₈in (1cm). Fold it again by the same amount to create a neat hem. To enclose the raw edge, pin the hem in place, checking that it is straight, then sew along the edge of the second fold to secure the hem. Repeat on the other piece of fabric.

8 Lay the pillow front, right side up. Place one of the back pieces on top, right side down, aligning its long, unhemmed edge with the top raw edge of the pillow front. Place the second back piece right-side down on top of the first, aligning its long, unhemmed edge with the bottom raw edge of the pillow front. The two back pieces should overlap. Pin along all four edges.

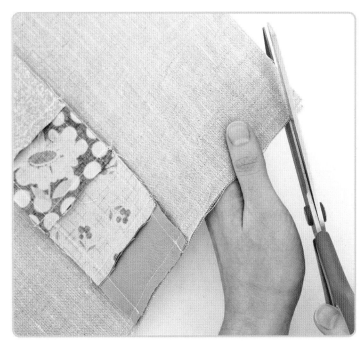

9 Leaving a ³⁄₈in (1cm) seam allowance, sew around all four edges of the pillow cover to secure the back pieces to the pillow front. Forward and backstitch over the hemmed, overlapping edges of the flaps to secure them in place. Remove the pins as you work.

10 Snip off all four corners, making sure not to cut through the stitches. Turn the pillow cover to the right side through the opening in the back. Iron, then insert the pillow cushion.

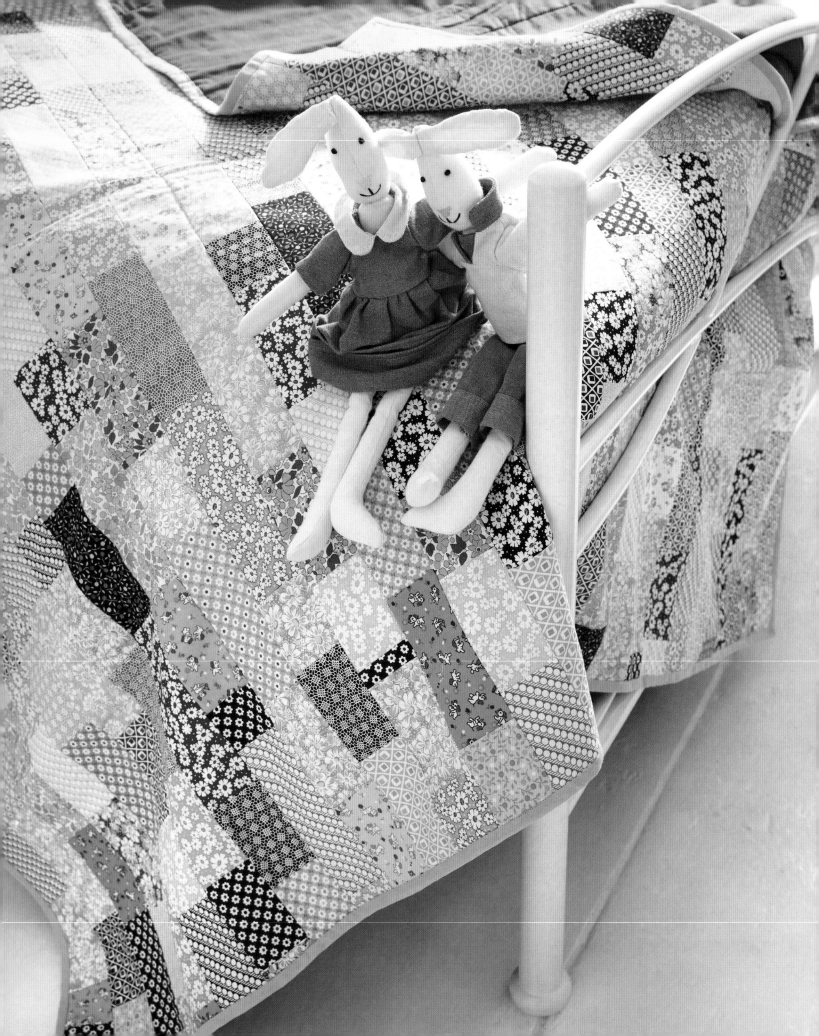

# Brick quilt

Piecing simple strips together is a great way for a beginner to get into patchwork. You get fast results without having to master any complicated techniques. This colorful single quilt is set off beautifully by its contrast backing and bias trim.

## Essential Information

**DIFFICULTY** Easy

**SIZE** 49 x 57in (125 x 145cm)

**TOOLS AND MATERIALS**
Measuring tape
Quilter's ruler
Rotary cutter
Cutting mat
Pins
Sewing machine
Threads to match your fabrics
Scissors
Iron and ironing board
Safety pins
Sewing needle

**FABRICS**
1 fabric Jelly Roll™
220in (560cm) pre-made bias binding or
    18 x 44in (46 x 112cm) fabric for double-fold
    binding
140 x 44in (356 x 112cm) backing fabric
55 x 64in (140 x 160cm) batting

**SKILLS**
Piecing strips (see p.62)
Chain piecing (see p.63)
Making a bigger backing (see p.47)
Binding (see pp.50–53)
Quilting in the ditch (see p.211)

**SEAM ALLOWANCE**
¼in (6mm) throughout, unless otherwise stated

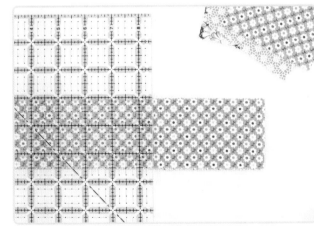

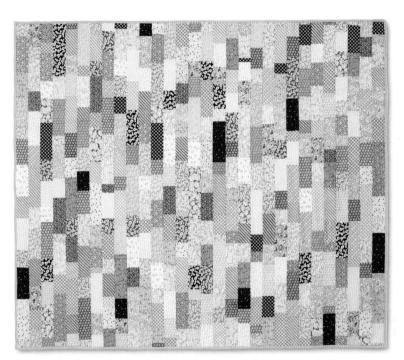

**1** Cut the Jelly Roll™ strips into a variety of random lengths of 2-10in (5-25cm), with most pieces about 5in (12cm) long. Use the quilter's ruler to make sure you cut them with straight, square edges. You can lay several strips on top of each other and cut them all at the same time.

Wrong side

Right side

Pin and sew along the shorter edge

2 With right sides together, pair each fabric strip with a strip of a different length and pattern. Align the short edges and pin together. When each piece has been paired, chain piece them together (see p.63).

3 Using scissors, cut the paired pieces apart by snipping through the short length of thread between them.

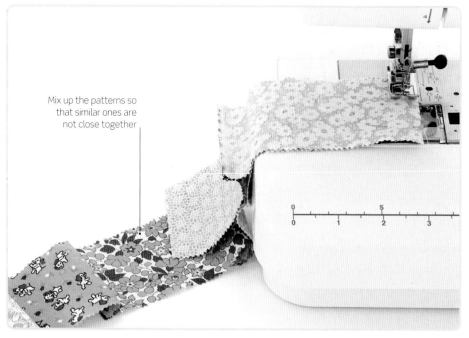

Mix up the patterns so that similar ones are not close together

4 With right sides together and aligning the short edges, sew each paired piece to another paired piece. Make sure that the same fabrics are not next to each other. Join all the paired pieces to form one long strip.

5 Press the strip. Using the measuring tape, cut the long strip into 49in (125cm) lengths. You should have about 30 strips, depending on the amount of fabric taken up by the seams.

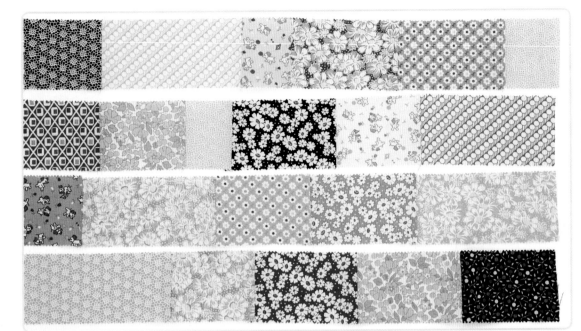

6 Lay the strips out on a large, flat surface and arrange them in a pleasing order in rows. Plan the layout of your pieces to make a quilt top that will be roughly 49 x 57in (125 x 145cm). Make sure the same fabrics are not placed together. When you are happy with the arrangement, turn each strip over and press the seams of each strip in the same direction.

7 Working from one edge of your arrangement and with right sides together, pin the first two strips together along their length. Sew them, leaving a ¼in (6mm) seam allowance. Join five strips together in this way, then repeat until you have about six pieces, each consisting of five joined strips. Your final number of pieces will depend on the number of strips you started with.

8 Join one piece to another, right sides facing, and sew them together. Repeat until all six pieces are joined. Turn the quilt over and press the seams open. The quilt top is now complete.

*The layout of the quilt is random so just arrange the strips in a pleasing order.*

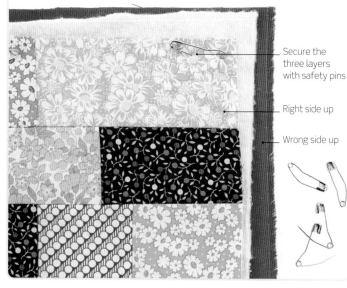

Secure the three layers with safety pins

Right side up

Wrong side up

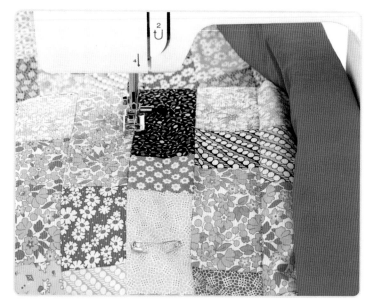

9 Lay the backing fabric on a large, clean, flat surface with the batting on top. Smooth out the two to make sure they are not bunched or folded, then lay the quilt top on the batting (see p.46). The batting and backing fabric will both extend slightly beyond the edges of the quilt top. Starting from the center and working outward, pin all three layers together using safety pins. Make sure that all the layers lie flat and check that the underside of the backing fabric also lies flat.

10 Quilt the top according to your preference. Here, we have quilted in the ditch (see p.211) along every sixth strip. Roll up the end of the quilt in the throat area of the sewing machine to keep it out of the way as you work. Remove any safety pins that get in the way as you work.

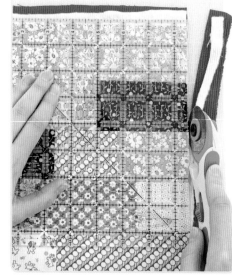

13 Fold the binding to the back of the quilt, pin it in place, then sew it by hand, slip stitching it in place (see p.51).

11 Using the quilter's ruler and the rotary cutter, trim away the excess batting and backing fabric from the edges of the quilt.

12 Attach the bias tape, if used, to the edge of the quilt following the instructions on pages 50–51. Or create a 3in (7.5cm) wide double-fold binding strip from fabric and attach it using the Double-fold binding technique on page 53.

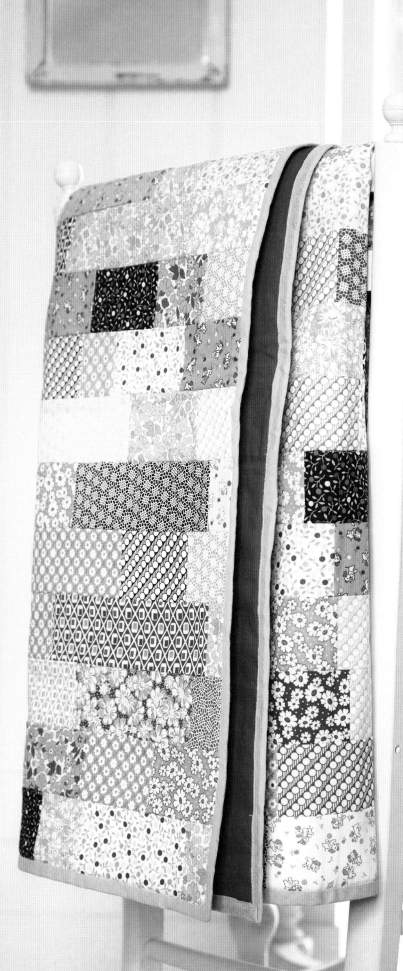

**Use a bright, solid color** for the backing fabric to contrast with the patchwork on top.

# Sewing intersecting seams

When sewing together any two pieces of patchwork, it is important to match the seams so that they align perfectly with the seams on the adjoining piece. By pressing the seams in opposite directions and fitting them into one another, known as nesting, you can create smooth, accurate seams without any gaps or misalignments.

## Matching straight seams

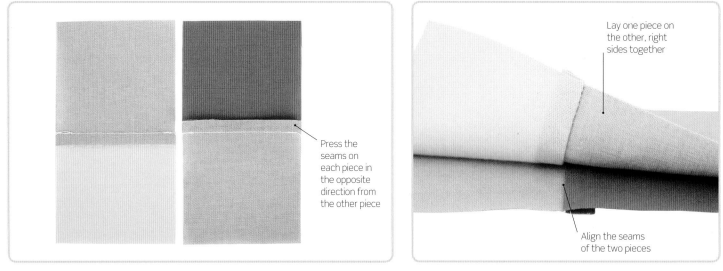

Press the seams on each piece in the opposite direction from the other piece

Lay one piece on the other, right sides together

Align the seams of the two pieces

1 After piecing plain squares or rectangles together, press the seams on each strip to be joined in the opposite direction from the seams on the strip it will be joined to.

2 Place the pieces right sides together, making sure to align the seams.

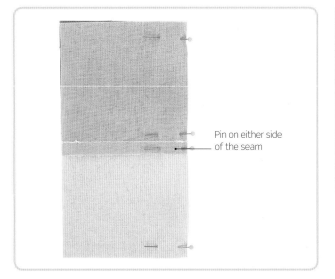

Pin on either side of the seam

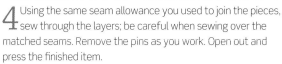

3 Nest the seams by running your finger over the spot where all four pieces of fabric meet, to feel for any gaps. Make sure that opposite seams butt right up against one another smoothly. Carefully pin on either side of the nested seams. If there are multiple joins along the two pieces, match each point, then work outward from each pinned seam, toward the ends.

4 Using the same seam allowance you used to join the pieces, sew through the layers; be careful when sewing over the matched seams. Remove the pins as you work. Open out and press the finished item.

# Matching seams with points

When joining pieces of patchwork that have points, it is important to match the seams correctly, so as not to lose the points in the seam.

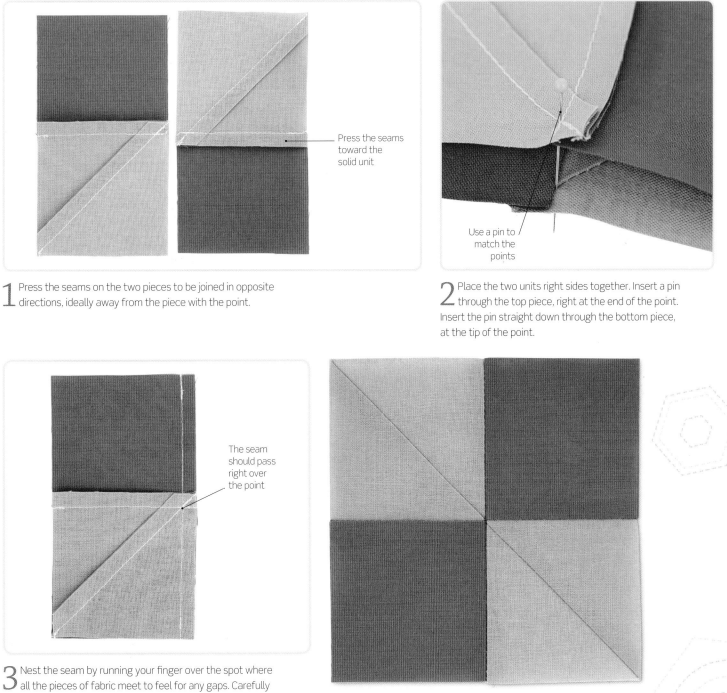

Press the seams toward the solid unit

1 Press the seams on the two pieces to be joined in opposite directions, ideally away from the piece with the point.

Use a pin to match the points

2 Place the two units right sides together. Insert a pin through the top piece, right at the end of the point. Insert the pin straight down through the bottom piece, at the tip of the point.

The seam should pass right over the point

3 Nest the seam by running your finger over the spot where all the pieces of fabric meet to feel for any gaps. Carefully pin on either side of the seam to be matched, then continue pinning, working outward. Sew along the seam using the same seam allowance previously used to join the pieces. Remove the pins as you work.

4 Open out the piece and press.

# Simple squares tote

This cheerful tote bag is perfect for running errands, heading to the beach, or carrying your quilting supplies while you are on the go. The bag is assembled using a simple, square patchwork pattern with no quilting needed.

## Essential Information

**DIFFICULTY** Medium

**SIZE** 12 x 8¾ x 6in (30 x 22.5 x 15cm)

**TOOLS AND MATERIALS**

Measuring tape
Rotary cutter or scissors
Cutting mat (optional)
Quilter's ruler
Pins
Threads to match your fabrics
Sewing machine
Iron and ironing board
Sewing needle
One 1⅜in (3.5cm) button

**FABRICS**

**A, B, C, D, E, F, G, H , I:** Assorted scraps of cotton fabric for the patchwork squares to make a total of 44 squares, each 3¾in (9.5cm)

**J:** 20in (50cm) of 44in (112cm) wide cotton fabric for the lining

**K:** 12in (30cm) of 44in (112cm) wide cotton fabric for the straps

**L:** 5½ x 7in (14 x 18cm) cotton fabric for the button flap

**SKILLS**

Piecing (see pp.60–62)
Sewing intersecting seams (see pp.74–75)

**SEAM ALLOWANCE**

⅜in (1cm) throughout, unless otherwise stated

### Front and back of bag (cut two batches of 18 squares)

| A | B | C | D | E | G | Top row |
|---|---|---|---|---|---|---|
| C | H | I | F | A | H | Middle row |
| E | F | D | H | G | I | Bottom row |

### Bottom of bag (cut one batch of 8 squares)

| A | E | B | D |
|---|---|---|---|
| H | F | I | G |

**Cut the patchwork squares** using the diagrams as a guide to how many squares of each fabric are needed and how to lay them out. Remember to cut squares for both the front and back of the bag. You only need to cut one batch of squares for the bottom of the bag.

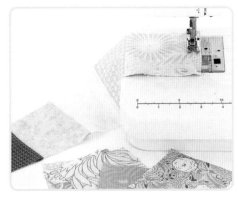

**1** Following the diagrams above, cut a total of 44 squares of fabric, each 3¾in (9.5cm) square. With right sides together, sew together the squares for the top and middle rows of the front and back of the bag making four strips of six squares each.

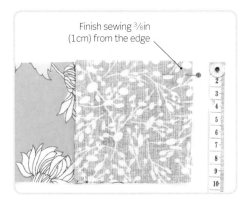

Finish sewing ⅜in (1cm) from the edge

**2** With the right sides together, sew together the squares for the bottom row of the front and the bottom row of the back of the bag. Mark with a pin ⅜in (1cm) from the lower edge of the first and last squares in each row and make sure not to sew beyond the pins.

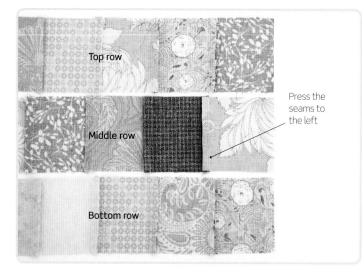

Top row

Middle row

Bottom row

Press the seams to the left

**3** With wrong sides facing up, press the seams of the top and bottom rows to the right, and of the middle row to the left.

**4** To make the front, with right sides together, pin, then sew the top and middle rows together, matching the seams. Pin and sew the bottom row to the middle row in the same way. Repeat to make the back. Press the seams of the front downward and the seams of the back upward.

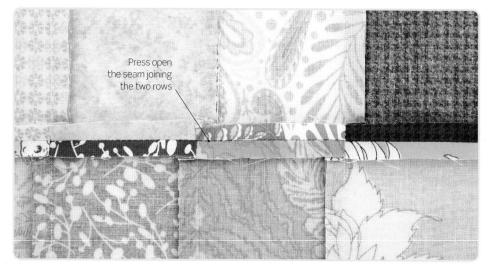

Press open the seam joining the two rows

**5** With right sides together, sew together the squares for the bottom in two rows of four squares. Pin, then sew the two rows together, matching the seams. With the wrong side facing up, press this seam open.

Do not sew beyond the first and last pins

**6** With right sides together, pin the lower edge of the front of the bag to one long edge of the base, matching the center seams. Sew together, making sure not to sew beyond the pins marked in Step 2. Sew the lower edge of the back of the bag to the other long edge of the bottom in the same way. Press the seams away from the bottom.

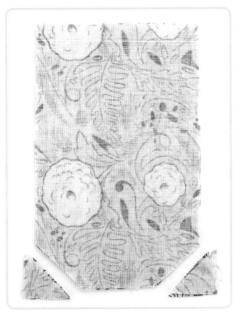

7 Cut a pair of button flaps from fabric L using the template (see p.292). With right sides together, pin, then sew them together, leaving the upper edge open. Clip the corners as shown above.

8 Turn the flap to the right side and press. Sew a buttonhole in the flap, large enough to accommodate your chosen button (see p.220).

9 Cut two 36 x 3½in (90 x 9cm) strips of fabric K to make the straps. With right sides together, fold the strips in half lengthwise and pin the raw edges together. Sew, then turn to the right side and press.

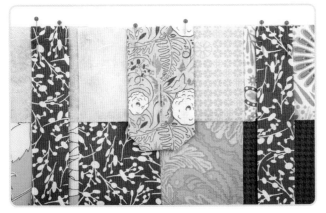

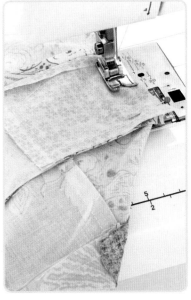

10 With right sides together, pin the open edge of the flap to the center of the upper edge of the back of the bag and pin the end of each strap 2¼in (5.5cm) on either side of the flap. Baste all the raw edges together.

11 With right sides together, fold the bag in half along the center seam of the bottom. Pin both sides of the front and back of the bag together, matching the seams. Sew the sides together, then press the seams open.

12 Bring the raw lower edges of the front and back of the bag to meet the short edges of the bottom. Match the bag's side seams to the center seam of the bottom. Pin, then sew between the ends of the seams that were sewn in Step 6. Turn the bag to the right side.

## Make the lining

Leave a 6¼in (16cm) gap on one side edge

**13** Cut two 18¾ x 12¾in (47 x 32cm) rectangles of lining fabric. Pin them together with right sides facing. Sew along one long side—the bottom edge—and along the two short sides, leaving a 6¼in (16cm) opening along one short side, 1½in (4cm) from the upper edge.

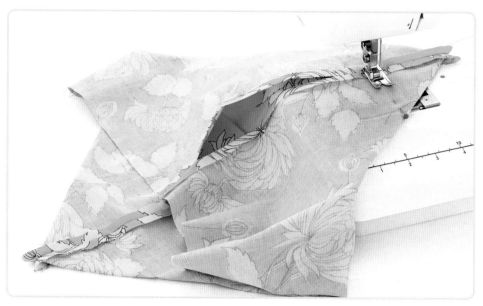

**14** To shape the lining to fit the bottom of the bag, with right sides of the lining facing, bring the lower part of one side seam to the adjacent part of the seam along the bottom of the lining. Starting at the corner where these seams intersect, measure and mark a point 6in (15cm) away. Sew across the lining, perpendicular to this mark, creating a triangle at the corner. Repeat on the opposite side of the lining.

**15** Trim the seam allowances to ⅜in (1cm) and cut off the triangles, as shown.

**16** Insert the bag into the lining with right sides facing. Pin the upper raw edges together, matching the side seams. Remove the base of the sewing machine, then slip the bag over the sewing machine bed and sew along the upper edge.

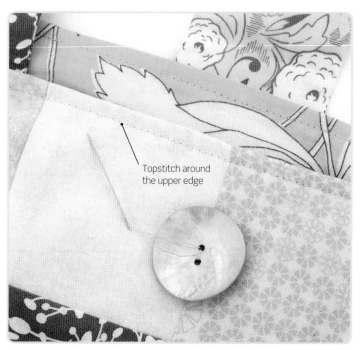

Topstitch around
the upper edge

**17** Turn the bag to the right side through the opening in the side of the lining. Slip stitch (see p.43) the opening in the lining closed. Press the lining to the inside.

**18** Topstitch the bag ¼in (6mm) below the upper edge to keep the lining inside the bag. Sew the button to the center seam of the top row of patchwork on the front of the bag, 1½in (4cm) below the upper edge.

**It's important to match** all the seams as you sew so that the patchwork squares align once your bag is complete.

# Triangles

Triangles form the basis of many patchwork units and, after squares and rectangles, are the next easiest and most versatile to work with. They can be combined with other triangle units or with plain units to create a wide range of blocks. Triangle units also make a wonderful impact when used in sashings and borders.

## Making a pair of half-square triangles

While a half-square triangle, which is a square made of two right-angled triangles, can be made by sewing two triangles together, a faster way is to start with two squares and use the method below.

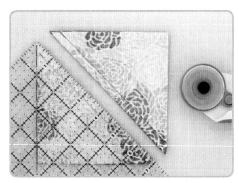
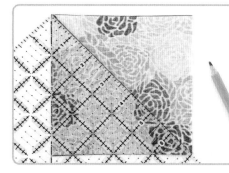

1 Cut two squares, each ⅞in (2.2cm) larger than the desired finished size and place them right sides together, with the lighter color on top.

2 Using a pencil, mark a diagonal line in one direction across the wrong side of the lighter-colored square.

3 Pin, then sew by machine along each side of the marked line, sewing ¼in (6mm) from the line.

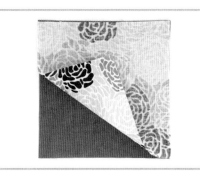
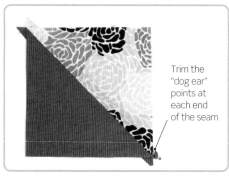

4 Using a rotary cutter or scissors, cut along the pencil line.

Trim the "dog ear" points at each end of the seam

5 Open out the pieces of fabric and press the seams, usually toward the darker fabric, to make two identical half-square triangles.

## Making multiple half-square triangles from strips

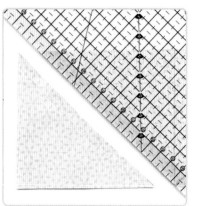

1 Start by cutting fabric strips that are the desired width plus ⅞in (2.2cm). Place them right sides together and mark squares on the wrong side of the lighter fabric. Draw a diagonal line across each square, alternating the direction of the line in each square.

2 Sew a ¼in (6mm) seam on each side of the marked diagonal lines. Cut along the marked diagonal and vertical lines to separate the half-square triangles. Press the seams toward the darker fabric.

## Making multiple half-square triangles from large pieces

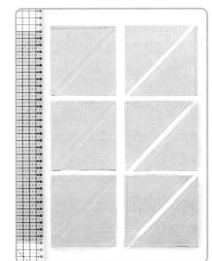

**1** You can also make multiple half-square triangles by placing two large pieces of fabric right sides together and marking a grid of squares, each ⅞in (2.2cm) larger than the finished size you want.

**2** Mark a diagonal in one direction across each square.

**3** Sew a ¼in (6mm) seam on each side of the marked diagonal lines. Cut along the marked diagonal and vertical lines to separate the half-square triangles. Then press all the seams toward the darker fabric.

## Making a pair of quarter-square triangles

Quarter-square triangles can be quickly made using the technique below. Start by making two half-square triangles using one of the techniques already described opposite and above. Begin with two squares each 1⅜in (2.75cm) larger than the desired finished size.

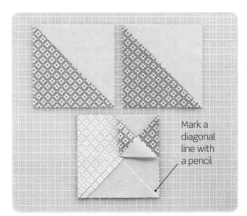

Mark a diagonal line with a pencil

**1** Place the two half-square triangles right sides together, with the seams aligned and the contrasting fabrics face to face.

**2** Using a pencil, mark a diagonal line from corner to corner in the opposite direction from the seam line that is on top. Sew a ¼in (6mm) seam on each side of the marked line.

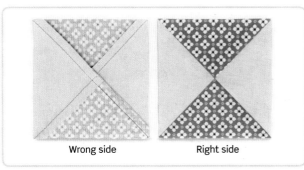

Wrong side          Right side

**3** Cut the units apart along the marked diagonal lines and press.

## Joining pieced and plain units

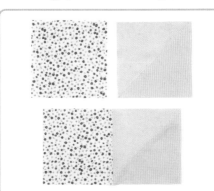

**1** Place one half-square triangle (the pieced unit) and one plain unit right sides together. Sew together, leaving a ¼in (6mm) seam allowance. On the right side, the corner of the half-square triangle will disappear in the seam allowance ¼in (6mm) from the raw edge. Repeat for the other pieced and plain unit.

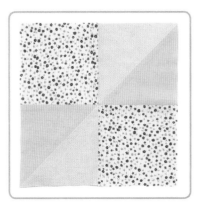

**2** Combining two pairs of joined pieced and plain units, as shown, will accommodate the seam allowances and their corners will meet exactly in the center of the four units.

# Equilateral triangles

Joining equilateral triangles requires slightly off setting each triangle using the "dog ears" left by the previous seam. This will ensure that the finished row is straight and even.

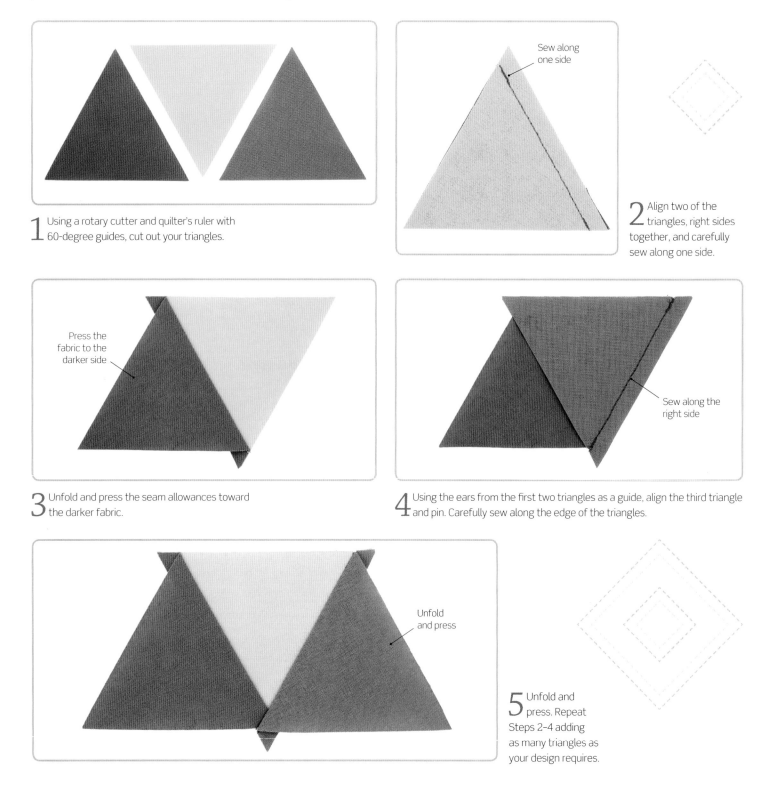

**1** Using a rotary cutter and quilter's ruler with 60-degree guides, cut out your triangles.

Sew along one side

**2** Align two of the triangles, right sides together, and carefully sew along one side.

Press the fabric to the darker side

**3** Unfold and press the seam allowances toward the darker fabric.

Sew along the right side

**4** Using the ears from the first two triangles as a guide, align the third triangle and pin. Carefully sew along the edge of the triangles.

Unfold and press

**5** Unfold and press. Repeat Steps 2–4 adding as many triangles as your design requires.

# Flying geese

Flying geese blocks are an easily adaptable and versatile design. They can be added to the borders of blocks to add more visual interest or can be used as a block on their own. They are often used to make star points in blocks.

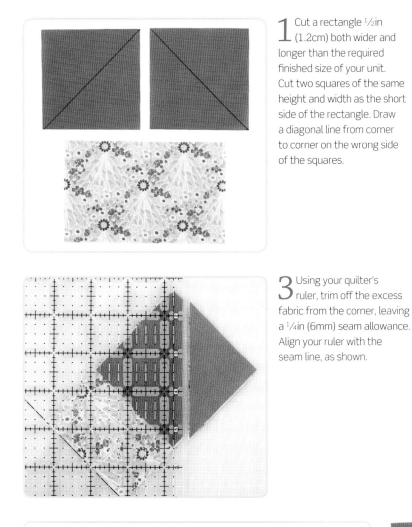

1 Cut a rectangle ½in (1.2cm) both wider and longer than the required finished size of your unit. Cut two squares of the same height and width as the short side of the rectangle. Draw a diagonal line from corner to corner on the wrong side of the squares.

2 Pin the square to the left side of the rectangle, right sides together, with the diagonal line positioned as shown. Carefully sew along the line.

3 Using your quilter's ruler, trim off the excess fabric from the corner, leaving a ¼in (6mm) seam allowance. Align your ruler with the seam line, as shown.

Unfold and press

4 Unfold and press the unit.

Sew through the line

5 Repeat the process on the right side of the rectangle, positioning the second square as shown. Pin in place and sew along the line.

Trim the excess and press

6 Trim away the excess as in Step 3 and press the seams open.

# Triangle corners

Triangle corners are made the same way as Flying geese (see p.85), but four corners are added around a square instead of two to a rectangle. This can be a good method of adding a border around a completed block, to tilt it on its point.

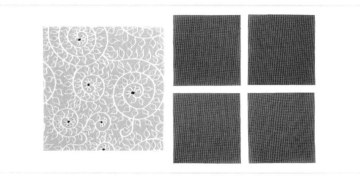

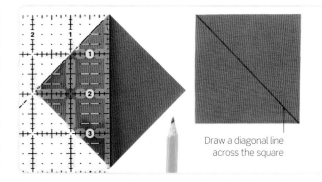

Draw a diagonal line across the square

1 Cut one large square from a fabric to the required size. Cut four squares, each half the size of the larger square, plus ¼in (6mm) extra, from another fabric. Here we have used a 3½in (9cm) large square and four 2in (5.1cm) small squares.

2 Draw diagonal lines on the wrong side of the smaller squares, as shown.

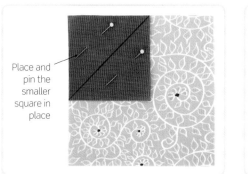

Place and pin the smaller square in place

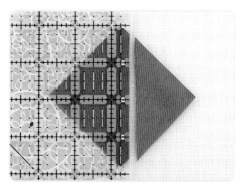

Sew through the diagonal line

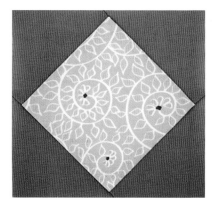

3 Place and pin the smaller square on the upper left corner of the larger square with the diagonal line as shown.

4 Carefully sew through the diagonal line of the smaller square.

5 Using a rotary cutter and quilter's ruler, trim off the excess fabric, leaving a ¼in (6mm) seam allowance.

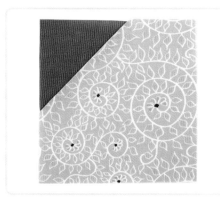

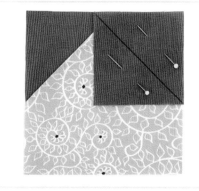

6 Unfold the smaller square and press into position.

7 Repeat the process on the remaining three corners, working clockwise.

8 With the right side facing up, press flat.

# Sewing triangles to squares

Attaching triangles to squares can be difficult, especially as the edges of the triangle may be cut on the bias. Follow Steps 2–4 below to attach one triangle to a square, but if you'd like to add them all around a square to create a block, complete the entire sequence.

Mark the middle of the triangle base

Mark the middle of the square edge

Trim off the excess fabric

Sew along the top edge

1 Cut a square of your required size, then cut triangles with a long side of the same width, plus ¼in (6mm) extra. Make marks in the center of all four sides of the square and the longest edge of each of the triangles.

2 With right sides together, place a triangle along the top edge of the square, aligning the center points. Make sure the triangle is centered along the edge so the side points overhang by equal amounts.

3 Carefully sew along the top edge using a ¼in (6mm) seam allowance. Trim off the excess fabric on the sides to square up the block.

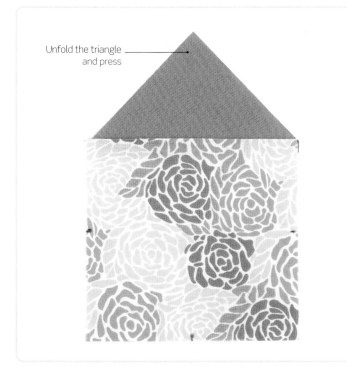

Unfold the triangle and press

Attach all the triangles and press flat

4 Unfold the triangle and press the seam toward the square.

5 Repeat the process, working clockwise, until all four sides of the center square have a triangle attached. Press flat.

# Star blocks

Star designs make up the largest group of patchwork patterns. They range from simple four-patch blocks to highly elaborate blocks with multiple star points. Making them combines many techniques. The following patterns are the starting points for numerous variations.

## Single star: Double four-patch

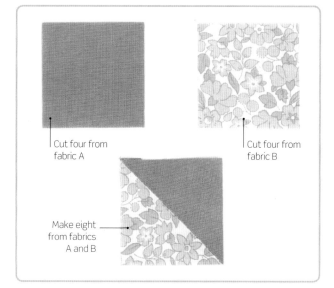

Cut four from fabric A

Cut four from fabric B

Make eight from fabrics A and B

**1** Divide the size of the finished block by four. Add seam allowances. Cut and make eight half-square triangles from fabrics A and B (see p.82). Cut an additional four squares each of fabric A and fabric B.

**2** Following the layout and with right sides together, sew the squares and half-square triangles together in rows of four, leaving a 1/4in (6mm) seam allowance.

**3** With right sides together, sew the rows together, matching the seams and leaving a 1/4in (6mm) seam allowance.

# Friendship star: Nine-patch

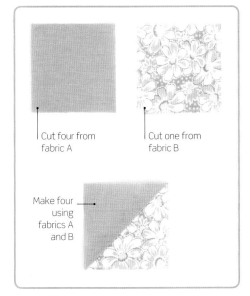

Cut four from fabric A

Cut one from fabric B

Make four using fabrics A and B

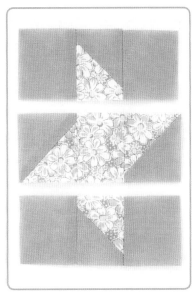

1 Divide the size of the finished block by three. Add seam allowances. Cut four squares from fabric A and one square from fabric B. Make four half-square triangles from fabrics A and B (see p.82).

2 Following the layout and with right sides together, sew the squares and half-square triangles together in rows of three, leaving a ¼in (6mm) seam allowance.

3 With right sides together, sew the rows together, matching the seams and leaving a ¼in (6mm) seam allowance.

# Ohio star: Nine-patch with quarter-square triangles

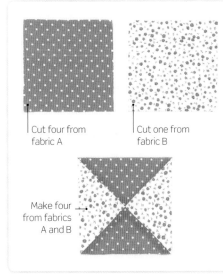

Cut four from fabric A

Cut one from fabric B

Make four from fabrics A and B

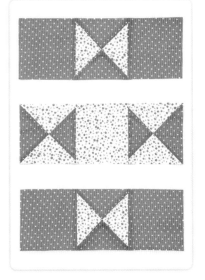

1 Divide the size of the finished block by three. Add seam allowances. Cut four squares from fabric A and one square from fabric B. Make four quarter-square triangles from fabrics A and B (see p.83).

2 Following the layout and with right sides together, sew the squares and quarter-square triangles together in rows of three, leaving a ¼in (6mm) seam allowance.

3 With right sides together, sew the rows together, matching the seams and leaving a ¼in (6mm) seam allowance.

# Hexagon star: 60-degree angles

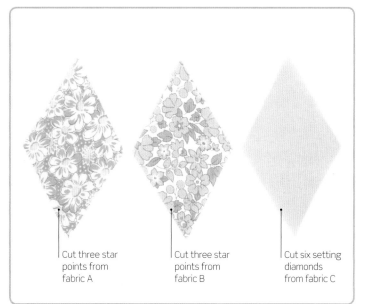

Cut three star points from fabric A

Cut three star points from fabric B

Cut six setting diamonds from fabric C

1 Cut twelve 60-degree-angle diamonds, as above. Those in fabrics A and B will be the points of the star, and those in fabric C will be the setting diamonds. Add a seam allowance all around each diamond.

2 With wrong sides together, sew the three star points together in units of three, alternating the fabrics as above.

3 With wrong sides together, sew the units together to make the star.

4 Set in the setting diamonds (see pp.100–101) to complete the block.

# Eight-point star: 45-degree angles

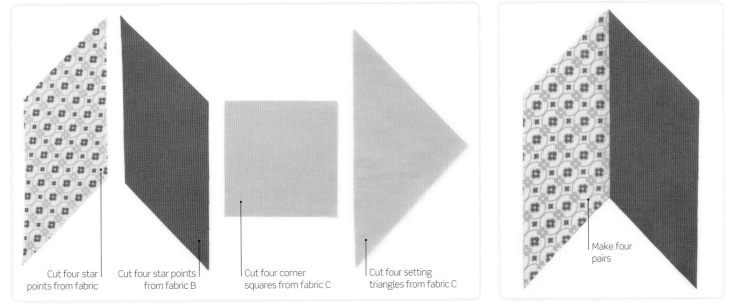

Cut four star points from fabric

Cut four star points from fabric B

Cut four corner squares from fabric C

Cut four setting triangles from fabric C

**1** Make templates to the desired size for the points of the star, the corner squares, and the setting triangles. Cut four 45-degree-angle diamonds (see p.39) each from fabrics A and B for the points of the star, and four corner squares (see p.37) and four setting triangles (see p.39) from fabric C.

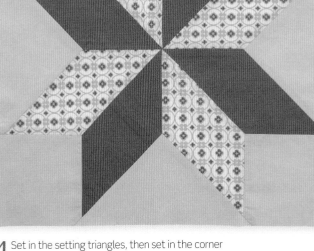

Make four pairs

**2** With right sides together, sew the star points together in four identical pairs, using one fabric A point and one fabric B point for each pair.

**3** With right sides together, sew two pairs together to make half the star, repeat to make the other half, then sew the two halves together to complete the star.

**4** Set in the setting triangles, then set in the corner squares (see pp.100–101) to complete the block.

# Triangle floor pillow

This floor pillow will show off your patchworking skills. It is easier to make than you might think, since it involves repeating the same techniques and building up the pattern a little at a time. It's simple to substitute colors and fabrics of your choice.

## Essential Information

**DIFFICULTY** Medium

**SIZE** 26 x 26in (65 x 65cm)

**TOOLS AND MATERIALS**
Tracing paper
Felt-tip pen
Pins
Quilter's ruler
Scissors
Rotary cutter
Cutting mat
Threads to match your fabrics
Sewing machine
Iron and ironing board
Contrasting thread for basting
Sewing needle
20in (51cm) zipper
26in (65cm) square pillow cushion

**FABRICS**
31½ x 44in (80 x 112cm) blue cotton fabric
16 x 44in (40 x 112cm) aqua cotton fabric
8 x 44in (20 x 112cm) pale green cotton fabric
8 x 44in (20 x 112cm) jade green cotton fabric

**SKILLS**
Sewing triangles (see pp.82-83)
Sashings and borders (see pp.108-113)

**SEAM ALLOWANCE**
⅜in (1cm) throughout, unless otherwise stated

**Pillow layout**

First sashing

Second sashing

Third sashing

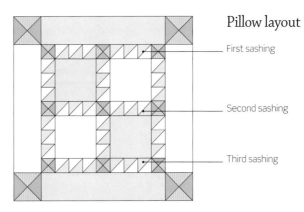

**1** Trace the templates (see p.292) onto the tracing paper and cut them out. From each of the blue and aqua fabrics, cut 36 medium triangles, two 6¾in (17cm) squares, and two 18¾ x 4¾in (47 x 12cm) rectangles for the borders. From each of the pale green and jade green fabrics, cut 18 small triangles and eight large triangles. Cut two 26¾ x 14in (67 x 35cm) rectangles from the blue fabric; these are the two back pieces of the pillow cover.

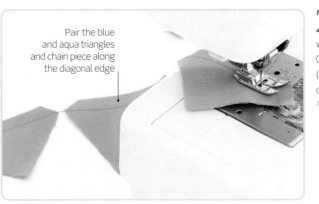

Pair the blue and aqua triangles and chain piece along the diagonal edge

**2** With right sides together, pair up a medium blue triangle with a medium aqua triangle. Chain piece them together (see p.63) along the long, diagonal edges, leaving a ⅜in (1cm) seam allowance.

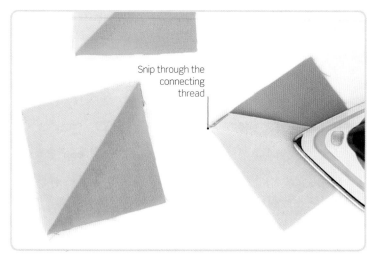

Snip through the
connecting
thread

**3** Using scissors, cut the paired pieces apart by snipping through the short length of thread between them. Press the seams toward the darker triangles. You will have 36 half-square triangles.

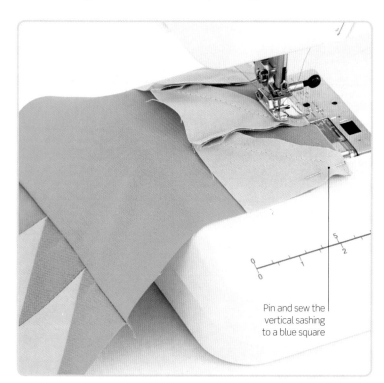

Pin and sew the
vertical sashing
to a blue square

**5** With right sides together, pin a vertical sashing to each of the two opposite sides of a blue square so the blue triangles of the sashing adjoin the blue square. Sew, leaving a ³⁄₈in (1cm) seam allowance, then press the seams toward the square.

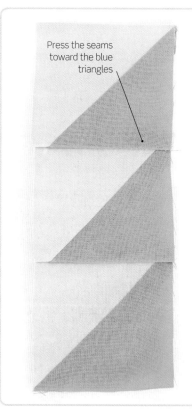

Press the seams
toward the blue
triangles

**4** Lay three of the half-square triangles in a vertical row with the aqua triangles on the left-hand side. With right sides together, sew the half-square triangles together, leaving a ³⁄₈in (1cm) seam allowance. Press the seams toward the darker triangles. Repeat to make a total of six rows. These are the vertical sashings.

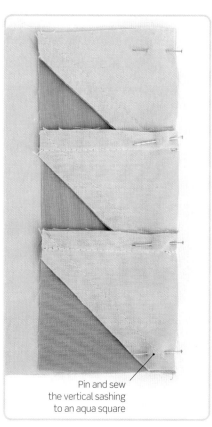

Pin and sew
the vertical sashing
to an aqua square

**6** With right sides together, pin a vertical sashing to the right-hand edge of an aqua square so the aqua triangles of the sashing adjoin the aqua square. Sew, leaving a ³⁄₈in (1cm) seam allowance, then press the seams toward the square.

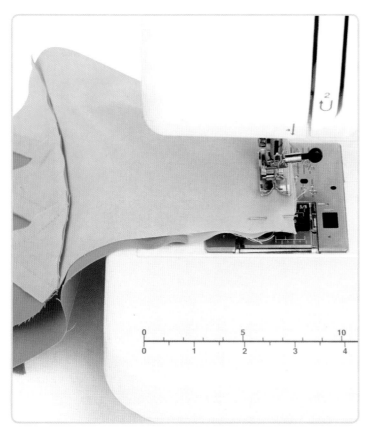

7 With right sides together and the sashings vertical, pin the left-hand raw edge of the aqua square to one of the vertical sashings attached to the blue square. Sew, leaving a ⅜in (1cm) seam allowance. Press toward the aqua square. Repeat Steps 5–7 to join the other blue and aqua squares in the same way, to make two patchwork rectangles.

8 To make the horizontal sashings, lay three of the remaining 18 half-square triangles in a horizontal row with the aqua triangles along the top edge. With right sides together, sew the half-square triangles together, leaving a ⅜in (1cm) seam allowance. Press the seams toward the darker triangles. Repeat to make a total of six horizontal sashings.

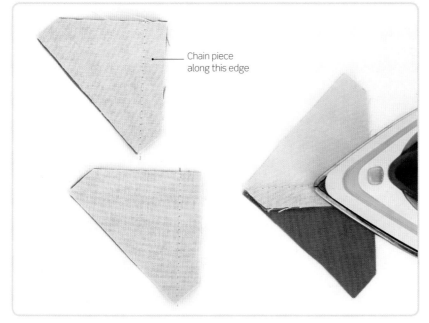

Chain piece along this edge

9 Place the small pale green triangles on top of the small jade green triangles with the points of the triangles top right, as shown. Chain piece the triangles together along the right-hand edges, leaving a ⅜in (1cm) seam allowance. Snip the triangles apart. Press the seams toward the jade green triangles.

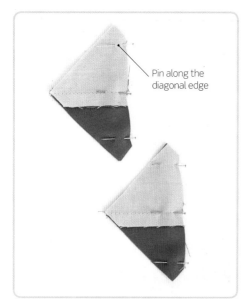

Pin along the
diagonal edge

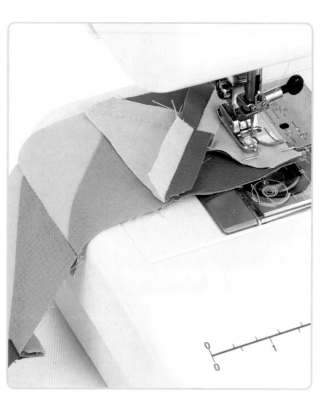

**10** With wrong sides together, pin the triangles together in pairs, matching the seams. Chain piece them together as in Step 9. Snip them apart, then open them to form nine small quarter-square triangles. Press the seams open.

**11** Lay a horizontal sashing so that its aqua triangles are along the top edge. With right sides together, pin a quarter-square triangle to each end of the sashing, so the small pale green triangles adjoin the sashing. Sew, leaving a ³⁄₈in (1cm) seam allowance. Press the seams toward the quarter-square triangles.

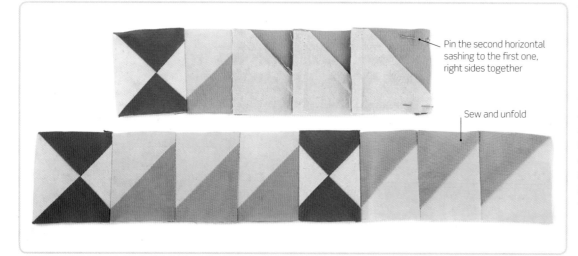

Pin the second horizontal
sashing to the first one,
right sides together

Sew and unfold

**12** Lay another horizontal sashing so that its aqua triangles are along the bottom edge. With right sides together, pin it to the right-hand edge (a small pale green triangle) of the quarter-square triangle that was attached in Step 11. Sew, leaving a ³⁄₈in (1cm) seam allowance. Press the seams toward the quarter-square triangles. Repeat steps 11–12 to complete another horizontal sashing. You now have the first and third sashings.

*Match the points of the sashings for a professional finish.*

Press the seams toward the quarter-square triangles

**13** To make the second sashing, lay one of the remaining horizontal sashings horizontally right-side up, with the blue triangles along the top edge. With right sides together, pin a quarter-square triangle to each end of the sashing, so the small pale green triangles adjoin the sashing. Pin the aqua triangle at the end of the remaining horizontal sashing to the small pale green triangle on the right-hand edge of the quarter-square triangle. Sew, leaving a ⅜in (1cm) seam allowance. Press the seams toward the small quarter-square triangles.

**14** With right sides together and leaving a ⅜in (1cm) seam allowance, pin and sew the small pale green triangles of the remaining three quarter-square triangles to the raw ends of all three horizontal sashings. Press the seams toward the quarter-square triangles. Note: the image shows the final quarter-square triangle being pinned to either the first or third horizontal sashing.

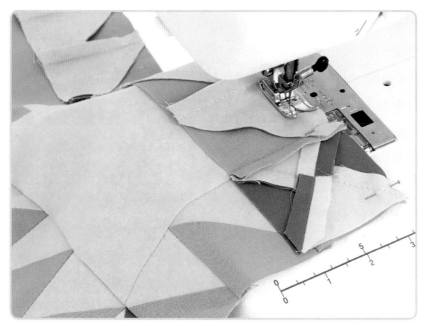

Sew, leaving a ⅜in (1cm) seam allowance

**15** With right sides together, pin the first and second horizontal sashings to the long edges of one of the patchwork rectangles made in Step 7. Place the blue triangles so they adjoin the blue square and the aqua triangles so they adjoin the aqua square. Sew, matching seams and leaving a ⅜in (1cm) seam allowance. Press the seams away from the sashings.

**16** With right sides together, pin the lower edge of the second sashing and one long edge of the third sashing to the long edges of the remaining patchwork rectangle. Place the aqua triangles so they adjoin the aqua square and the blue triangles so they adjoin the blue square. Sew, matching seams and leaving a ⅜in (1cm) seam allowance. Press the seams away from the sashings. The center block of the pillow cover is now complete.

**17** With right sides together, pin and sew an aqua border to each of the two opposite sides of the center block, leaving a ⅜in (1cm) seam allowance. Press the seams toward the borders.

**18** Using the large pale green and jade green triangles and following Steps 9 and 10, make four large quarter-square triangles. With right sides together, pin one quarter-square triangle to each end of the two blue borders, matching the pale green triangles to the short edges. Sew the short edges, leaving a ⅜in (1cm) seam allowance. Press the seams toward the borders.

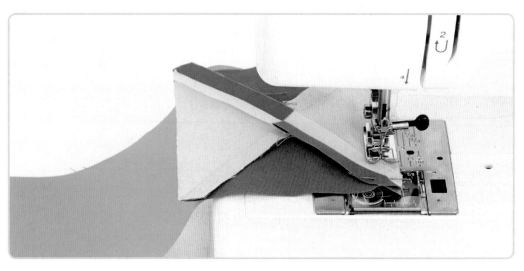

**19** With right sides together and matching the seams, pin the blue borders to the center block and their attached quarter-square triangles to the short edges of the aqua borders. Sew, leaving a ⅜in (1cm) seam allowance. Press the seams toward the borders and the large quarter-square triangles. The front of the pillow cover is now complete.

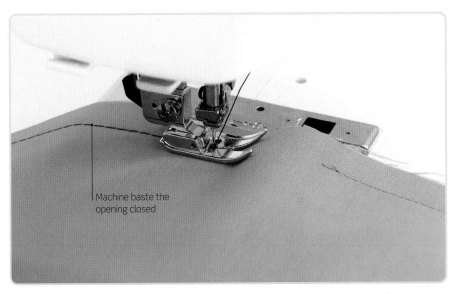

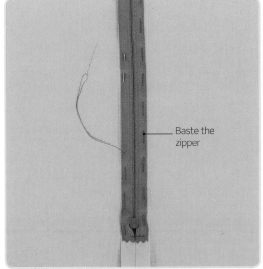

**20** With right sides together, pin and sew the back pieces of the pillow together along one long edge, leaving a ⅝in (1.5cm) seam allowance and a 20in (51cm) opening at the center. Baste the opening closed by machine or by hand. Press the seam open.

Machine baste the opening closed

**21** On the wrong side of the back, pin and hand baste the zipper, facedown, in the center of the opening (see p.221).

Baste the zipper

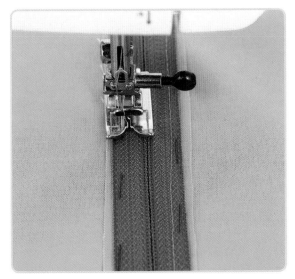

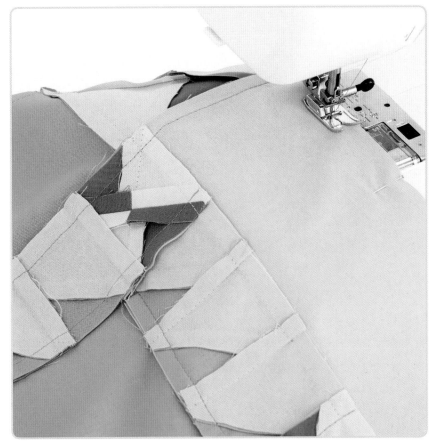

**22** On the wrong side, use a zipper foot to sew around the zipper, ¼in (6mm) from the edges of the zipper, and straight across the ends. Remove the basting stitches. Undo the zipper in readiness for turning the pillow cover to the right side.

**23** With right sides together, pin the front and back of the pillow cover together. Sew around the outer edge, leaving a ⅜in (1cm) seam allowance. Turn the pillow cover to the right side, insert the pillow cushion, and close the zipper.

# Set-in seams

Most patchwork involves joining straight seams, but in some cases you will need to join three pieces of fabric into one corner. This is called a set-in seam or a Y-seam. You will need to measure, mark, and sew carefully, starting and finishing the distance of your seam allowance away from each set-in corner.

## Setting in by hand

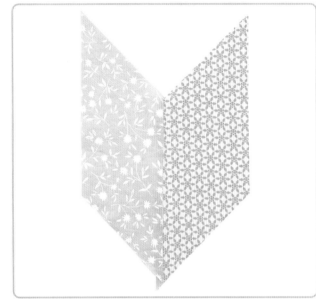

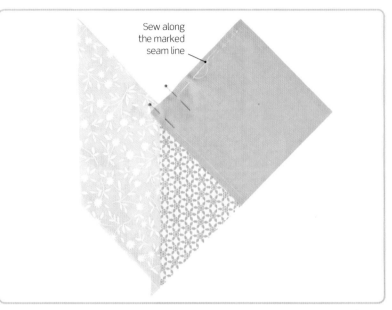

Sew along the marked seam line

**1** Diamonds and triangles sometimes meet at oblique angles. Setting a piece into the resulting space requires careful pinning and sewing. Here, a square is set in the space between two diamond shapes. Cut the square to size and mark ¼in (6mm) seam lines. Mark the starting and finishing points ¼in (6mm) from the edges.

**2** Match one corner of the square to the inner point on the first diamond and pin, right sides together. Match the outer point and pin. Pin the edges together along the seam line. Sew along the marked seam line from the outer point to the inner, removing pins as you work. Take a few small backstitches into the seam at the inner corner, avoiding the seam allowance. Make sure not to cut the thread.

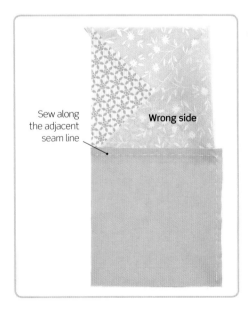

Sew along the adjacent seam line

**Wrong side**

**3** Match the adjacent side of the square to the corresponding side of the diamond. Pin and then sew as in Step 2.

**4** Press the seam allowances on the square toward the two diamonds.

# Setting in by machine

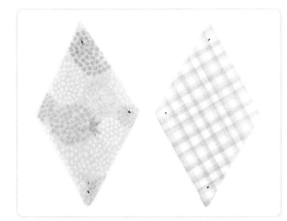
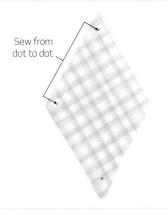

1 Using a light pencil or water-soluble marker, mark a dot ¼in (6mm) in from each end of the two pieces that are to be joined first. This marks the point where you start and finish sewing. Do not sew to the very end of the seam.

2 Place the shapes right sides together and sew from dot to dot, backstitching at each end. Do not overshoot the dots. Press the seam toward the darker fabric.

Sew from dot to dot

3 On the wrong side of the piece that is to be set in, mark a dot ¼in (6mm) in at the three set-in corners of the piece.

Dot

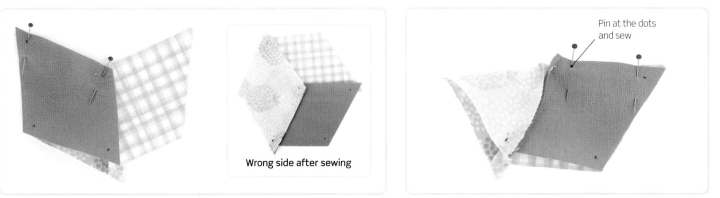

Wrong side after sewing

Pin at the dots and sew

4 Match the middle marked corner of the piece that is to be set in with the corresponding dot on one of the two pieces that have already been sewn together. Pin the seam at each end and sew from the inside corner to the outer dot.

5 Match the outer dot on the second side of the piece that is to be set in with the outer dot on the free edge of the other piece. Pin them together at the dot and sew, again sewing from the inside corner to the outer dot.

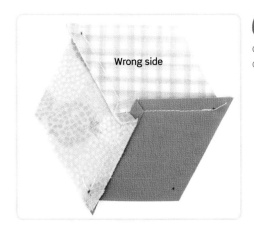

Wrong side

6 Press the seams flat in one direction. Snip off the corners.

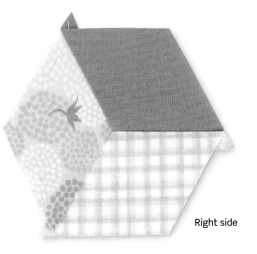

Right side

# Diamond coasters

These coasters can be whipped up in no time and are perfect for practicing set-in seams. They can easily be made from odd scraps of fabric that you might have around the house. Make them as a house-warming gift—or to keep for yourself.

## Essential Information

**DIFFICULTY** Easy

**SIZE** 4½in (11.5cm) diameter approximately

**TOOLS AND MATERIALS**
Tracing paper
Pencil
Scissors
Quilter's ruler
Rotary cutter
Cutting mat
Sewing machine
Threads to match your fabrics
Pins
Sewing needle

**FABRICS**
Three 6 x 3½in (15 x 19cm) pieces of
    coordinating fabric scraps per coaster
6 x 6in (15 x 15cm) backing fabric
6 x 6in (12 x 12cm) batting (optional)

**LAVENDER BAG VARIATION**
6¼in (16 cm) of thin ribbon
Dried lavender

**SKILLS**
Set-in seams (see p.101)

**SEAM ALLOWANCE**
¼in (6mm) throughout, unless otherwise stated

1 Trace the diamond template (see p.292) onto the tracing paper and cut out the diamond pattern piece. Be sure to add the ¼in (6mm) seam allowance lines to the pattern piece. Place the pattern piece on a piece of scrap fabric and, using the quilter's ruler and the rotary cutter, cut a fabric diamond. When cutting, align the marked seam allowance with the ¼in (6mm) mark on the quilter's ruler to ensure that you do not make the pattern piece smaller each time you cut.

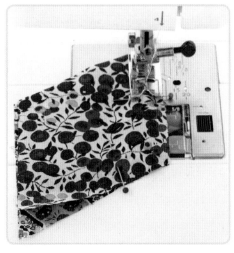

2 To prepare to sew set-in seams (see p.101), mark a dot ¼in (6mm) inside each corner on the back of each fabric diamond. Pin two diamonds, right sides together, along one edge. Sew the diamonds together between the two marked dots, making sure not to sew beyond the dots.

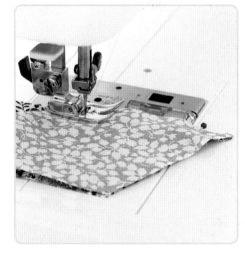

3 Following the same technique, set in the third diamond to complete the coaster top. Press the seams at the back to one side.

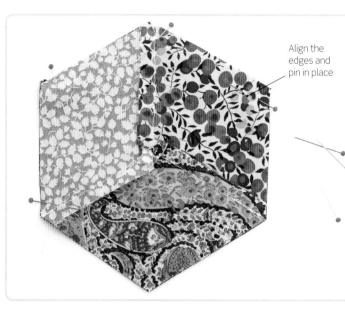

**4** Lay the coaster top on the backing fabric. Using the quilter's ruler and the rotary cutter, cut a piece of the backing fabric to match.

**5** With right sides together, lay the coaster top on the backing fabric. Align the edges and pin all around.

*Wrong side of backing fabric*

*Align the edges and pin in place*

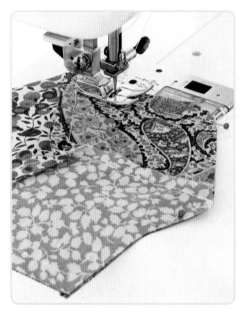

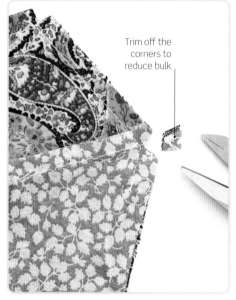

**6** Sew around the edges, leaving an opening of approximately 2in (5cm) along one edge for turning through.

**7** Clip into each corner, making sure not to cut through the stitches.

**8** Turn the coaster to the right side through the opening and pick out the corners with a pin. Iron thoroughly. If you would like a more padded and absorbent coaster, cut a piece of batting smaller than the coaster and insert it through the opening. Press the batting flat.

*Trim off the corners to reduce bulk*

*While trimming the corners, make sure not to cut through the stitches.*

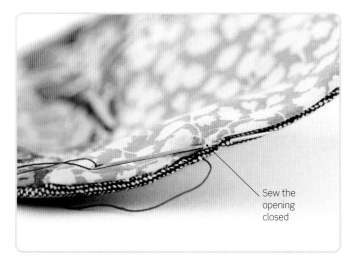

**9** Whipstitch (see p.43) the opening in the edge of the coaster closed, picking up a few threads from each side of the opening as you go.

Sew the opening closed

**10** Leaving a ³⁄₈in (1cm) seam allowance, topstitch around the edges of the coaster with coordinating thread. You can quilt the coaster in any pattern you wish to help hold the batting in place, if used.

# Lavender bag variation

By slightly altering the pattern, you can turn the coaster into a lavender bag for your closet, for keeping moths at bay. You can also make the lavender bag without a ribbon and use it as a lavender-filled sachet to keep in a drawer.

**1** Follow Steps 1–4 of the coaster. At Step 5, pin the length of ribbon between the coaster top and the backing. Center the ribbon on one corner. Complete Steps 6–8 of the coaster, securing the ends of the ribbon in place in Step 6.

**2** Stuff the lavender bag with dried lavender, then sew up the opening in the edge, as in Step 9 of the coaster. Your lavender bag is now complete.

**Keep moths at bay in your closet** by looping these pretty patchwork lavender bags on your hangers. Thanks to the natural properties of lavender, the bags will act as moth-repellents.

# Settings

The way quilt blocks are arranged in a finished top is called the set, or setting. The following section can give only an outline of the virtually infinite possibilities for putting blocks together. The way to work out the best setting for a quilt is to lay out all of the blocks and view them from a distance.

## Quilt layouts

Many quilt blocks, even fairly simple ones, can create interesting secondary patterns when they are joined, and rotating or reversing blocks makes a quilt look entirely different.

**The simplest sets** are rows of repeating blocks sewn together edge to edge, referred to as "straight set."

Straight sets

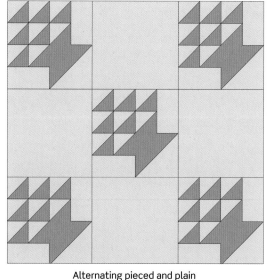

**Alternating a pieced block** with a plain block means there are fewer blocks to put together. It allows for large, open areas, perfect for showcasing elaborate quilting.

Alternating pieced and plain

**Blocks can be set** "on point" (turned on the diagonal), with setting triangles around the edges and at each corner.

On point: Solid set

**This setting needs plain blocks** between the pieced blocks as well as triangles added to each corner and along each side to fill the edges.

On point: Alternating pieced and plain blocks

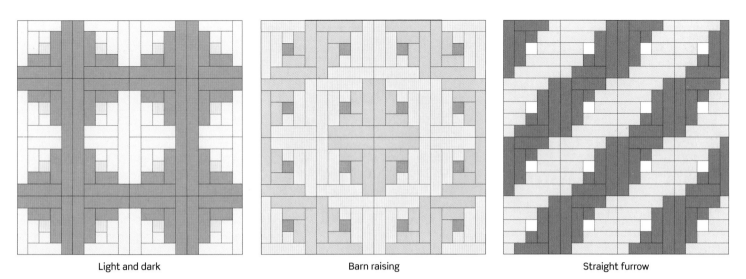

| Light and dark | Barn raising | Straight furrow |

## Log cabin

There are so many possible sets for log cabin designs that each version has its own name. The examples above all have the same number of identical log cabin blocks. In each case, the way each block is turned determines the final over-all effect.

### Frame settings

**Also known as medallion settings,** these have a central block, sometimes an elaborate appliqué, surrounded by several borders of various widths, some pieced, some plain. The center can be set square or on point, as here.

### Stripped set

**When blocks are arranged vertically,** a stripped set results. The first stripped quilts were usually simple strips of fabric joined to make the width of a quilt, but beautiful stripped quilts can be made from pieced blocks, too.

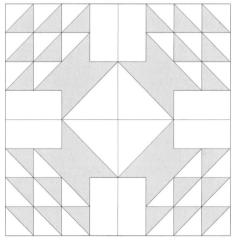

### Rotating blocks

**This setting creates** new patterns once several blocks are set, particularly with asymmetrical patterns.

# Sashing

Sashing is strips of fabric placed between blocks to frame them. Sampler quilts and star blocks usually have sashing to give each block the chance to shine. The width of the sashing is flexible: try out different widths before you cut the strips. Plain or pieced squares (known as setting squares or cornerstones) can be placed at the corners of a block to make the pattern even more interesting.

**Straight-set simple continuous sashing** Each block in this piece is framed by straight-set simple sashing.

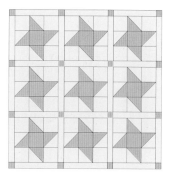

**Straight-set sashing with setting squares** Adding a square in each corner between the blocks creates more pattern. The setting squares can also be pieced; simple pinwheel, four-patch, and nine-patch designs work well.

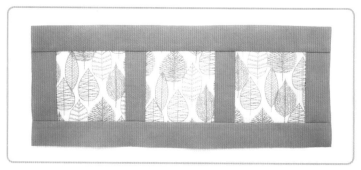

**Vertical or horizontal set sashing** Blocks can be assembled in rows with the sashing between them running vertically or horizontally.

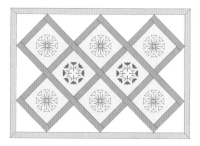

**Diagonal set (on point) with sashing** Blocks set on point can be framed by sashing and assembled in strips with extra triangles added around the edges to give a chevron effect.

## Simple continuous sashing

1 Cut sashing strips to the desired width plus a ½in (1.2cm) seam allowance, and to the same length as one side of the blocks.

2 With right sides together and leaving a ¼in (6mm) seam allowance, alternate strips and blocks to make a row. Press the seams toward the strips. Repeat to make as many rows as needed.

3 Cut two more sashing strips to the desired width plus a ½in (1.2cm) seam allowance, and the same length as the joined row.

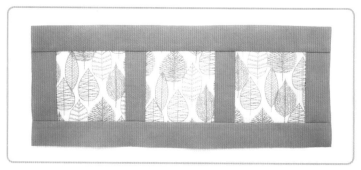

4 With right sides together and leaving a ¼in (6mm) seam allowance, sew the two strips either side of the row. Press the seams toward the sashing. Continue alternating sashing strips and rows of blocks with strips until the quilt top is the required size.

## Sashing with setting squares

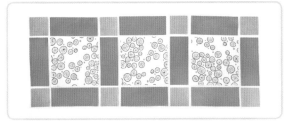

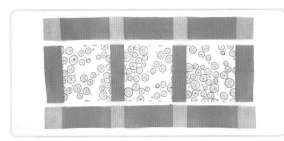

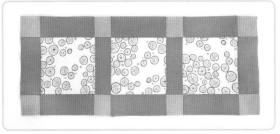

1 Repeat Steps 1 and 2 of Simple continuous sashing (opposite) to make a row of blocks. For the sashing, cut strips the same length as the width of a block, and setting squares the same width as the strips.

2 With right sides together and leaving a 1/4in (6mm) seam allowance, alternate squares and strips to make two long sashing strips.

3 With right sides together and leaving a 1/4in (6mm) seam allowance, sew the long sashing strips along the top and bottom edges of the row of blocks. Ensure that the corners of the blocks and the setting squares match up. Continue alternating rows of sashing strips and blocks until the quilt is the required size.

## Tilted block setting

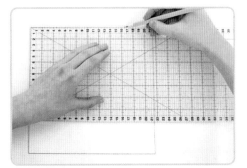

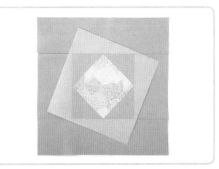

1 First make the central block, then frame it with a wide border made from four pieces of sashing, as shown left.

2 Create a template for the block by measuring and marking its size on tracing paper, adding 1/2in (1.2cm) seam allowances.

3 Center the template on top of the block that was made in Step 1, then angle the template to the desired tilt.

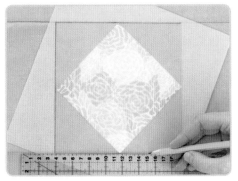

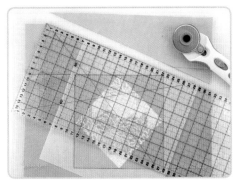

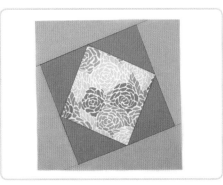

4 To be able to tilt subsequent blocks at the same angle, use a ruler and pencil to mark the outline of the central block on the template.

5 Cut away the fabric around the template. To reuse the template, ensure that all central blocks in the project align with the block marked on the template.

6 When the finished block is placed so its outside edges are perpendicular, the central block will be tilted.

# Borders

The outside edges of most quilts are finished with strips that make up the border. This frames the piece and protects the edges. Borders can be single or multiple, wide or narrow, pieced or plain. Whatever type you choose, the border should complement and enhance the overall design of the quilt. If possible, strips should be cut along the lengthwise grain, in one long piece and with the selvages removed. Never cut borders on the bias.

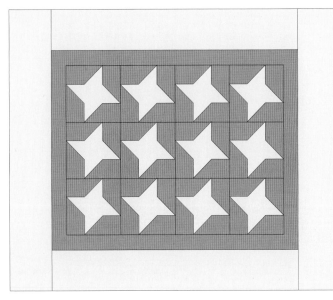

**Straight borders** Adding a plain, straight border is an easy, popular choice. When made from solid-colored fabric, it gives an uncluttered look and is especially effective when framing a complex design.

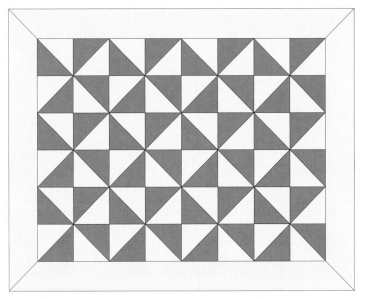

**Mitered borders** More complex than straight borders, well executed mitered borders look very professional and neat. The corners are sewn at a 45-degree angle to the sides of the quilt.

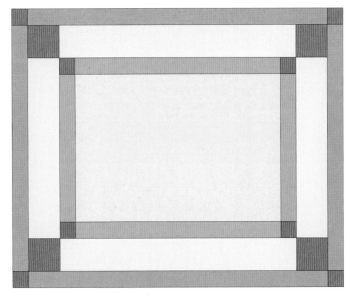

**Multiple borders with setting squares** You can add several borders to a quilt, together with setting squares in the corners. The effect is a little like a series of "retreating" picture frames.

**Pieced inner border with straight outer border** Another variation on multiple borders uses a straight outer border framing an inner border made of pieced patchwork.

# Making straight borders

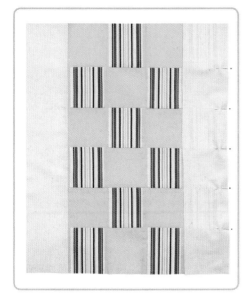

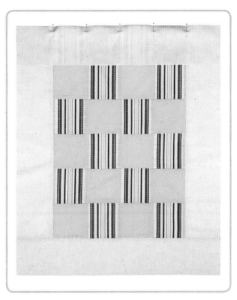

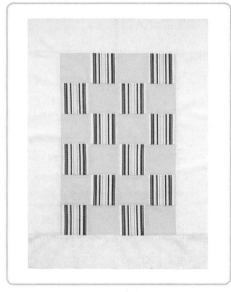

**1** Cut or piece two strips of the desired width, plus ¹⁄₂in (1.2cm) for seam allowances, and the same length as the sides of the quilt. Mark the center of each strip and of the sides of the quilt. Pin the strips to the quilt, right sides together and matching the marks. Sew together, leaving a ¹⁄₄in (6mm) seam allowance.

**2** Press the seams toward the border strips. Measure the top and bottom edges of the quilt plus borders, and cut two strips to that length. Mark the center of each strip and of the top and bottom edges, as in Step 1. Pin with right sides together, matching the marks. Sew together, leaving a ¹⁄₄in (6mm) seam allowance. Press the seams toward the border strips.

**3** The quilt top is now completed and ready to be quilted (see pp.202–205, 210–213).

# Joining strips to make a border

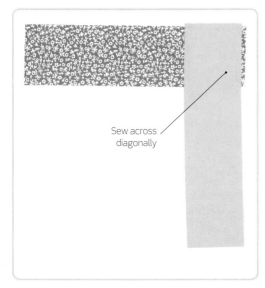

Sew across diagonally

**1** Place two strips at right angles with right sides together with the ends overlapping by at least ¹⁄₄in (6mm). Mark a line across the diagonal and pin. Sew along the line, as shown.

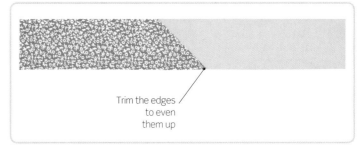

Trim the edges to even them up

**2** Trim the seam to ¹⁄₄in (6mm), then open out the joined strips to the right side. Trim the edges of the strip, if needed. Press the seam to one side.

# Making a straight border with setting squares

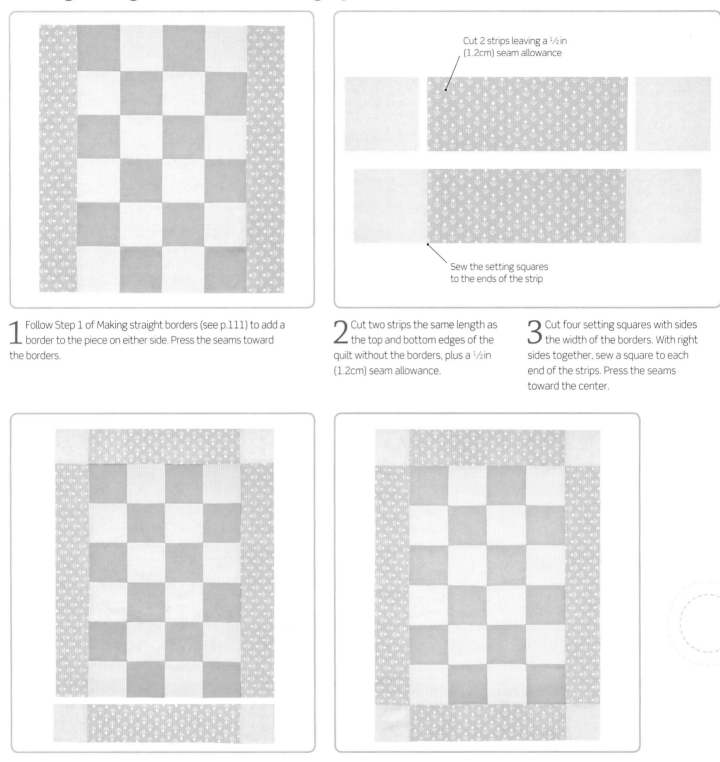

Cut 2 strips leaving a ½ in (1.2cm) seam allowance

Sew the setting squares to the ends of the strip

1 Follow Step 1 of Making straight borders (see p.111) to add a border to the piece on either side. Press the seams toward the borders.

2 Cut two strips the same length as the top and bottom edges of the quilt without the borders, plus a ½ in (1.2cm) seam allowance.

3 Cut four setting squares with sides the width of the borders. With right sides together, sew a square to each end of the strips. Press the seams toward the center.

4 With right sides together, sew the pieced strips to the top and bottom edges of the quilt. Press the seams toward the border.

5 The quilt top is now completed and ready to be quilted (see pp.202-205, 210-213).

# Making a mitered border

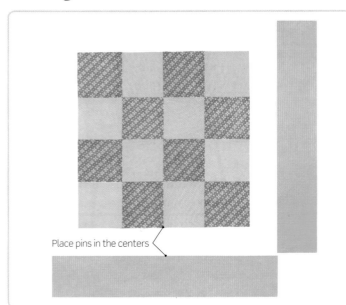

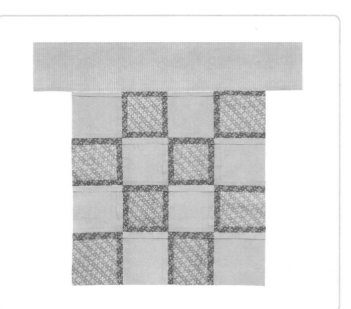

1 Square up the quilt top. Cut the border strips to the desired width plus ½in (1.2cm) for seam allowances. Measure the length of the quilt top sides, then add two times the width of the border, plus 6in (15.5cm).

2 Place a pin in the center of each side of the quilt top and each border. Aligning the center pins, position the borders right side together with the corresponding side and pin in place. Position a pin ¼in (6mm) from each corner to mark your starting and stopping points for sewing.

Place pins in the centers

3 Join the border strips to all sides of the quilt, leaving a ¼in (6mm) seam allowance. Do not sew into adjoining border strips. Press the seams toward the borders.

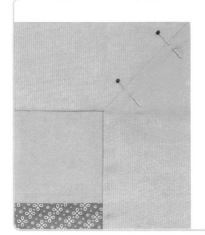

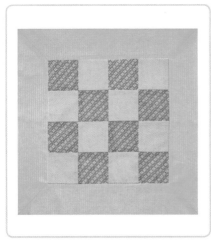

## Multiple mitered borders

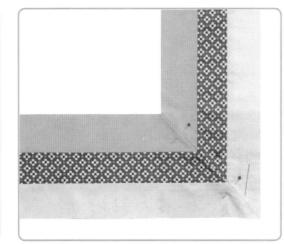

4 Place the quilt right side up on a flat surface and fold under the ends of each strip at a 45-degree angle. Pin the folds in place from the right side, ensuring that the angle is correct. Press the folds and remove the pins.

5 Working from the wrong side, re-pin the miter along the pressed fold. Baste in place if desired. Hand sew the fold together from the quilt edge to the outside corner. Trim the seam allowance and press it open. Repeat to miter all corners.

If you are using multiple borders, join them together in straight rows and attach them to the quilt top all at once. Miter the corners as in Steps 4 and 5, making sure you match the borders through the miter.

# Simple sashings pillow

A simple block pattern framed by sashing can be a nice addition to any chair in the room. If using fabrics with a directional pattern, be sure to cut and sew them so that they're the correct way up on the pillow front.

## Essential Information

**DIFFICULTY** Easy

**SIZE** 16 x 16in (40 x 40cm)

**TOOLS AND MATERIALS**
Rotary cutter
Cutting mat
Quilter's ruler
Pins
Thread to match your fabrics
Sewing machine
Scissors
16in (40cm) square pillow cushion

**FABRICS**
**A:** 11 x 11in (28 x 28cm) patterned flower fabric
**B:** 11 x 11in (28 x 28cm) patterned dotted fabric
**C:** 2½ x 2½in (6.5 x 6.5cm) patterned bird fabric
**D:** 5 x 5in (13 x 13cm) patterned triangle fabric
**E:** 23½ x 27½in (60 x 70cm) solid gray fabric
**F:** 4 x 10in (10 x 26cm) patterned fabric, for the back inset detail

**SKILLS**
Sashing and borders (see pp.108–113)

**SEAM ALLOWANCES**
¼in (6mm) throughout, unless otherwise stated

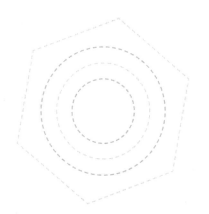

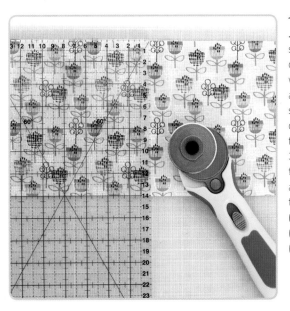

1 Cut four 5½in (14cm) squares from fabric A; four 2½ x 5½in (6.5 x 14cm) strips from fabric B (if you are using a directional pattern for the sashing you will need to cut two strips with the pattern across the width of the strip and two strips with the pattern across the height of the strip); four 2½in (6.5cm) squares from fabric D; four 2½ x 12½in (6.5 x 32cm) strips (cutting two strips with the pattern across the width of the strip and two strips with the pattern across the height of the strip), one 16½ x 10in (42 x 26cm) rectangle, one 4½ x 10in (12 x 26cm) rectangle, and one 8½ x 10in (22 x 26cm) rectangle from fabric E.

2 Lay out all your pieces for the pillow front on a flat surface. With right sides together, pin and sew the first fabric B strip (with the pattern running height-wise to the first fabric A square). Open up the seam and sew the second fabric A square to the opposite side of the strip.

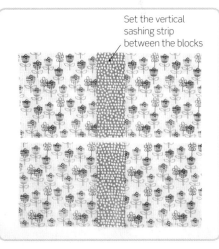

Set the vertical sashing strip between the blocks

3 Repeat using the second height-wise fabric B strip and the remaining two fabric A squares to create the two front strips. Make sure that all of the patterns on the fabrics are running the same way—in this case that all the flowers are upright. Open up and press the seams toward the darker fabric.

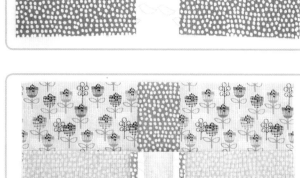

Make sure the sashing strip is straight—trim if needed

4 Take the two remaining fabric B strips and the fabric C square and sew them together with the square in the center to create the central sashing. Press the seams open.

5 Pin and sew the central sashing to the bottom edge of the top front strip, being sure to match the seams on all the pieces (see p.74). Make sure that when the strip is sewn and opened up that the pattern is the same way up on all the pieces.

6 Pin and sew the bottom front strip to the bottom edge of the central sashing, matching the seams as you pin. Make sure all of the patterns are the right way up. Press open the seams to create the main pillow front.

7 Pin and sew one of the fabric E strips with the pattern running height-wise to the right edge of the main pillow front, right sides together.

8 Pin and sew the second height-wise fabric E strip to the left edge of the main pillow front. Open out and press the seams just sewn toward the darker fabrics.

9 Sew two fabric D squares to either end of one of the remaining fabric E strips, as shown, to create the first border. Repeat using the remaining two fabric D squares and final fabric E strip to create the second border. Press the seams toward the darker fabric.

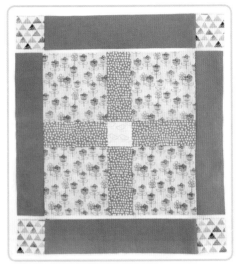

**10** Pin and sew the two borders to the top and bottom of the main pillow front, matching the seams and making sure all of the patterns are the right way up. Press the seams open.

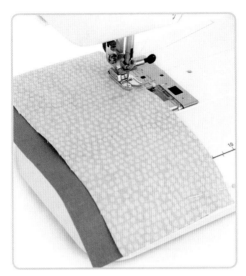

**11** Pin and sew the 4 x 10in (10 x 26cm) fabric F rectangle right sides together with the 4½ x 10in (12 x 26cm) fabric E rectangle. Pin and sew the 8½ x 10in (22 x 26cm) fabric E rectangle to the opposite side of the fabric F rectangle to create a 16½ x 10in (42 x 26cm) strip.

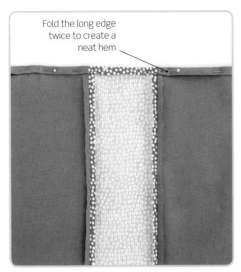

Fold the long edge twice to create a neat hem

**12** You now have two 16½ x 10in (42 x 26cm) strips—one plain and one with a strip of fabric F running through it—these are the back flaps. Turn over one of the long raw edges of one flap by ⅜in (1cm) to the wrong side using a seam guide if needed, then the same again to create a hem. Pin in place. Repeat on the second flap.

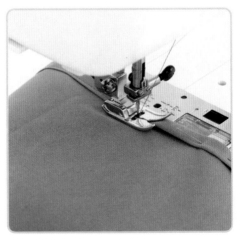

**13** Using a matching thread, topstitch along the inner fold to secure the hem. Repeat on the second flap.

**14** Lay the pillow front out, right-side up. Then lay the plain back flap on top, right side down, with the raw edges aligning with the top of the pillow front. Lay the second flap on top of this, right side down, with the raw edges aligning with the raw edges of the bottom of the pillow front. Pin all around.

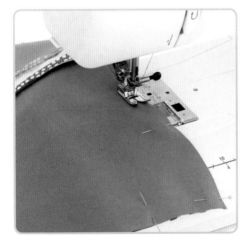

**15** Sew around the entire perimeter of the pillow. Forward and reverse stitch over the area where the flaps overlap to reinforce the seam. Carefully snip off all four corners, being sure not to cut through any of the stitches. Turn the pillow cover right-side out, carefully pushing out the corners and insert the pillow cushion.

# Curves

Patchwork patterns based on curves are less common than those with straight seams, which are easy to cut and sew. But although curves can be tricky, they give more options and, with careful preparation at every stage from template making to cutting and pinning, they are straightforward to sew. Many people find curves easier to work by hand, but it is not difficult to machine sew them.

## Sewing curved seams by hand

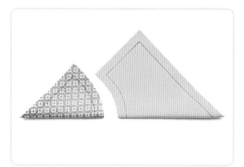

**1** Mark the seam lines and any pattern marks, especially the center point, on the wrong side of each piece. If the center isn't marked on the pattern, fold each piece in half, finger press it at the center seam line, and use the crease as the center mark.

**2** Place the smaller convex piece right sides together on the concave one, aligning the center points. Pin the center point through both pieces. Pin the end points of the marked seam line. Then pin along the seam line every ³⁄₈in (1cm) or so, manipulating the fabric to eliminate creases.

**3** Take out the pin at one end and take the needle through the matching points. You may use a double backstitched loop (see p.42) in the seam line to secure the thread. Do not sew into the seam allowance. Take several short running stitches along the seam line, then pull the needle through. Repeat along the length of the seam, removing pins as you work. Secure the seam further by making a small backstitch each time you bring the needle through.

**4** Check the back to make sure your sewing is on the line on both sides and stop at the matching point at the end. Do not sew into the seam allowance, but use a double backstitched loop to secure the thread. Do not clip the seam allowance. Press the seam toward the convex piece. If your sewing is accurate, the piece will lie flat.

## Sewing curved seams by machine

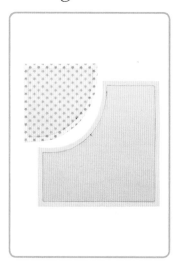

**1** Make templates and mark the center of the curve on each one. Cut out the fabric pieces, adding a ¹⁄₄in (6mm) seam allowance. Center the templates on the wrong side of your fabric pieces, draw around them to mark the seam allowances, then mark the center point of the curve on the fabric pieces.

**2** Pin the two fabric pieces together at the center point on the seam allowance, then pin at each end. Pin along the edge to stabilize the curve.

**3** Sew along the marked curve without stretching or pulling. Remove the pins as you sew. Press the seam toward the convex piece. It should lie flat without being clipped.

# Reducing seam bulk

Sometimes you may need to reduce the bulk in curved seams to help your patchwork lie flat. This is usually used on 3-dimensional objects.

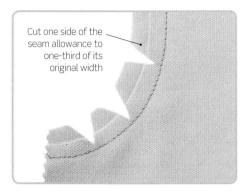

Cut one side of the seam allowance to one-third of its original width

**Reducing bulk on an inner curve** Layer the seam by cutting along one side of the seam allowance to reduce it to one-third of its original width. Then cut out "V" notches to reduce the bulk. Do not cut through the seam.

Clip into the seam allowance

**Reducing bulk on an outer curve** Layer the seam and clip through the seam allowances to reduce bulk.

# Fans

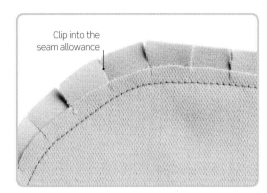

Cut 1 from fabric D

Cut 3 from fabric A

Cut 3 from fabric B

Cut 1 from fabric C

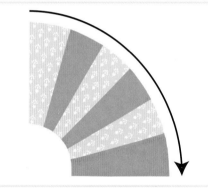

1 Transfer the outlines to cardboard or template plastic and cut out the shapes. Make two sets of templates—set 1 for the cutting lines, and set 2 with the seam allowances trimmed off the curved edges for the seam line.

2 For a six-blade fan, cut three blades each from fabrics A and B. Cut a small corner piece from fabric C and a background from fabric D.

3 Join the fan blade pieces, alternating the colors and taking a ¼in (6mm) seam allowance. Press the blades in the same direction.

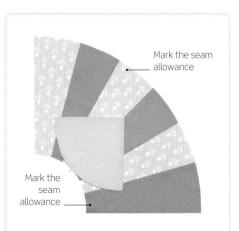

Mark the seam allowance

Mark the seam allowance

4 Mark the seam allowances on the top and bottom edges of the fan unit.

5 Mark the seam allowance on the small corner piece and pin it to the lower edge of the fan unit. Join them as in Steps 5 and 6 of Drunkard's path (see pp.120–121). Press toward the fan.

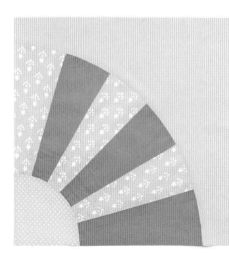

6 Mark the seam allowance on the background piece and pin the background piece to the upper edge of the fan unit. Join them as before. Press toward the background.

# Drunkard's path

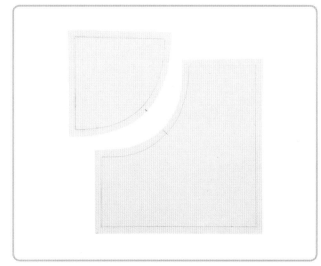

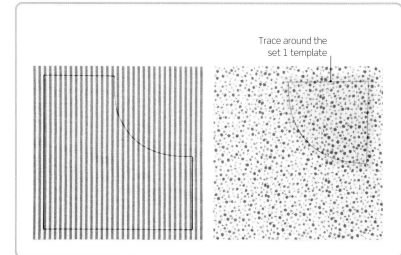

Trace around the
set 1 template

**1** Make two sets of templates from cardboard or plastic—set 1 for the cutting lines, and set 2 with the seam allowances trimmed off the curved edges for the seam line. Place the pattern marks precisely on both sets.

**2** Trace the larger outlines onto the wrong side of the chosen fabrics. Make sure the pattern marks are transferred accurately.

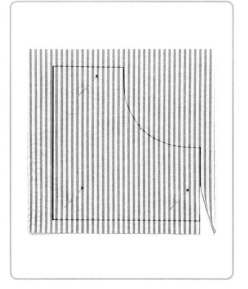

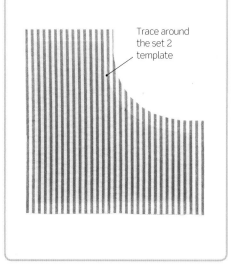

Trace around
the set 2
template

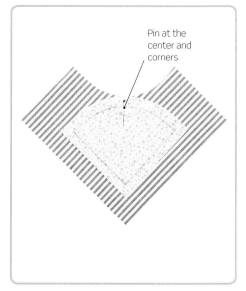

Pin at the
center and
corners

**3** Cut out the shapes. If you are using scissors, cut around the curve, not into it. If you prefer to cut with rotary equipment, use the smallest size blade (1in/25mm) and a perfectly smooth cutting mat for best results.

**4** Separate the cutout shapes and, using the set 2 templates, trace the seam lines and pattern marks onto the wrong side of each fabric piece.

**5** Pin one of each shape and fabric right sides together, with the convex piece on top of the concave one. Match and pin the center marks first, then pin the corners.

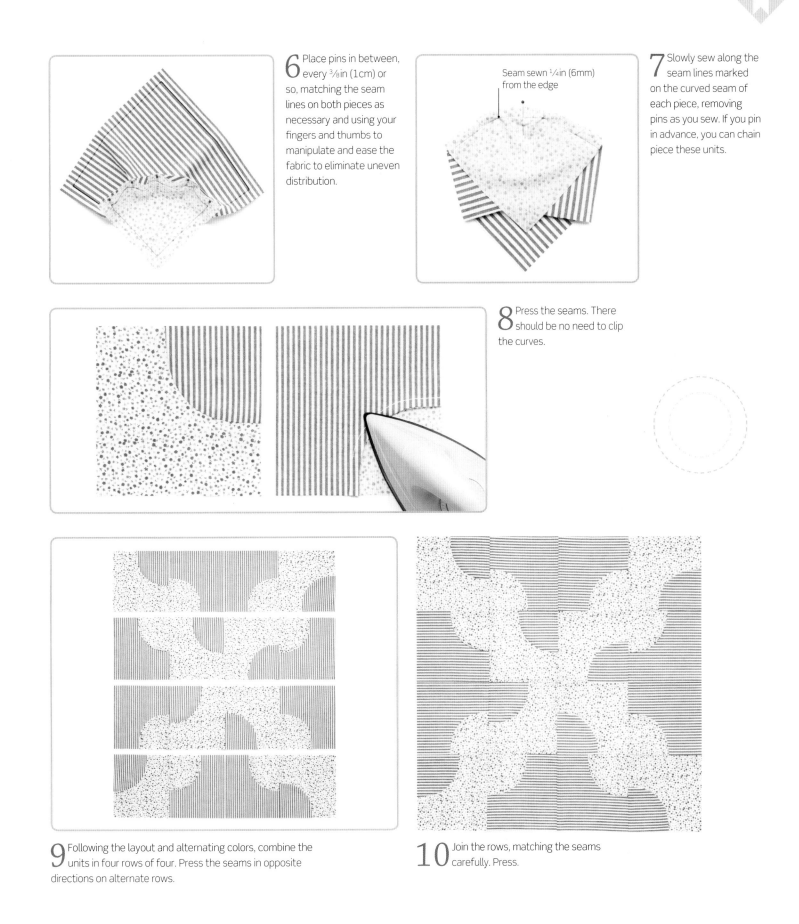

**6** Place pins in between, every ³⁄₈in (1cm) or so, matching the seam lines on both pieces as necessary and using your fingers and thumbs to manipulate and ease the fabric to eliminate uneven distribution.

Seam sewn ¹⁄₄in (6mm) from the edge

**7** Slowly sew along the seam lines marked on the curved seam of each piece, removing pins as you sew. If you pin in advance, you can chain piece these units.

**8** Press the seams. There should be no need to clip the curves.

**9** Following the layout and alternating colors, combine the units in four rows of four. Press the seams in opposite directions on alternate rows.

**10** Join the rows, matching the seams carefully. Press.

# Dresden plate pillow

This round pillow features a traditional Dresden plate patchwork block. Many variations of the Dresden plate block exist, but this one is a multi-petaled flower. Once the "plate" is complete, it is hand-sewn to the front of the pillow.

## Essential Information

**DIFFICULTY** Medium

**SIZE** 15in (38cm) in diameter x 4in (10cm) deep

**TOOLS AND MATERIALS**
Tracing paper
Measuring tape
Pencil
Pins
Threads to match your fabrics
Sewing machine
Scissors
Iron and ironing board
Sewing needle

**FABRICS**
19¾ x 33½in (50 x 85cm) solid white fabric
  for the circle for the pillow front and for
  the two semicircles for the pillow back
A selection of seven patterned blue fabrics
  for the petals and the flower center
9½ x 24½in (24 x 62cm) blue fabric, cut
  into two rectangles, each 4¾ x 24½in
  (12 x 62cm) for the pillow sides
Toy filling, batting, or a 15in (38cm) diameter
  x 4in (10cm) deep round pillow cushion

**SKILLS**
Chain piecing (see p.63)
Curves and fans (see pp.118–119)

**SEAM ALLOWANCE**
¼in (6mm) throughout, unless otherwise stated

1 Using the template on page 293, cut two petals from each of six differently patterned blue fabrics, giving a total of 12 petals. Arrange the petals in a circle, with matching petals directly opposite each other, as shown. Cut the remaining pieces for the pillow using the templates and instructions on page 293.

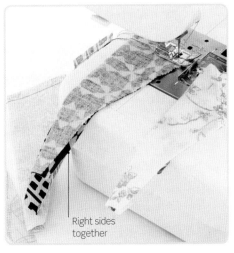

Right sides together

2 Fold the wider end of each petal in half, right side to right side, and pin. Chain piece all the petals together (see p.63).

Snip off the corners on the folded side

3 Cut the petals apart and snip off the inside, folded corner of each petal.

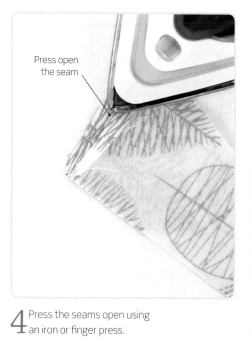

Press open
the seam

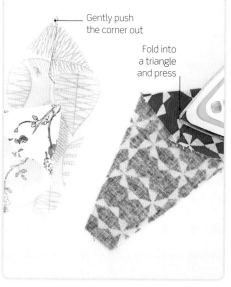

Gently push
the corner out

Fold into
a triangle
and press

Start sewing
from here

4 Press the seams open using
an iron or finger press.

5 Turn each petal to the right side and gently
push the corner out. Fold the wider end of the
petal to the wrong side to form a symmetrical
triangle. Press in place. Lay the petals out in the
correct order again.

6 Pin two adjacent petals together, right sides
together, along the long edge. Starting at the
triangular end, sew along the edge. Stop sewing
¼in (6mm) from the narrow end of the petals.
Press the seam open.

Fold the narrow
ends to the
wrong side and
baste in place

7 Continue adding the remaining petals in the same way,
pressing the seams open as you go, until you have a full
circle or "plate" of joined petals.

8 Fold over ¼in (6mm) of the narrow ends of the petals to the wrong
side of the fabric, then press and baste.

Make small pleats as you baste to reduce bulk

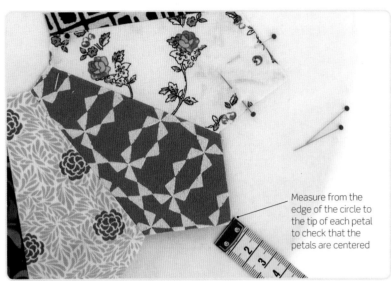

Measure from the edge of the circle to the tip of each petal to check that the petals are centered

**9** To make the flower center, pin the flower center pattern piece to the wrong side of the flower center fabric. Fold the seam allowance over the pattern piece and baste together, making small pleats in the fabric to reduce the bulk. Press to set the pleats.

**10** Lay the white circle of fabric for the front, right-side up. Measure and mark the center, then place the completed "plate" of petals on top, right-side up and centered. Measure from the edge of the circle to the tip of each petal to ensure the petals are centered.

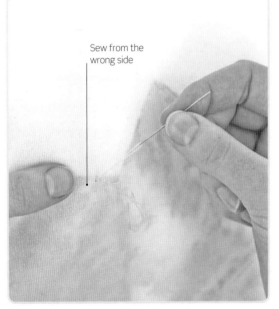

Sew from the wrong side

**11** Pin the plate in place along its inside and outside edges. As you pin, make sure that the mark in the center of the white circle remains in the center of the plate and that the tips of the petals remain equidistant from the edge of the white circle.

**12** Using small slip stitches and matching thread (see p.43), and working from the wrong side, sew the outside and inside edges of the plate to the white circle, making the stitches as invisible as possible.

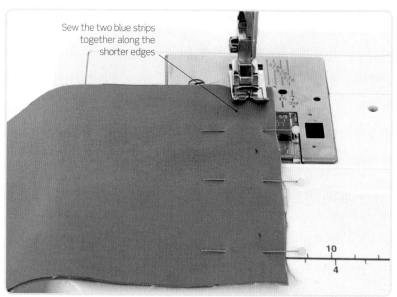

Sew the two blue strips together along the shorter edges

**13** To complete the pillow front, unpick the basting stitches from the flower center and gently remove the paper pattern piece. Pin the wrong side of the flower center to the center of the plate. Slip stitch in place.

**14** To make the sides of the pillow, place the two blue strips right sides together. Pin their shorter edges together at both ends, then sew them together, leaving a ³⁄₈in (1cm) seam allowance. Press the seams open. You will now have a loop of fabric.

Pin the blue strip around the edge

**15** With the right sides together, pin one long edge of the blue loop all around the edge of the pillow front.

**16** Sew all around the pinned edge, leaving a ³⁄₈in (1cm) seam allowance.

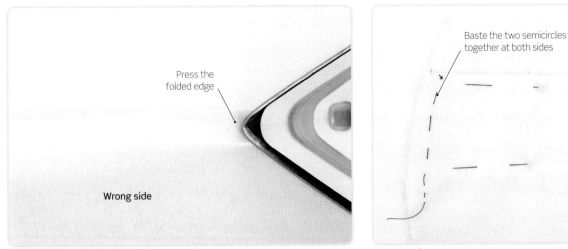

Press the
folded edge

Wrong side

Baste the two semicircles
together at both sides

**17** To make the back of the pillow, lay out the bigger white semicircle wrong-side up. Fold the straight edge over by ³⁄₈in (1cm) and press, then fold it over again to create a neat hem and to enclose the raw edge. Press again, then topstitch together. Repeat on the straight edge of the smaller semicircle.

**18** With right sides faceup and with the larger semicircle on top, lay the two semicircles together to form a full circle. Overlap the hemmed edges by about 1⁵⁄₈in (4.5cm). Pin along both sides of the overlap, then baste the two overlapped semicircles together at both sides, inside the ³⁄₈in (1cm) seam allowance. Remove the pins along the overlapped edges.

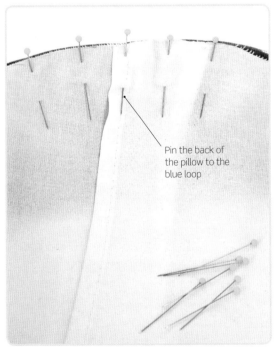

Pin the back of
the pillow to the
blue loop

Turn the pillow
to the right side
through the opening

**19** With right sides together, pin the back of the pillow to the remaining long edge of the blue loop. Remove the basting stitches from the back of the pillow, then sew all around the pinned edge, leaving a ³⁄₈in (1cm) seam allowance.

**20** Turn the pillow to the right side through the opening in the back and press the seams that join the sides of the pillow to the front and back. Stuff the pillow with toy filling, batting, or a pillow cushion.

# Bird toy

This delightful bird is the perfect gift for a special little one, and it's just the right size for small hands to grasp. You can adapt the project if you like, perhaps by using a different fabric for the belly, or by putting a child-safe rattle inside.

## Essential Information

**DIFFICULTY** Moderate

**SIZE** 4in (10cm) in diameter

**TOOLS AND MATERIALS**
Tracing paper
Felt-tip marker
Pins
Scissors
Sharp pencil
Black embroidery thread
Sewing needle
Sewing machine
Threads to match your fabrics
Iron and ironing board
Bodkin
Contrasting thread for basting
2oz (35g) polyester toy filling

**FABRICS**
**A:** 6 x 6in (15 x 15cm) cotton fabric for the face
**B:** 12 x 12in (30 x 30cm) cotton fabric for the body
**C:** 8 x 8in (20 x 20cm) cotton fabric for the wings
**D:** 10 x 10in (25 x 25cm) cotton fabric for the legs and feathers
6 x 4in (15 x 10cm) lightweight batting

**SKILLS**
Curved seams (see p.118)

**SEAM ALLOWANCE**
³⁄₈in (1cm) throughout, unless otherwise stated

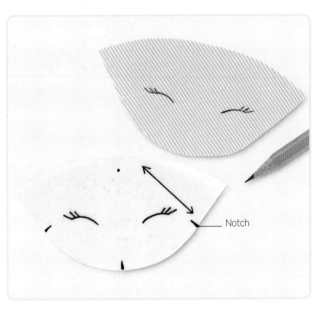

Notch

1 Trace the templates (see p.294) onto the tracing paper and cut them out. Pin the pattern pieces to the fabrics. Cut out one face and one pair of beaks from fabric A, three bellies and three backs from fabric B, and two pairs of wings from fabric C. Cut one pair of wings from the batting. Snip into the notches. Use a pencil to trace the eyes and eyelashes onto the face pattern piece, as well as the dot that marks the top of the head. To transfer these markings to the fabric face, place the pattern, penciled-side down, on the right side of the fabric face, and trace over the eyes and eyelashes again.

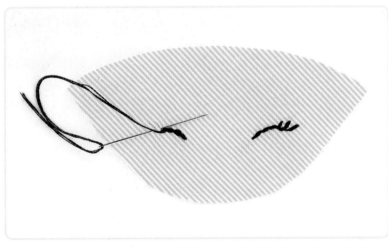

2 Embroider the eyes and eyelashes with three strands of black embroidery thread, knotting the end of the thread to start and finish. To stem stitch the eyes, work from left to right. Bring the needle to the right side of the fabric, then insert it ¹⁄₈in (3mm) along the marked line to the right. Bring the needle back to the right side of the fabric about halfway back toward your starting point, keeping the thread below the marked line. Reinsert the needle ¹⁄₈in (3mm) to the right and bring it back to the right side of the fabric at the end of the first stitch. Embroider the eyelashes with single stitches.

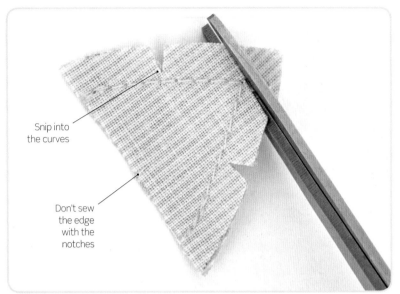

Snip into the curves

Don't sew the edge with the notches

3 With right sides together, pin the pair of beaks together. Sew around the edge, leaving the notched side open. Clip the curves, making sure not to cut through the stitches, then clip off the corner. Turn to the right side through the open side, then press the beak flat.

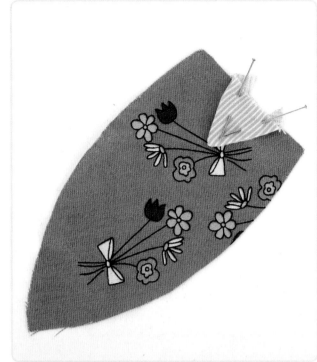

4 With right sides together, pin and baste the beak to one belly piece, matching the notches. This is the middle belly.

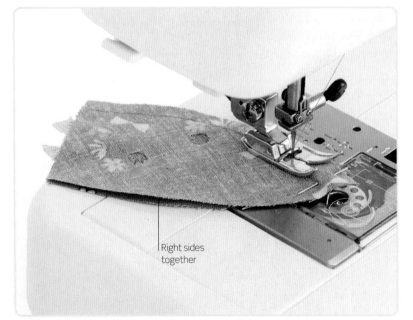

Right sides together

5 With right sides together, pin and sew one long edge of one of the remaining bellies to one long edge of the middle belly. Clip the curves, making sure not to cut through the stitches, then press the seam away from the middle belly.

6 In the same way, pin and sew one long edge of the remaining belly to the other long edge of the middle belly. As before, clip the curves, then press the seam away from the middle belly.

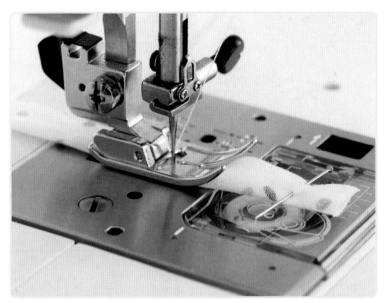

**7** To make the body front, with right sides together, pin and sew the face to the upper edge of the bellies, matching the notches. Clip the curves, then press the seam toward the face.

**8** From fabric D, cut one 8⅝ x 1in (22 x 2.5cm) bias strip for the feathers and one 8 x 1½in (20 x 3.5cm) bias strip for the legs (see p.38). With right sides together, fold the strips in half lengthwise and pin the raw edges together. Sew the long edges. Trim the seam allowance of the feathers to ⅛in (3mm). Using a bodkin, turn the feather strip and the leg strip to the right side.

**9** Cut the feather strip into one 3⅛in (8cm) length and two 2¾in (7cm) lengths. Fold the lengths in half to form loops. Pin the ends of the longest loop to the right side of the face at the marked dot, matching the raw edges. Pin the other loops on either side.

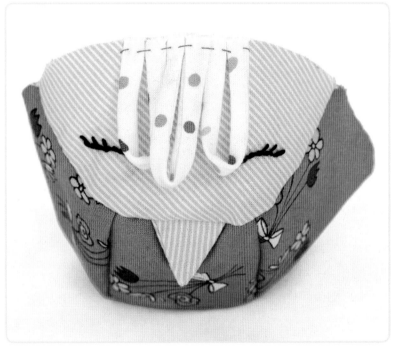

**10** After pinning the feather loops, baste them in place, then remove the pins.

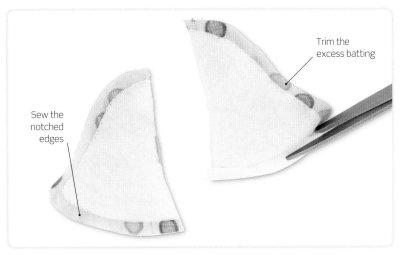

Trim the excess batting

Sew the notched edges

**11** Cut the leg strip in half, turn one end of each half to the inside, and slip stitch it closed (see p.43). Knot the legs, ⅝in (1.5cm) above the closed ends. Cut each leg to 1½in (3.5cm) above the knots. Pin and baste the open ends of the legs to the bottom of the body front, ¼in (6mm) on each side of the intersection of the belly seams.

**12** Pin a batting wing to the wrong side of a fabric wing. Pin a second fabric wing on top of the first fabric wing, right sides together. Repeat for the second wing. Sew around the notched edges, then carefully trim away the batting in the seam allowance. Clip the curves.

**13** Turn the wings to the right side and press lightly. With right sides together, pin and baste the wings to the body front, with their upper tips adjacent to the seam joining the face to the body.

**14** With right sides together, pin and sew one long edge of a back to one long edge of a second back. The second back will now be the middle back. Clip the curves, making sure not to cut through the stitches, then press the seam away from the middle back.

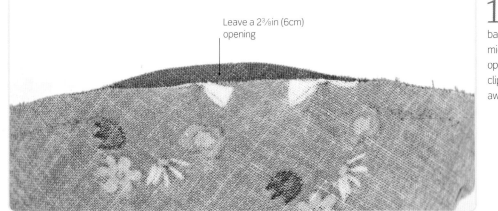

Leave a 2³⁄₈in (6cm) opening

**15** In the same way, pin and sew one long edge of the remaining back to the other long edge of the middle back, leaving a 2³⁄₈in (6cm) opening for turning through. As before, clip the curves, then press the seam away from the middle back.

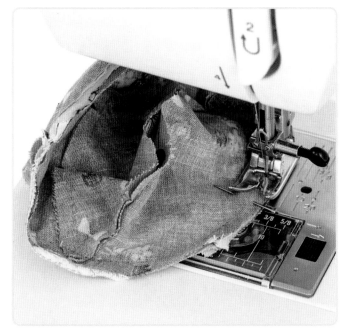

**16** With right sides together, match the intersections of the belly and back seams at the bottom, and the dot on the head to the seam intersection at the top of the back. Pin the front and back of the bird together and sew around the edges. Clip the curves and press the seam open.

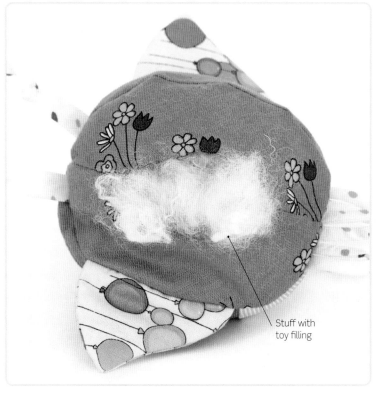

Stuff with toy filling

**17** Turn the bird to the right side through the opening left in Step 15. Stuff the bird firmly and evenly with the toy filling. If you'd like to add a child-safe rattle to the toy, add it now, settling it in the middle of the toy filling. Turn under the raw edges of the opening, then slip stitch the opening closed (see p.43).

*Stuff the bird firmly to get the desired shape.*

# English paper piecing

This is a traditional method for making a quilt of mosaic shapes. The fabric pieces—hexagons, honeycombs, diamonds, and triangles, all of which have at least two bias edges—are basted to precut paper templates the size of the finished element. The technique is usually done by hand. The backing papers can be cut from virtually any heavy paper, but freezer paper can be ironed on quickly and is easy to remove.

## Basic paper-piecing technique

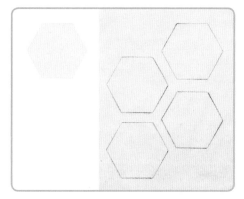

1 Unless you are using precut paper shapes, make a template. Draw around it to make the necessary number of shapes. Using paper scissors, carefully cut out the backing papers.

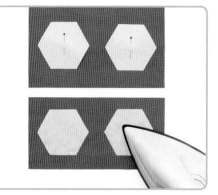

2 Pin a plain-paper shape or iron a freezer-paper shape (paper side up) to the wrong side of the fabric. Leave enough space for seam allowances.

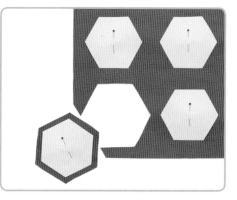

3 Cut out each shape from fabric, leaving a ¼in (6mm) seam allowance all around. You can use scissors or a rotary cutter, but be careful to keep at least one side of the shape along the straight grain of the fabric.

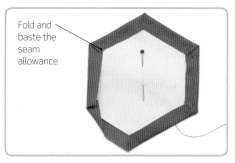

Fold and baste the seam allowance

4 Turn the seam allowance to the wrong side over the edge of the paper shape. Fold the seam allowance in each corner neatly and place a few basting stitches through the wax paper and fabric, holding it securely in place.

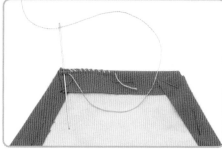

5 To join patches into units, place two shapes right sides together. Make a backstitched loop (see p.42), and whipstitch to the corner as close to the fold as possible. Do not sew through the backing papers.

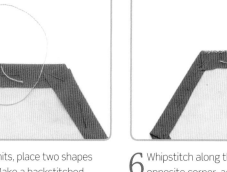

6 Whipstitch along the same edge to the opposite corner, again taking small stitches. When you reach the corner, backstitch in the opposite direction for ¼in (6mm).

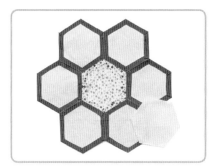

7 Continue adding shapes until complete. If you want to reuse papers, you can remove them once all the shapes adjoining a particular piece have been added by clipping the basting stitches and carefully pulling the paper out.

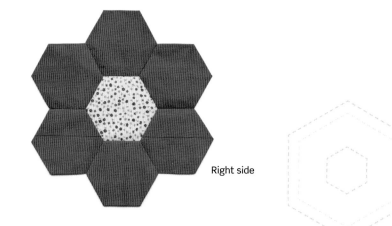

Right side

# Setting in hexagons

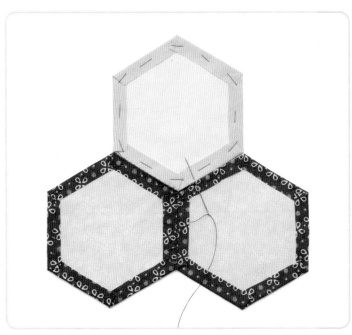

**1** To set in a third hexagon, whipstitch one side of the seam, starting at the center point.

**2** Align the second sides to be joined at their outer points, folding back the pieces as necessary, and sew as before.

## Neat folds

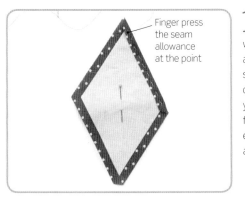

Finger press the seam allowance at the point

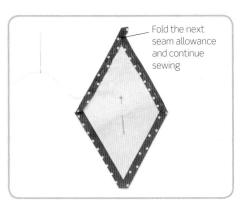

Fold the next seam allowance and continue sewing

**1** To make a neat fold at the sharp points when basting diamonds and triangles, start sewing in the middle of one side. When you reach the point, finger press the extended seam allowance.

**2** Fold over the allowance from the next side neatly. Take a stitch through the fold and continue. Do not trim off the fabric extensions.

## Neat seams

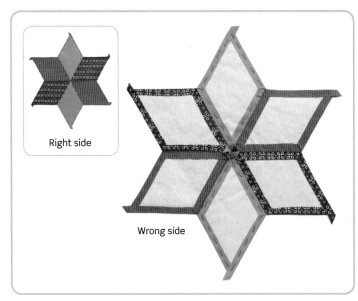

Right side

Wrong side

**To make a neat seam** when you sew pieces together, fold the extension to the side so that you don't stitch through it. Where several come together, the unsewn extensions will form a spiral around their meeting point and lie flat.

# Electronic device cover

You can make this project to fit any electronic device, whether it's a laptop, tablet, or even a phone. Just remember to adjust all of the fabric requirements and flower template size, as needed. You can use a paper clip to hold the template and fabric pieces together.

## Essential Information

**DIFFICULTY** Medium

**SIZE** To fit the device of your choice

**TOOLS AND MATERIALS**

Paper
Paper clip (optional)
Pins
Needle
Threads to match the fabrics
Quilter's ruler
Cutting mat
Rotary cutter
Tailor's chalk or water-soluble pen
Scissors
Velcro® for the closure. You will need enough to fit across the width of your device

**FABRICS**

5 x 7½in (12 x 18cm) petal fabric
2½ x 2½in (6 x 6cm) flower center fabric
Calculate the main fabric requirements for your device by following the instructions in Step 4
You will need enough batting to fit around the circumference of your device, plus 6in (15.5cm) extra in both dimensions
Bias tape to fit the edges of your device ([length + height of device] x 2)

**SKILLS**

English paper piecing (see p.134–135)

**SEAM ALLOWANCE**

¼in (6mm), unless otherwise stated

1 Copy and cut out seven paper hexagons using the template on page 292. Using the English paper piecing technique (see p.134), create six hexagons in the petal fabric and one hexagon from the flower center fabric.

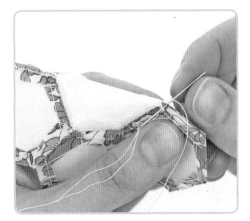

2 Join the hexagons into a flower shape, whipstitching the petals to the center hexagon, then the sides of the petals to one another (see p.134).

3 Once the petals are joined, press the finished flower to set the folds. Set aside.

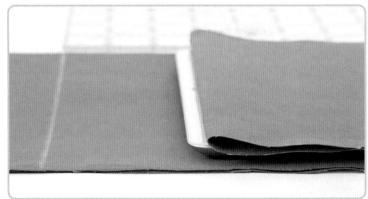

4 Measure the circumference of the width of your device, divide by two, then add 1in (2.5cm) to the total. Next, measure the circumference of the height of your device, add 6in (15.5cm), then multiply by two. Measure and cut a strip of fabric with these dimensions.

5 Fold the strip in half lengthwise. The folded edge will be the top, front edge of the cover. Place the device on the strip and then fold the folded edge up and over the front of the device so that it sits just below the top edge of the device, as shown. Measure and mark a line approximately 2½in (6.5cm), or the length of your choice, from the top of the device to create the flap. Cut along the line just marked. Mark a second line where the top of the device sits.

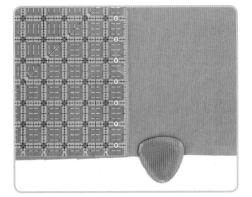

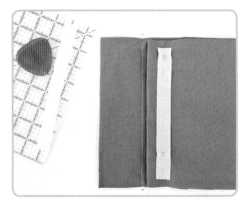

6 Open up the fabric strip and measure and mark a line in the center of the fabric, where it was previously folded.

7 Cut a piece of batting to fit on one half of the fabric strip, from the halfway line just marked to the opposite edge. Trim it slightly smaller all around so that it sits just inside the edges of the fabric. Fold the other side of fabric lengthwise over the batting, on the marked line, aligning all of the edges.

8 Fold the folded edge of the strip up to just below the line that marks the top of the device. Pin on the line. Cut a piece of Velcro® slightly shorter than the width of the fabric strip. Pin the rough side of the Velcro® just below the folded edge, on the front.

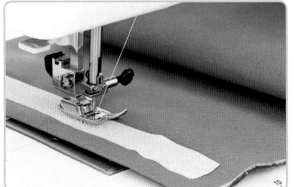

9 Using a matching thread, topstitch around all four edges of the rough Velcro® piece to attach it to the front of the cover.

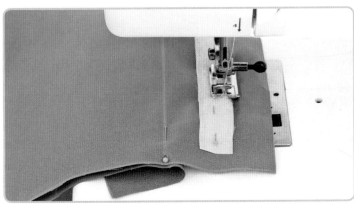

**10** Pin the soft side of the Velcro® to the inside of the flap, only through the inside piece of fabric and batting, so that when the flap is folded over the two halves of Velcro® will meet one another. Place your device inside the roughly constructed cover to ensure the placement is correct. Topstitch the piece of Velcro® in place, being sure not to sew through the outer fabric flap.

**11** Carefully remove the paper from your flower and pin the flower on the front of the cover, in the location of your choice.

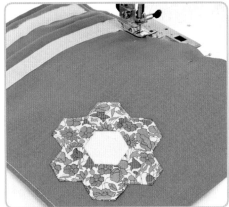

**12** Using a matching thread, topstitch around the outer edges of the flower to attach it to the front of the cover only.

**13** Fold the front of the cover back up in place so that the folded front edge sits just below the line. Pin around the three raw edges of the cover.

**14** Starting in the bottom, left corner, sew around the three raw edges using a ¼in (6mm) seam allowance.

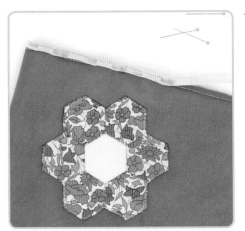

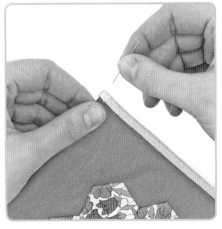

**15** Pin the bias tape around the three raw edges, mitering the corners and folding under the raw edges of the bias tape at either end.

**16** Using a needle and matching thread, attach the bias tape to the edges. We've used a running stitch, weaving back and forth through all the layers at one time.

# Strip piecing

Strip piecing is a good way to build blocks quickly. In principle, several long strips are joined—or pieced—and then cut apart before being sewn together again in a different sequence. It is the method by which many blocks can be made, including log cabin (see pp.142–143) and Seminole patchwork (see pp.153–155).

## Strip-pieced blocks: Rail fence

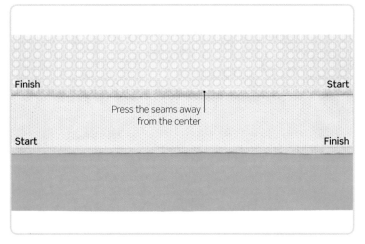

Finish      Start

Press the seams away from the center

Start      Finish

**1** Cut three strips of equal width from three contrasting fabrics. With right sides together, sew them lengthwise, leaving a ¹⁄₄in (6mm) seam allowance. To prevent the pieced strip from bowing, join strips 1 and 2, then reverse the direction of sewing to add strip 3. Press the seams to one side, away from the center.

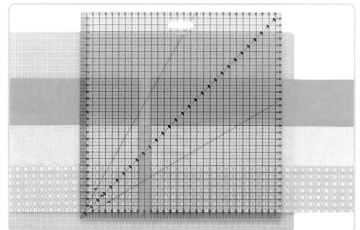

**2** Using a rotary cutter and quilter's ruler, measure the width of the pieced strip and cut across it to make squares the same size on each side as this measurement.

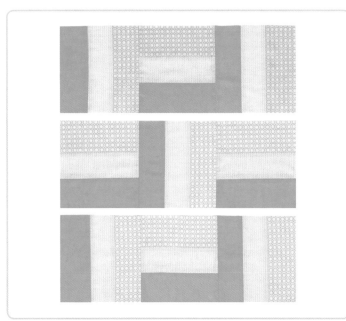

**3** Following the layout, arrange the squares in rows of three. With right sides together, join the squares to make three rows, leaving a ¹⁄₄in (6mm) seam allowance. Press, alternating the direction in each row.

**4** With right sides together, join the rows, matching the seams and leaving a ¹⁄₄in (6mm) seam allowance.

# String piecing

String piecing is similar to strip piecing, but the lengths of fabric are not necessarily straight strips and are referred to as "strings." The string-pieced blocks can be combined to make larger units. If using a paper foundation block for Method 2, use a stitch length of around 1.5 to perforate the paper making it easier to remove.

## Method 1

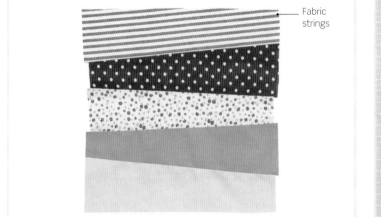

Fabric strings

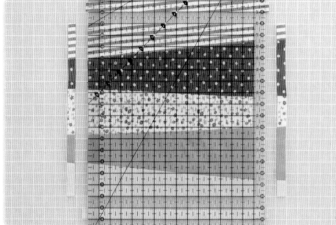

1 Select "strings" of fabric with plenty of color and pattern contrast. With right sides together, sew them together lengthwise, leaving a ¼in (6mm) seam allowance. Alternate the angle as you add each piece and alternate the direction of sewing each time to prevent bowing.

2 Press the seams to one side. Using a rotary cutter and quilter's ruler, trim the piece to the desired size and shape.

## Method 2

Machine sew along one edge

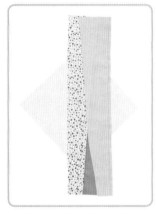

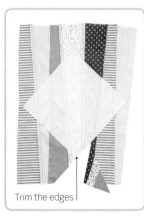

Trim the edges

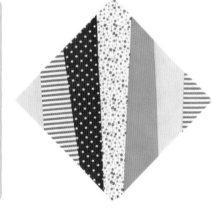

1 Cut a muslin or paper foundation block, plus seam allowances. Place the first string right side up in the center of the block and lay the second string right side down on top. Make sure both strings are longer than the block at its widest point. Machine sew along one edge of the strips through all layers. Flip the joined pieces open and press.

2 Turn the foundation block, then add a new string, right-side down, to the free edge of the first string. Flip the joined pieces open and press.

3 Continue to add strings, flip, press, and sew, until the foundation block is covered. Trim the edges level with the foundation. If you have used a paper foundation, leave a ¼in (6mm) allowance when you trim.

4 Carefully tear away the paper foundation, if used. A muslin foundation will remain in place. Press.

# Log cabin

Log cabin is a very versatile block design, usually featuring fabric strips surrounding a small central square, as shown here, although some log cabin blocks have other shapes in the center. Blocks can be made individually or chain pieced. Always leave a ¼in (6mm) seam allowance unless otherwise stated. Log cabin is stunning in simple two-color versions and the blocks can be set in many ways to create secondary patterns (see p.107).

## Method 1: Individual blocks

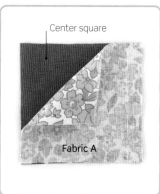

Center square

Fabric A

**1** Cut a center square of the desired size, plus seam allowances. Cut a second square the same size from fabric A and, with right sides together, sew them together along one edge to make a pieced unit. Press open.

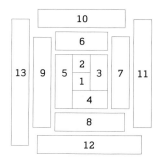

Sew along the long side

**2** Cut a strip from fabric A the width of the center square and the same length as the pressed pieced unit. With right sides together, sew this strip to the long side of the unit.

Fabric B

**3** Add two strips from fabric B in the same way, working in a clockwise direction to ensure that the center square remains in the middle.

**4** Continue adding strips, two from fabric A and two from fabric B, or two each from different fabrics. Always work in a clockwise direction until the block reaches the desired size.

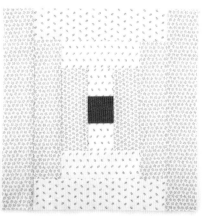

## Method 2: Courthouse steps variation

Fabric A

Fabric A

**1** Cut a center square. From fabric A, cut two squares the same size as the center and with right sides together, join them to opposite sides of the center square to make a pieced unit. Press the seams away from the center.

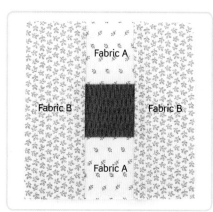

Fabric A

Fabric B

Fabric B

Fabric A

**2** Cut strips the same width as the center square from fabric B, and add one strip to each long side of the pieced unit. Trim to the same length as the pieced unit. Press away from the center.

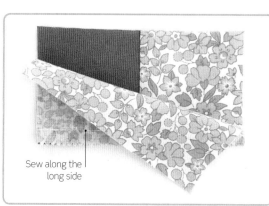

**3** Continue adding strips—first two strips of fabric A to the top and bottom, then two of fabric B to the sides, or two each from different fabrics— until the block reaches the desired size. Press each strip away from the center.

# Method 3: Chain piecing

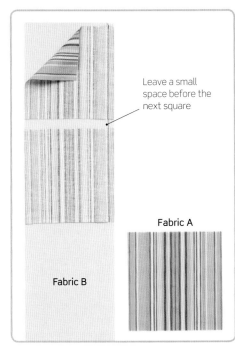

Leave a small space before the next square

Fabric A

Fabric B

1 Cut the required number of identical center squares from fabric A. Cut strips from fabric B the same width as the fabric A squares. Place one center square at one end of a strip with right sides together. Sew, leaving a ¼in (6mm) seam allowance.

2 Without raising the machine needle or breaking the thread, leave a small gap and add a second fabric A square in the same way. Continue adding squares until you reach the end of the strip and have a chain of units.

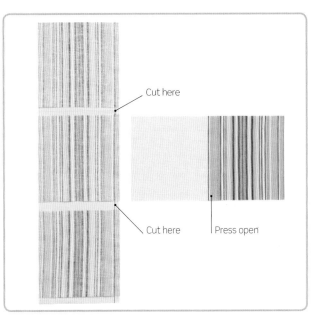

Cut here

Cut here

Press open

3 Snip the units apart and, if necessary, trim the squares so they are the same size. Flip them open and press.

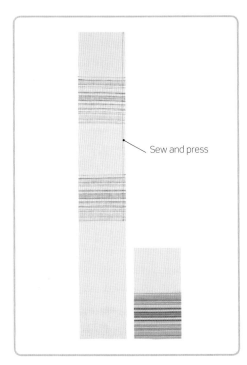

Sew and press

4 Place the pieced units on a second fabric B strip, with right sides together and with the fabric A squares below the fabric B squares. Sew and press, then cut across the strip below each fabric A square to make a number of three-part units.

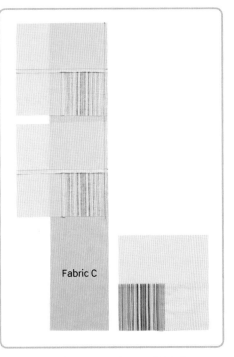

Fabric C

5 Place the three-part units on a fabric C strip with right sides together, again with the fabric A squares at the bottom. Sew, press, and trim, as before.

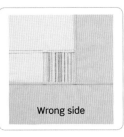

Wrong side

6 Repeat to add the fourth strip (fabric C) along the unsewn edge of the fabric A square, always working clockwise. Continue adding strips—two B, and then two C, or two each from different fabrics—until the blocks are the desired size.

# Log cabin pillow

This pillow uses four log cabin blocks, each with light fabrics radiating from one corner and dark fabrics from the other. This light and dark contrast is traditional in log cabin blocks, and the greater the contrast, the more dramatic the effect.

## Essential Information

**DIFFICULTY** Easy

**SIZE** 16 x 16in (40 x 40cm)

**TOOLS AND MATERIALS**
Rotary cutter
Cutting mat
Quilter's ruler
Pins
Sewing machine
Threads to match your fabrics
Iron and ironing board
Curved safety pins or a sewing needle
Scissors

**FABRICS**
**A:** $3\frac{1}{2}$ x $3\frac{1}{2}$in (9 x 9cm)
**B:** $3\frac{1}{2}$ x $3\frac{1}{2}$in (9 x 9cm)
**C:** 7 x $2\frac{3}{4}$in (18 x 7cm)
**D:** 7 x $2\frac{3}{4}$in (18 x 7cm)
**E:** 7 x $4\frac{1}{4}$in (18 x 10.5cm)
**F:** 7 x $4\frac{1}{4}$in (18 x 10.5cm)
**G:** 7 x 6in (18 x 14cm)
**H:** 7 x 6in (18 x 14cm)
**I:** 7 x $6\frac{3}{4}$in (18 x 17.5cm)
**J:** 7 x $6\frac{3}{4}$in (18 x 17.5cm)
**K:** 7 x $8\frac{1}{2}$in (18 x 21cm)
**L:** 7 x $8\frac{1}{2}$in (18 x 21cm)
**M:** 7 x $9\frac{1}{2}$in (18 x 24.5cm)
18 x 40in (46cm x 100cm) backing fabric
$16\frac{1}{2}$ x $16\frac{1}{2}$in (42 x 42cm) batting
16in (40cm) square pillow cushion

**SKILLS**
Log cabin (see pp.142–143)

**SEAM ALLOWANCE**
$\frac{1}{4}$in (6mm) throughout, unless otherwise stated

Make sure the fabric aligns on all four edges

**1** Cut your fabric pieces to size, starting with a $1\frac{3}{4}$in (4.5cm) square for the center of each block. Cut each strip to $1\frac{3}{4}$in (4.5cm) wide by the required length (see p.37).

Right sides together

**2** Create a block following the instructions on page 142. With right sides together, join piece A to piece B, then continue adding the pieces in order until the block is complete. Press the seams as you work (see pp.44–45).

**3** Repeat to create four identical blocks. Use your quilter's ruler to square up the block and trim off any uneven or messy edges.

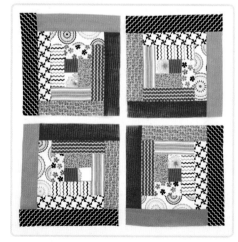

**4** Arrange the four blocks as you would like them to appear on the pillow front. Here a traditional light and dark color contrast has been used, but you can choose any arrangement you wish for your pillow (see p.107).

5 With right sides together, pin together, then sew the top two blocks of your design and the bottom two blocks. Here the blocks have been joined so that the darker colors are adjacent to each other. Press the seams open.

6 To complete the pillow front, with right sides together, pin, then sew the top pair of blocks to the bottom pair of blocks. Keep the seams joining the strips aligned between one pair of blocks and the other. Press the seam open.

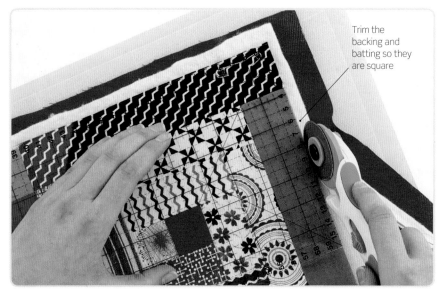

Trim the backing and batting so they are square

7 Lay out a piece of backing fabric and place the batting on top. Place the pillow front on top of the batting, right side faceup. Use safety pins or baste all three layers together. Use the quilter's ruler and rotary cutter to trim the batting and backing fabric square with the edges of the pillow front.

8 To make the pillow back, cut two pieces from the backing fabric, each 16½ x 10¼in (42 x 26cm). Fold one of the long edges of one piece to the wrong side of the fabric by ⅜in (1cm). Fold it again by the same amount to create a neat hem and to enclose the raw edge. Pin the hem in place.

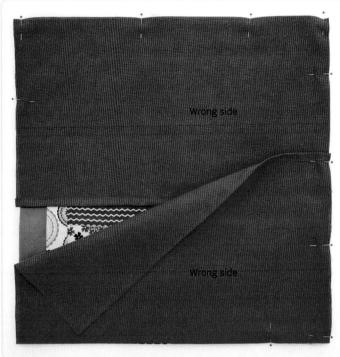

9 Check that the hem is straight, then sew along the edge of the second fold to secure the hem. Repeat Steps 8 and 9 on the other piece of fabric to make the second back piece.

10 Lay the pillow front, right-side up. Place one of the back pieces on top, right-side down, aligning its long, unhemmed edge with the top raw edge of the pillow front. Place the second back piece right-side down on top of the first, aligning its long, unhemmed edge with the bottom raw edge of the pillow front. The two pillow back pieces should overlap. Pin along all four edges.

11 Leaving a ³⁄₈in (1cm) seam allowance, sew around all four edges of the pillow cover to secure the back pieces to the pillow front. Remove the pins as you work.

12 Snip off all four corners, making sure not to cut through the stitches. Turn the pillow cover to the right side through the opening in the back. Iron and insert the pillow cushion.

# Working on a foundation

Several patchwork techniques are worked on a foundation, also known as stitch-and-flip. Crazy patchwork uses random shapes and is a great way to use up scraps. It is best made on a lightweight foundation fabric, such as muslin.

Reverse-pieced foundation piecing ensures accuracy and is a quick way to make blocks. You can make patterns for each segment, or cut the shapes with generous seam allowances.

## Foundation piecing: Top pieced

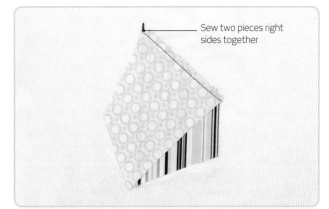

Sew two pieces right sides together

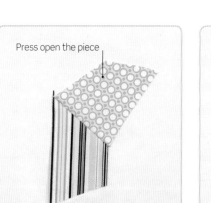

Press open the piece

Sew a third piece along one edge

1 Cut a foundation of lightweight muslin the size you want the finished block to be plus a 1in (2.5cm) seam allowance all around.

2 Gather a selection of straight-sided pieces of various shapes and colors. Starting in the center, place two pieces right sides together, on top of the foundation, and sew along one side through all three layers. Take a ¼in (6mm) seam allowance, whether you are working by hand or machine.

3 Press or finger press the pieces open.

4 Add piece 3 along one edge of the combined shape made in Step 1. Open and press. If necessary, trim the seam allowance level with scissors before you add the next piece. Snip off the thread ends.

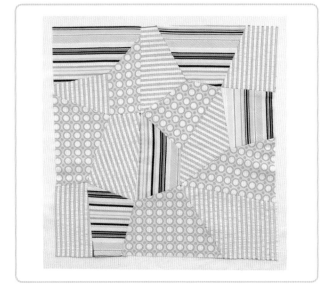

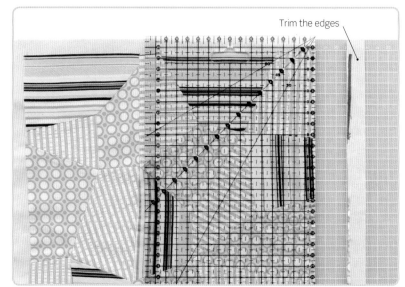

Trim the edges

5 Continue clockwise around the center piece until the foundation is completely filled. Keep the arrangement random and avoid parallel lines. Run the seams in different directions and vary the angles. Press each piece open as you work.

6 Trim the edges level with the edges of the foundation fabric. Embellish the finished piece if you wish.

# Foundation piecing: Reverse pieced

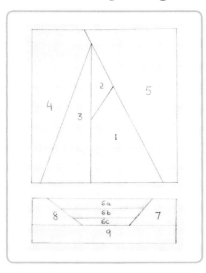

**1** Cut the chosen foundation (use paper, muslin, batting, or nonwoven interfacing) to size, with a generous amount added all around.

**2** Trace or transfer the design to the foundation. Number the piecing order clearly on the foundation. You will be sewing from the back of the foundation, so the block will be the reverse of the foundation itself.

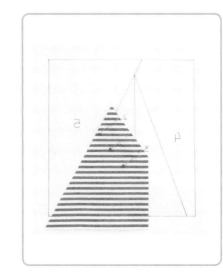

**3** Cut out piece 1 and pin it right side up on the reverse side of the foundation. Make sure that it extends beyond the seam lines; you can check this by holding it up to the light.

**4** Cut out piece 2 and place it right sides together on piece 1, along the seam to be sewn. Pin through all layers.

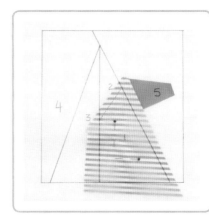

**5** Turn the foundation right-side up and re-pin carefully to keep from catching any pins in the feed dogs of your sewing machine.

**6** Sew the seam, joining pieces 1 and 2. If your foundation is made of paper, use a short 1.5 stitch length to make it easier to remove. If necessary, trim the seam allowance to ¼in (6mm).

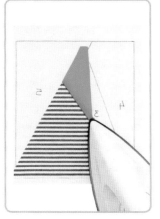

**7** Turn the foundation fabric right-side up, remove the pins, open the pieces, and press.

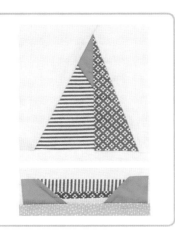

**8** Cut piece 3 and align it next to piece 2. Pin it on top, then turn under and sew as in Steps 3–7 until the top is complete. Make the bottom section in the same way.

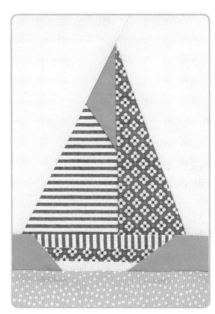

**9** Join the sections. Then trim the foundation level with the edges of the patchwork design. If the foundation is removable, carefully tear it away.

# Folded patchwork

There are a number of specialized patchwork techniques that involve manipulating fabric by folding it in specific ways before joining pieces together. They can all be used to make quilts, but because they are, by definition, made from more than one layer, they are also good for making household items, such as placemats.

## Cathedral window

Fold the seam allowance to the wrong side and press

**1** Decide the size of the finished square (4in/10cm) and multiply the measurement by 2 (8in/20cm). Add ½in (1.2cm) seam allowance and cut four squares this size from the background, fabric A.

**2** Fold the seam allowance down and press each side of the square flat. Diagonally fold one way and press, then fold along the other diagonal and press firmly to mark the exact center. Open out.

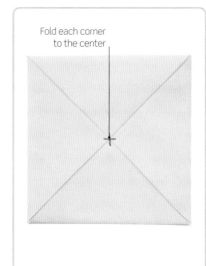

Fold each corner to the center

**3** Fold each corner of each square to the center and press the folds firmly. Make sure that the new corners are sharply defined.

**4** Take a small cross-stitch across the center into each point, through all the layers to hold the points in place.

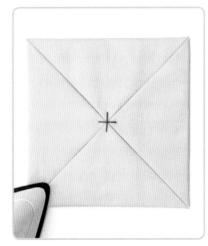

Sew two squares along one edge

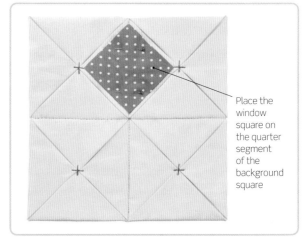

Place the window square on the quarter segment of the background square

**5** Fold each corner to the center again and press firmly. Take a small cross-stitch as before through all the layers to hold the points in place. The square is now half the size of that cut in Step 1.

**6** With folded edges together, join the four squares in pairs, whipstitching with tiny stitches along the edge. Then join the two pairs to make a square. If you are making a large piece, you can also work in rows that are joined before the windows are added.

**7** Cut four contrasting window squares from fabric B. Each window square should just fit inside a quarter segment of the background square; to work out the size, measure the distance from the center of one folded square to the outside corner.

**8** Place the first window square over a seam, on the diagonal. Pin in place. If necessary, trim the edges slightly to make it fit.

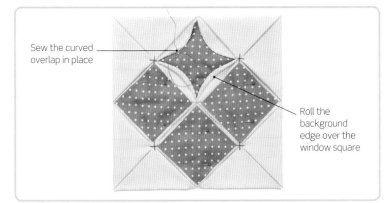

Sew the curved overlap in place

Roll the background edge over the window square

**9** Roll one folded edge in the background square over the raw edge of the first window square.

**10** Matching the thread to the background fabric, sew the rolled, slightly curved overlap in place with tiny stitches, catching in the raw edge completely. Do not sew through the background fabric. Repeat to catch in the other three edges of the window.

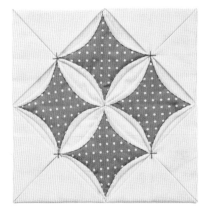

**11** Repeat Steps 7 to 9 to fill the other spaces in the square. If you work in rows, add windows after you join rows together.

## Secret garden

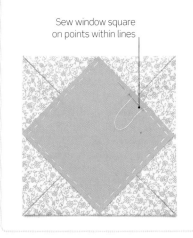

Sew window square on points within lines

**1** Make a folded square as for Steps 1 to 3 of Cathedral window (see opposite). Fold and press the corners, as in Step 4, but do not sew in place. Cut a window square the size of the finished square.

**2** Open the pressed corners and place the window square on point within the lines. If necessary, trim the raw edges to fit and anchor with small basting stitches.

Pin ¼in (6mm) in from each corner

**3** Fold the four corners of the background square into the center. Press. Anchor each corner in the center with a small cross, sewing through all layers.

**4** Pin ¼in (6mm) in from each corner through all layers to stabilize the square.

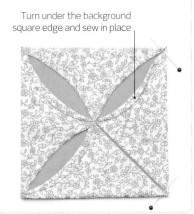

Turn under the background square edge and sew in place

**5** Turn under one edge of the background square to form a curving "petal" shape. Sew in place, working outward from the center and using thread to match the background fabric.

**6** Repeat on all eight folded edges of the background square, removing the pins and securing each corner with a double basting stitch.

# Folded star

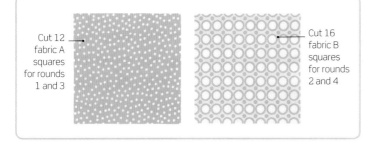

Cut 12 fabric A squares for rounds 1 and 3

Cut 16 fabric B squares for rounds 2 and 4

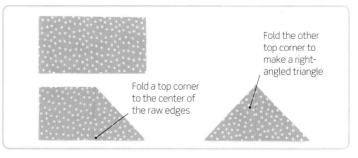

Fold a top corner to the center of the raw edges

Fold the other top corner to make a right-angled triangle

1 The star consists of a calico foundation square with four rounds, or layers, of triangles on top. Cut the calico to the finished size plus 2in (5cm) on all sides. For rounds 1 and 3, cut twelve 4in (10cm) squares from fabric A. For rounds 2 and 4, cut sixteen 4in (10cm) squares from fabric B.

2 For the triangles, with wrong sides together, press each square in half. Fold one top corner of the resulting rectangle to the center of the raw edges and press. Repeat, folding the other top corner to the raw edges to make a right-angled triangle with raw edges along its long side.

**Foundation square**

Place four fabric A triangles on the (square) foundation and baste in place

3 To make guidelines, fold the foundation square in half horizontally and vertically and press. Fold in half again along the diagonals and press again. Open the square out.

4 For round 1, place the four fabric A right-angled triangles along the pressed guidelines, so their points meet in the center and the folded edges are on top. Pin or baste in place along the raw edges. Secure each point with a small hidden stitch.

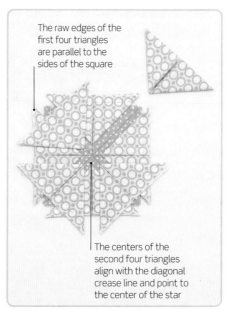

The raw edges of the first four triangles are parallel to the sides of the square

The centers of the second four triangles align with the diagonal crease line and point to the center of the star

5 For round 2, place four fabric B right-angled triangles with their points ³⁄₈in (1cm) from the center, and with their raw edges parallel with the sides of the foundation square. Secure as in Step 4, then add four more fabric B triangles in the gaps, aligning their raw edges with the diagonal guidelines on the foundation square. Secure as before. Measure ³⁄₈in (1cm) from the points and mark.

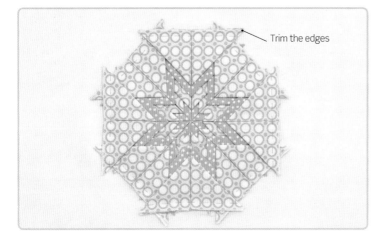

Trim the edges

6 Add eight fabric A triangles for round 3 in the same way as the eight were added for round 2, followed by eight fabric B triangles for round 4. Remove the basting and trim and finish all the edges as desired.

# Seminole patchwork

Used by the Seminole tribe of American Indians in Florida, this type of strip-pieced patchwork is useful for borders or blocks. The method often involves cutting pieced strips at an angle and rejoining them.

## Method 1: Straight band

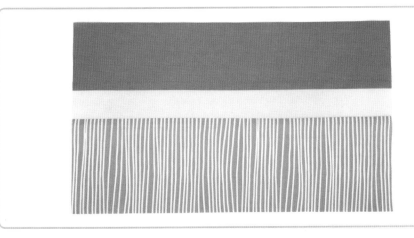

1 Cut strips from three contrasting fabrics. Here the width of the strips from top to bottom of the picture is in the ratio of 2:1:3, plus seam allowances, which ensures that the white will be evenly offset either side of the center line of the finished patchwork. With the narrowest strip in the center and with right sides together, join the three strips, leaving a ¼in (6mm) seam allowance. Press the seams toward the darker color.

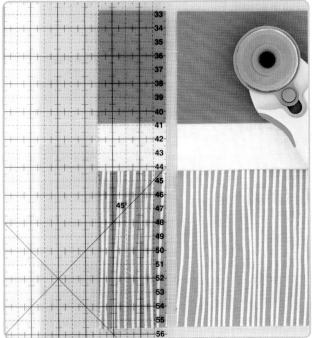

2 Using a rotary cutter and quilter's ruler, cut across the joined strips to make pieced strips of the desired width.

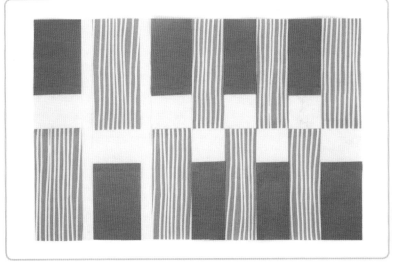

3 Alternating the top and bottom of each adjacent strip and with right sides together, sew the strips together again, leaving a ¼in (6mm) seam allowance. Press all the seams in the same direction.

# Method 2: Angled band

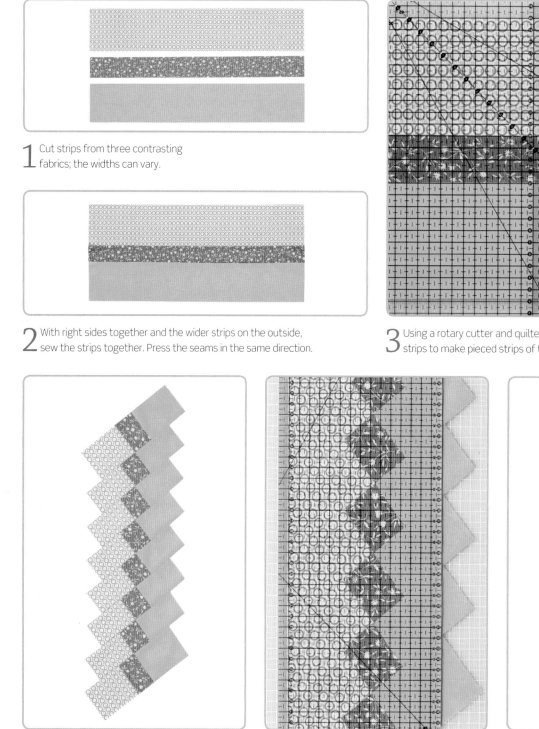

1 Cut strips from three contrasting fabrics; the widths can vary.

2 With right sides together and the wider strips on the outside, sew the strips together. Press the seams in the same direction.

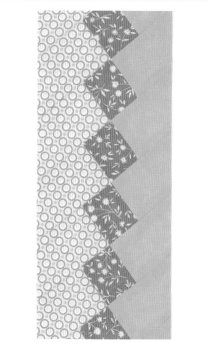

3 Using a rotary cutter and quilter's ruler, cut across the joined strips to make pieced strips of the desired width.

4 Sew the strips back together, leaving a ¼in (6mm) seam allowance and offsetting the center squares each time you join one strip to the next. Press the seams in the same direction.

5 Using a rotary cutter and quilter's ruler, trim off the points at either edge of the pieced strip.

6 Square up both ends to make a neat pieced strip.

# Method 3: Chevron band

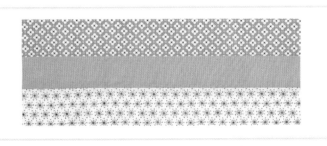

1 Cut strips the same width from three contrasting fabrics. With right sides together, sew the strips together and press the seams in the same direction. Make a second identical pieced strip.

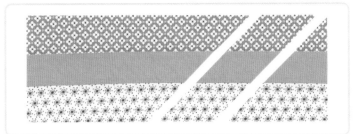

2 Using a rotary cutter and quilter's ruler, cut one of the pieced strips several times at a 45-degree angle in one direction (see p.38) to make angled strips.

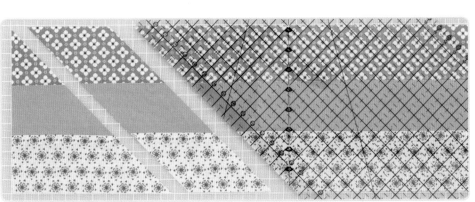

3 Repeat on the second pieced strip, using the same angle but reversing the direction of the cut.

4 Match the seams of an angled strip from the first pieced strip to the seams of an angled strip from the second pieced strip. Sew together, leaving a ¼in (6mm) seam allowance. Repeat to join in pairs.

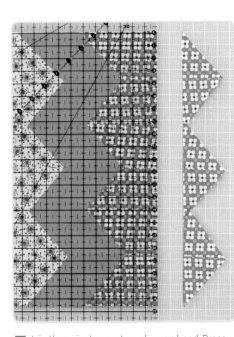

5 Join the pairs to create a chevron band. Press the seams in the same direction. Using a rotary cutter and quilter's ruler, trim off the points at either edge of the pieced strip.

6 The result is a chevron pattern running through the whole of the pieced strip.

# Chevron quilt

Create a visually appealing chevron pattern by using bold, contrasting fabrics for the stripes, or choose similar colors for a more subtle quilt. You can try adding more rows, for more chevrons, or even fill the entire quilt top with chevrons.

## Essential Information

**DIFFICULTY** Medium

**SIZE** 38½ x 53in (98 x 135cm)

**TOOLS AND MATERIALS**
Measuring tape
Quilter's ruler
Rotary cutter
Cutting mat
Scissors
Sewing machine
Threads to match your fabrics
Iron and ironing board
Safety pins
Pins
Sewing needle

**FABRICS**
**A:** 17 x 44in (44 x 112cm) white fabric
**B:** 12 x 44in (31 x 112cm) orange fabric
**C:** 44 x 44in (112 x 112cm) main fabric
44 x 55in (112 x 140cm) backing fabric
16 x 44in (40 x 112cm) binding fabric
44 x 59in (110 x 150cm) batting

**SKILLS**
Chevron band (see p.155)

**SEAM ALLOWANCE**
¼in (6mm) throughout, unless otherwise stated

1 Cut 10 strips of fabric each 2½ x 44in (6.5 x 112cm); six from fabric A and four from fabric B.

2 Pin, then sew, the first two strips—one of fabric A and one of fabric B—together along the long edges. Repeat to attach five strips together, alternating so you have A, B, A, B, and A. Sew in opposite directions when attaching each strip, to help prevent distortion (see p.62).

3 Repeat, sewing the remaining five strips together to create a second pieced strip.

4 Iron the finished pieced strips pressing the seam allowances toward the darker fabric.

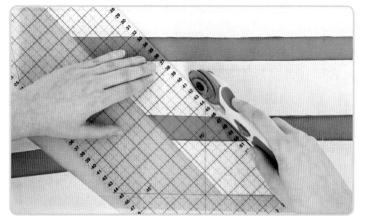

5 Cut the first pieced strip into 2½in (6.5cm) segments on a 45-degree angle. Cut until the entire strip has been cut (see p.155, Step 2).

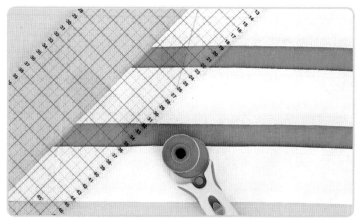

6 Cut the second pieced strip in the same way, but changing the direction of the angle to the opposite way (see p.155, Step 3).

7 Lay out 19 cut pieces, alternating one from each directional group, to create the chevron pattern.

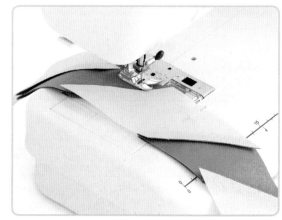

8 Pin and sew the pieces together in pairs. Then, pin and sew the pairs and extra piece together to create one long strip.

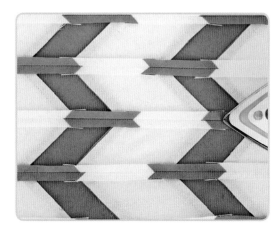

9 Press the seams open at the back of the pieced chevron strip.

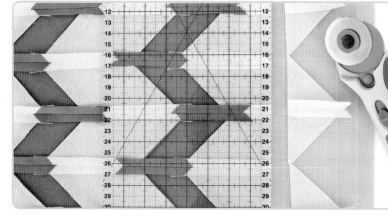

10 Trim off the pointed edges of the chevron strip to even both edges (see p.155, Step 5). Make sure to trim each edge the same amount, so that the chevron design is centered in the strip.

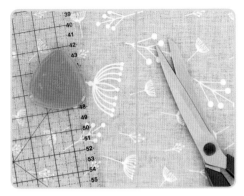

**11** Cut the two pieces of front fabric from the main fabric—one 39 x 29in (100 x 74cm) piece for the top and one 39 x 14in (100 x 35.5cm) piece for the bottom.

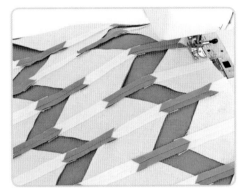

**12** Pin and sew one long edge of the chevron strip right sides together with the bottom edge of the top main fabric piece. Then, pin and sew the other long edge of the chevron strip to the top edge of the bottom main fabric piece to create the quilt top. Press the seams toward the main fabric.

**13** Lay out the backing fabric right-side down, then the batting, and then the quilt top right-side up. Smooth all of the layers, then pin or baste them together to create the quilt sandwich (see p.46).

**14** Quilt the quilt sandwich using the quilting method and pattern of your choice (see pp.204-205, 210-213).

**15** Trim the batting and backing fabric even with the quilt top, squaring up all of the edges.

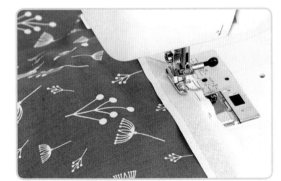

**16** Create a 2½in (6cm) wide binding strip from the binding fabric (see pp.48-49) and attach the binding using the Double-fold binding method (see p.53), or the method of your choice (see pp.50-53).

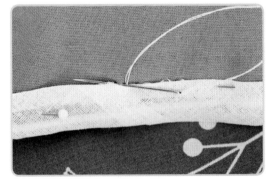

**17** Finish the binding at the back by hand, slip stitching it in place with a needle and thread.

# Frayed patchwork

Seams do not always have to be hidden. By sewing pieces wrong sides together the seams will show on the outside of the patchwork piece. While there are more involved ways of sewing frayed seams, the method shown below is the easiest. Do not quilt over the frayed seams, since it will flatten the fluffy edges; only quilt inside the seams.

**1** Piece your patchwork in the normal way, but sew all of the pieces wrong sides together. Carefully snip into the seam allowance and use a pin to tease out a few threads from the edge.

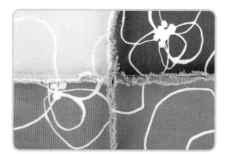

**2** Putting the piece through a wash and dry cycle will really fluffy up the raw edges. When the patchwork is complete it will create a lovely chenille effect, which is great for baby quilts.

# Yo-yos

Yo-yos, also called Suffolk puffs, are fabric circles that have been gathered to make two layers. They are widely used as decorations in appliqué and can be further embellished. Joined edge to edge, they can be made into tablecloths, pillow covers, or openwork bedcovers. Yo-yo projects are a great way to use up small scraps of fabric.

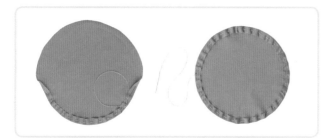

**1** Cut circles of fabric twice the desired finished size. Knot a length of strong thread, doubled if necessary, and secure it close to the edge on the wrong side of the circle. Turn the raw edge ¼in (6mm) to the wrong side and take small gathering stitches through both layers all around the edge to make a single hem. Finish next to where you started.

Gently pull the thread to gather the circle

**2** Do not remove the needle or cut the thread, but pull the thread gently to gather the circle into a smaller one, with pleats around the center. The raw edge will disappear inside the circle. Secure the thread with a couple of basting stitches or backstitches, then knot. Cut the thread. Flatten the circle by gently finger pressing the edges. The gathered side is usually the front, but sometimes the back is used instead.

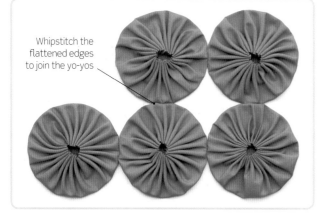

Whipstitch the flattened edges to join the yo-yos

**3** To join yo-yos, place them gathered sides facing and whipstitch the flattened edges for a short distance, taking small, tight stitches. Join yo-yos together until you have a row that is the desired length; join rows together in the same way.

# Pictorial blocks

Most pictorial quilt blocks are appliquéd, but there are a number of representational blocks, traditional and modern, that are pieced. Many of them, such as flowers and leaves, derive from nature, and most look best if they are spaced out on a quilt, not set together edge to edge. Sashing (see pp.108–109) can be used to separate blocks to show them off, or they can be alternated with plain, solid blocks.

## Maple leaf: nine-patch

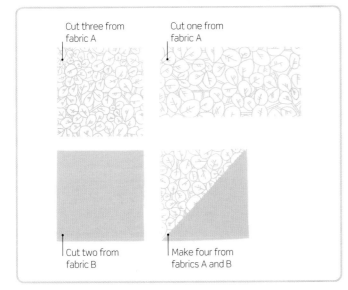

Cut three from fabric A

Cut one from fabric A

Cut two from fabric B

Make four from fabrics A and B

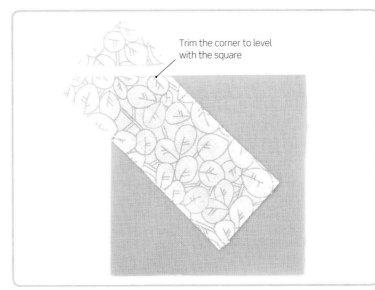

Trim the corner to level with the square

1 Divide the size of the finished block by three. Add seam allowances. Cut three squares that size from fabric A and two from fabric B. From fabric B cut a strip 1½in (4cm) wide and long enough to fit across the diagonal of one square for the "stem." Make four half-square triangles of the same size (see p.82) from fabrics A and B.

2 Place the stem strip diagonally across one of the fabric B squares. Turn under the raw edges on the long edges and one short edge. Topstitch along the edges through the fabrics. Trim the other edges level with the corner of the square.

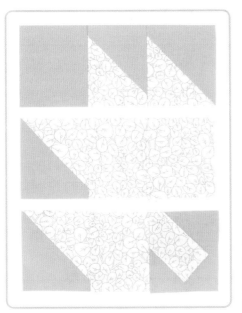

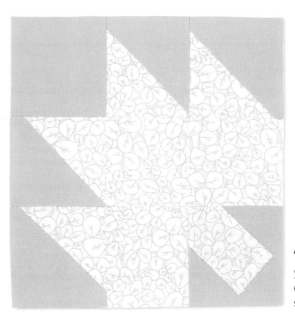

3 Following the layout, join the units to make three rows of three blocks each.

4 Join the rows, making sure you catch the raw edge of the "stem" strip in the seams.

# Lily: eight-point star

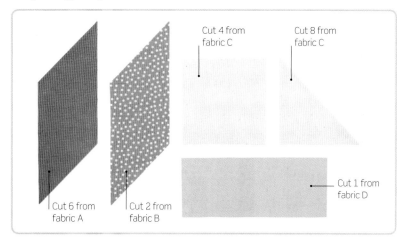

Cut 4 from fabric C

Cut 8 from fabric C

Cut 1 from fabric D

Cut 6 from fabric A

Cut 2 from fabric B

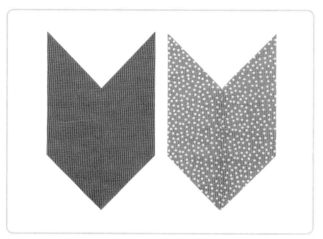

**1** Cut six 45-degree angle diamonds for the "petals" from fabric A, two petals from fabric B, and four corner squares and eight right-angled triangles from fabric C (see p.39). Make sure to cut half the petals in reverse, to form pairs. From fabric D, cut a strip 1in (2.5cm) wide and long enough to fit across the diagonal of one fabric C square for the "stem."

**2** Matching the prints, join the "petals" in pairs as shown above. Apply the fabric D strip diagonally across one of the fabric C squares. Turn the raw edges under on the long edges and level both short ends even with the corners of the square (see Maple leaf, p.161). Topstitch $\frac{1}{16}$in (2mm) from the folded edge to square C.

Sew 2 triangles to the sides

**3** Sew a right-angled triangle to both long sides of each pair of "petals."

Attach the corner square

**4** Set in the corner squares to make four units. Make sure you catch the raw edges of the "stem" square in the seams.

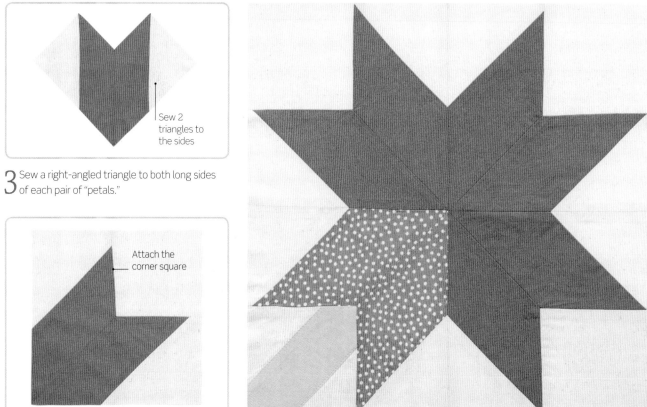

**5** Sew together the units in pairs, then sew together the pairs, manipulating the seams in the center to help them lie flat.

# Cake stand basket: five-patch

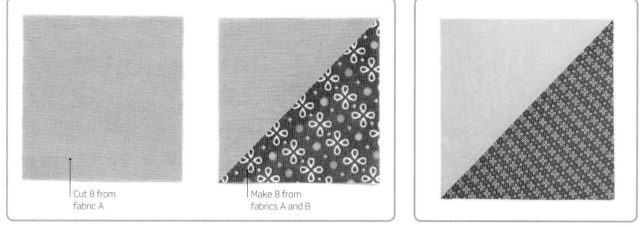

Cut 8 from
fabric A

Make 8 from
fabrics A and B

1 Divide the size of the finished block by five. Add seam allowances.
Cut eight squares this size from fabric A. Make eight half-square triangles
(see p.82) from fabrics A and B.

2 The finished center half-square triangle is
three times the size of the outside squares.
Cut one triangle from fabric A and one from
fabric B to this size and sew them together
on the diagonal.

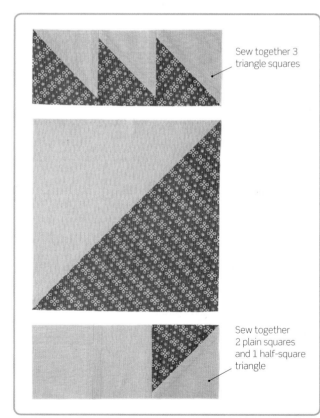

Sew together 3
triangle squares

Sew together
2 plain squares
and 1 half-square
triangle

3 Sew together three small half-square triangles,
then sew one small half-square triangle to two
small plain squares. Sew the strips to opposite sides,
top and bottom, of the center half-square triangle.

4 Following the layout above, sew the remaining small squares into
two strips and sew the strips to opposite, left and right, sides of the
large unit. Match all of the seams carefully.

# Ship: Double four-patch

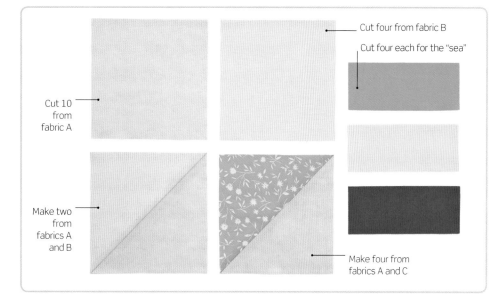

Cut 10 from fabric A

Cut four from fabric B

Cut four each for the "sea"

Make two from fabrics A and B

Make four from fabrics A and C

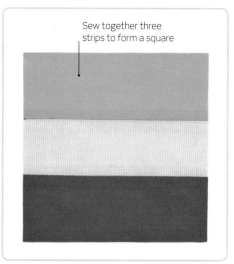

Sew together three strips to form a square

**1** The fabric requirements given here make a 12in (30.5cm) square block. Divide the size of the finished block by four (3in/7.6cm). Add seam allowances to each side (3½in/8.8cm ). Cut 10 squares this size from fabric A, four from fabric B, and four from fabric C. Set aside four from fabric A and two from fabric B to use as squares. The others will be made into half-square triangles. Divide the finished mini block by three (3in ÷ 3 [7.6cm ÷ 3]) and add ½in (1.2cm) seam allowance to determine the size of the strips that make up the "sea" (3½ x 1½in [8.8 x 3.7cm]). Cut four strips in each of three "sea" colors to that measurement.

**2** Sew together the 3½ x 1½in (8.8 x 3.7cm) sea strips to make four units the same size as the solid-colored squares 3½in (8.8cm). You can also make the "sea" from three long strips if you prefer. The length of each strip would be the same as the finished measurement of the block (12in [30.5cm]) and the width should be the width determined in Step 1 (1½in/3.7cm).

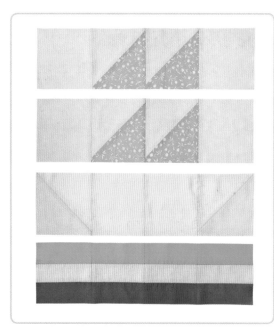

**3** Following the layout, sew the half-square triangle units together by drawing a diagonal line from corner to corner and sewing along that line. Piece together the rows using a ¼in (6mm) seam allowance.

**4** Sew the four rows together, aligning the points to complete the block.

# House

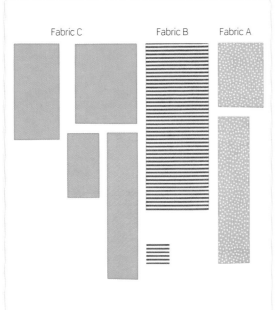

1 From fabric A, cut five 2½ x 3½in (6.5 x 9cm) rectangles and four 1½ x 8½in (4 x 21.5cm) strips.
From fabric B, cut one 3½ x 12in (9 x 30.5cm) strip and one 1½in (4cm) square.
From fabric C, cut two rectangles 2 x 3½in (5 x 9cm), one 3¼ x 1½in (8.25 x 4cm), and one strip 8¼ x 1½in (21 x 4cm), two rectangles 3½ x 4½in (9 x 11.5cm), and one 2½ x 5½in (6.5 x 14cm).

2 On each of the two 2 x 3½in (5 x 9cm) fabric C rectangles, draw a diagonal line from corner to corner on the wrong side of the fabric. Place a rectangle in each of the corners of the fabric B 3½ x 12in (9 x 30.5cm) rectangle, lining up the corners. Sew through the lines and trim to a ¼in (6mm) seam allowance to create the "roof."

3 Make the chimney strip from the smallest square (fabric B) and the two narrow fabric C strips, as shown.

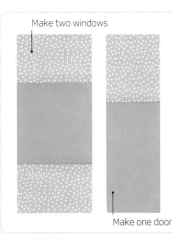

Make two windows

4 Make two window units by adding a 2½ x 3½in (6.5 x 9cm) fabric A rectangle to the short ends of each 3½ x 4½in (9 x 11.5cm) fabric C rectangle.

Make one door

5 Make the door unit by sewing together the remaining fabric A rectangle to the 2½ x 5½in (6.5 x 14cm) fabric C rectangle.

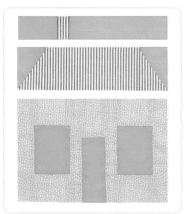

6 Sew together the window and door units by adding the remaining four fabric A strips to the long edges. Then sew together the chimney and roof elements.

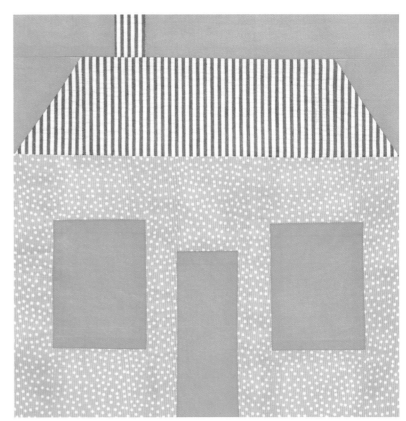

7 Sew the roof and house together to complete the 12in (30.5cm) square block.

# Appliqué

# Appliqué

Appliqué is a decorative technique in which shapes are cut from one fabric and applied to a background fabric. It has been used in quilting for centuries and is found on many other items, from clothing to pillows. Hand appliqué is the traditional method, but working by machine can be just as effective.

## Stitches for appliqué

Appliquéd shapes can be attached to the background in two ways, either hidden (using blind stitch) or calling attention to themselves as part of the design. Machine appliqué is almost always worked with decorative stitches such as zigzag or satin stitch, or with one of the many stitches programmed into modern sewing machines.

## Blind stitch or slip stitch

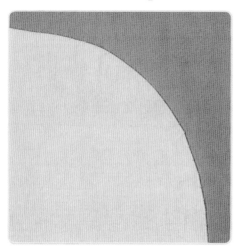

Bring the needle up on the right side of the background fabric, next to the turned-under edge of the shape being applied. Insert a few threads into the folded edge. Go back through the background fabric and continue taking tiny stitches 1/8in (3mm) apart around the entire shape.

## Blanket stitch

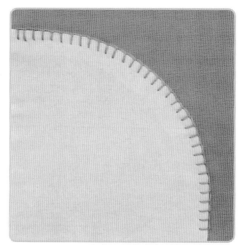

Bring the needle up on the right side of the background fabric, next to the turned-under edge of the shape being applied. Take a stitch into the shape 1/8–1/4in (3–6mm) to the right and perpendicular to the edge. Bring the needle out at the edge and loop the thread under the point. Pull tight and repeat.

## Tips for appliqué

• Blanket stitch (above, right) is the most popular decorative stitch for hand appliqué, but many basic embroidery stitches can be used as decoration, including cross-stitch, herringbone, chain stitch, and feather stitch.

• Make sure that decorative stitches sit tight against the turned-under edge and are in proportion with the size of the applied pieces.

• In most appliqué techniques, a seam allowance has to be added to the shapes. The secret is to make an allowance that is wide enough to keep fraying at bay and narrow enough to be undetectable once it has been stitched.

• Most seam allowances for appliqué can be cut by eye, following the outline of the shape. Remember that you can trim away any excess as you work, but you can't add it once it has been removed. The ideal seam allowance is around 1/8in (3mm).

• If you need only one piece of a particular shape, draw it on tracing paper and cut it out. Pin the tracing paper shape to the fabric and cut it out, in the same way as a dressmaking pattern.

• Appliqué designs usually have a right and a wrong side. When transferring a design, make sure that the right side of the fabric will be the right way around when the shape is cut out and applied.

• Some methods call for the outline of a design to be marked on the background fabric. In this case, make sure that the outline will be covered or can be removed when the sewing is completed.

Draw the design lightly on the right side of the fabric or baste around the outlines.

• When basting, make sure that any knots are on the wrong side of the background fabric, as this will make it easier to remove the thread later.

• If the fabric is light or you have access to a lightbox, you may be able to trace from an original pattern directly onto the fabric.

• When working machine appliqué, work a practice row or two using the same fabrics as the design to make sure your settings are correct.

# Dealing with peaks and valleys

Both "peaks" (shapes that come to a sharp point) and "valleys" (sharp points between two sides of a shape) can be pointed or curved, and both can be difficult to work neatly. The points of peaks should, of course, be pointed, but you risk creating a lump under the point where you turn the edges under. The seam allowance in valleys needs to be clipped to make the edge neat.

## Peaks

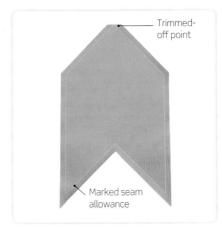

Trimmed-off point

Marked seam allowance

Fold the seam allowance and press

1 Trim the tip of the point a few threads shy of the seam allowance.

2 Fold the sides of the point along the seam allowance. Make sure that the raw edge at the point is hidden. Press the edges.

## Valleys

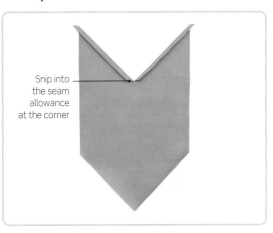

Snip into the seam allowance at the corner

At the bottom of the valley, clip to within a few threads of the marked seam allowance. Fold the edges to the wrong side. When applying the piece, take several tiny stitches in the valley to secure the cut threads.

# Dealing with curves

Curves can be difficult to keep smooth. The raw edge of an outward (convex) curve is slightly longer than the folded-under edge and can cause bunching under the fold unless the seam allowance is clipped. Inward (concave) curves will sometimes stretch smoothly, but shallow curves may need to be clipped before being sewn.

## Convex curves

Cut notches into seam allowance

1 Cut tiny V-shaped notches into the seam allowance to remove excess fabric.

2 When it is turned under, the curved edge will lie flat.

## Concave curves

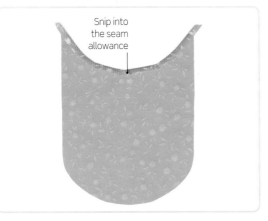

Snip into the seam allowance

Clip straight cuts into the seam allowance as you work, one section at a time. The clips will form notches that will spread open and allow the edge to lie flat.

# Machine appliqué general techniques

Machine appliqué is quick and will stand many washes, especially if you use a tightly woven fabric and finish the edges with zigzag or satin stitch. Before you begin, it is a good idea to practice on scraps of the fabrics you will be using. Try out different stitch widths and lengths to see what works best.

## Outer corners

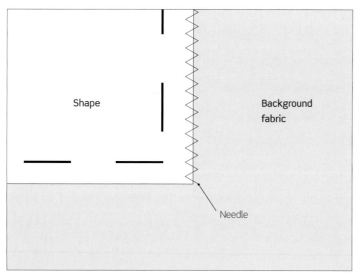

To work outer corners, stop with the needle outside the shape on the right-hand side. Lift the foot, turn the work, and continue.

## Inner corners

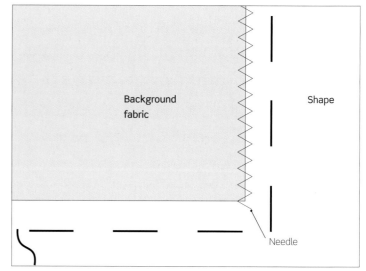

To work inner corners, stop with the needle inside the shape on the left-hand side. Lift the foot, turn the work, and continue.

## Convex curves

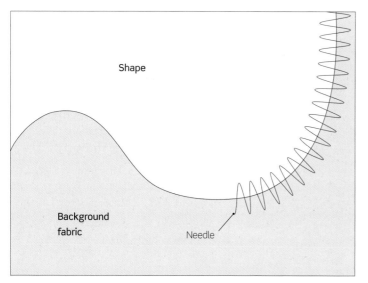

When approaching convex (outer) curves, stop with the needle just outside the shape. Lift the foot, turn the work to align it with the direction you're sewing, and continue.

## Concave curves

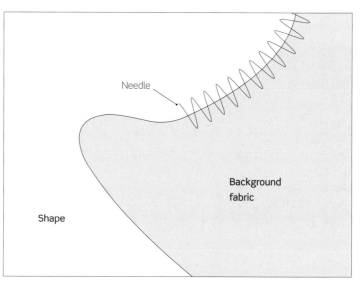

When approaching concave (inner) curves, stop with the needle inside the shape. When working any kind of curve, you may need to stop frequently to turn the work slightly, then take a few stitches, then stop, and turn again.

# Using appliqué templates

There are many ways to make appliqué templates (see p.30), but the principle is the same for most. If you will be using the same shape over and over, it is best to use stiff card or template plastic. If you will only be using it once, use paper or tracing paper. Templates can be created for almost any shape. You can trace a preexisting shape, or create your own hand-drawn shapes.

1 With a marker or pencil, draw or trace your shape onto the template material of your choice.

2 Using a sharp pair of scissors, but not your fabric scissors, carefully cut out the shape.

3 Position the template on the fabric and trace around it with a water-soluble pen. We've used a pencil here so the lines can be easily seen.

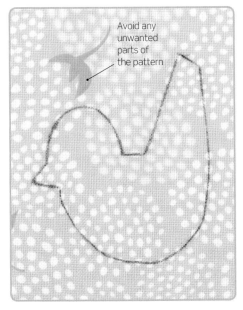

Avoid any unwanted parts of the pattern

4 Be careful in positioning the template on the fabric to avoid any unwanted part of the fabric pattern on your appliqué piece.

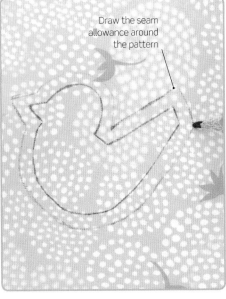

Draw the seam allowance around the pattern

5 Add a ⅛–¼in (3-6mm) seam allowance to the outside of the traced line.

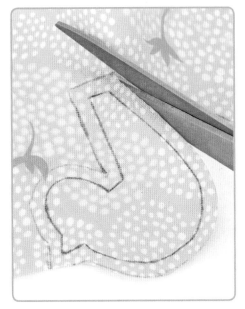

6 Using a sharp pair of fabric scissors, cut out your design along the seam allowance line.

# Needle-turned appliqué

Needle-turned or turned-edge appliqué is the traditional method for applying shapes to a background. We've used a pencil here for clarity, but you should use a water-soluble pen or other removable method to mark your fabric.

1 Make templates for the appliqué shapes. Transfer the shapes to the right side of the appliqué fabric and cut them out, adding a scant ⅛–¼in (3–6mm) seam allowance all around.

2 Wash and press the background fabric, then lay it out flat, right side up. Place the pattern on the background fabric and trace it out.

3 Place the appliqué piece in position on the background fabric and pin in place right-side up.

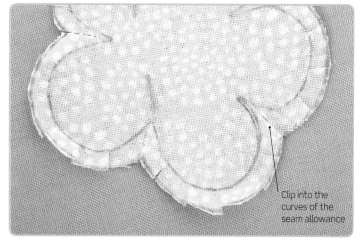

Clip into the curves of the seam allowance

4 With the appliqué piece pinned in place, clip into the curves, peaks, or valleys at regular intervals along the seam allowance (see p.169).

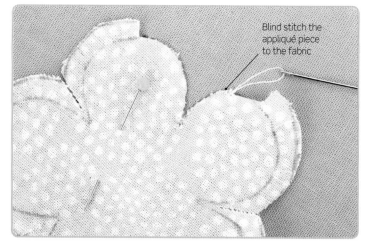

Blind stitch the appliqué piece to the fabric

5 With the point of the needle, turn under a small section of the seam allowance and blind stitch the appliqué piece to the background, using thread to match the appliqué fabric.

# Freezer paper appliqué

Freezer paper is a stiff, white paper coated on one side with a film that can be ironed onto fabric and easily removed without leaving residue. The paper side is ideal for drawing patterns onto. It can be found in craft stores, at some supermarkets, and online. Seam allowances can be pressed over the edge to the wrong side to give a hard crease that makes it easy to sew the shapes in place.

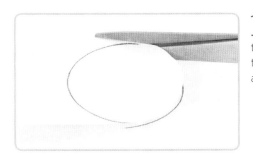

**1** Trace the templates in reverse on the matte side of the freezer paper and cut out.

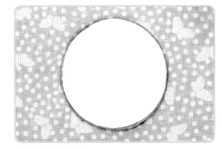

**2** Place the freezer paper template on the wrong side of the appliqué fabric, shiny side down, and trace around it.

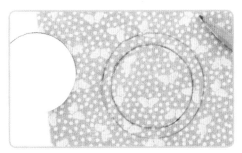

**3** Add a ⅛–¼in (3–6mm) seam allowance all around, then iron the template in place. Cut around the shape on the marked seam allowance.

**4** Clip or notch any peaks, valleys, or curves up to the paper (see p.169). Press the seam allowance to the wrong side, using the edge of the freezer paper as a guide. Remove the freezer paper and blind stitch the shape to the background fabric.

# Raw-edge appliqué

Nonwoven fabrics, such as felt and felted wool, that won't fray can be used effectively in decorative appliqué, but remember that they cannot be laundered. No seam allowances are needed.

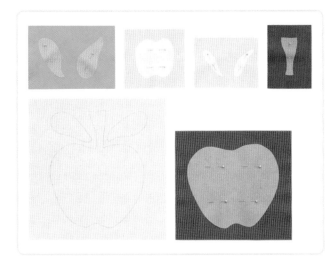

**1** Trace your entire pattern onto the background fabric. Then trace the pattern pieces separately onto tracing paper. Cut out each paper pattern and pin to the fabrics.

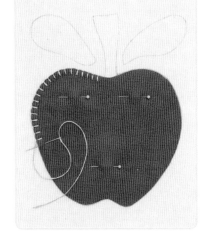

**2** Cut out the appliqué pieces (without a seam allowance). Pin the first piece to the background and stitch in place, using a decorative stitch.

**3** Add pieces in order. Remove all the pins and press from the wrong side.

# Hawaiian appliqué

Hawaiian appliqué originated in Hawaii when women native to the islands were taught to sew by early missionaries. The patterns are usually square and cut as eight-sided motifs from a single piece of folded fabric. The designs are traditionally based on flora indigenous to the Pacific Islands, but six-sided snowflake motifs can also be used. Finished pieces are usually echo quilted (see p.211).

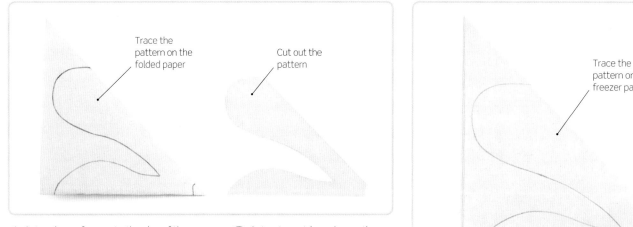

Trace the pattern on the folded paper

Cut out the pattern

Trace the pattern on the freezer paper

**1** Cut a piece of paper to the size of the finished block. Fold the paper in half twice, then along the diagonal once to make a triangle. Draw on the triangle or cut freestyle through all the layers, with the main part of the design on the folded edge.

**2** Cut out one triangular section and transfer it to card to use as a template in Step 3.

**3** Cut a square of freezer paper the same size as the original paper pattern. Fold it in half twice, paper side out, then fold it once along the diagonal to make a triangle. This matches the template. Transfer the template outline to the paper, making sure that the fold of the paper matches the fold on the template.

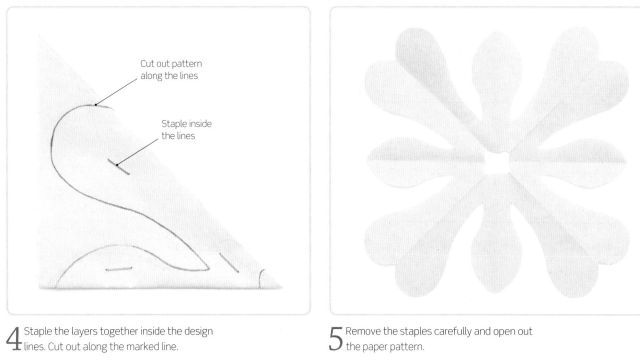

Cut out pattern along the lines

Staple inside the lines

**4** Staple the layers together inside the design lines. Cut out along the marked line.

**5** Remove the staples carefully and open out the paper pattern.

6 Cut a square of the appliqué fabric and one of the background fabric, both 2in (5cm) larger than the pattern square. Fold both in half twice to find the center and position them, wrong side of the appliqué fabric to right side of the background fabric.

7 Center the freezer paper pattern on the right side of the appliqué fabric, sticky-side down, and iron it in position.

8 Baste the layers together ¼in (6mm) from the inside edge of the paper pattern.

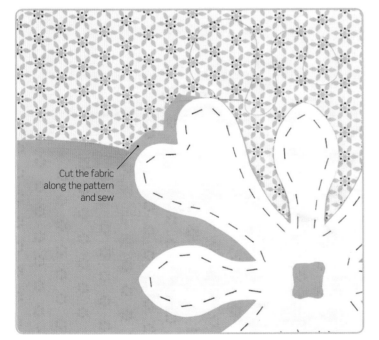

Cut the fabric along the pattern and sew

9 Work a small section at a time by cutting away the appliqué fabric along the edge of the pattern, leaving a ¼in (6mm) seam allowance. Turn the seam allowance under so that it's level with the edge of the pattern and blind stitch the fabric to the background.

10 Continue cutting and sewing until the entire pattern has been applied to the background (see p.169 for dealing with curves). Remove the basting stitches and peel the pattern away.

# Broderie perse

Persian embroidery, or broderie perse, is a technique in which motifs are cut from one printed fabric and applied to a different background. Several motifs, not necessarily from the same fabric, can be layered and rearranged to create a new design.

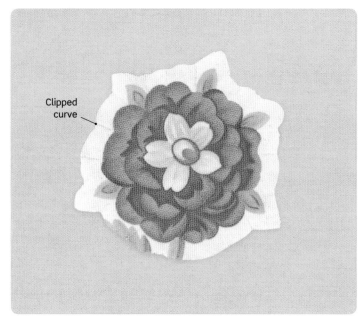

**1** Cut out the motif with a generous ¼in (6mm) seam allowance. Clip any curves inside the seam allowance. If there are areas that are too small to cut away, leave the background fabric in place.

**2** Pin the motif in position on the background and baste it ½in (1.2cm) inside the outline. For narrow areas such as stems, baste along the center. Trim outside seam allowances to reduce bulk wherever possible.

**3** Using the needle tip, turn the seam allowance under and blind stitch the motif to the background, using thread to match the motif, or use a decorative stitch and contrasting thread, as shown.

**4** This appliqué technique allows you to make a small piece of expensive printed fabric go a long way, since individual motifs can be applied over a larger and less-costly background fabric.

# Stitch and cut appliqué

In this quick machine method, the motif is marked on the appliqué fabric and then sewn along the marked line before being cut out along the line of stitches. The edges can then be finished by machine or by hand.

1 Make templates for the shapes. Draw around each shape on the right side of the fabric and add a ½in (1.2cm) seam allowance all around. Cut out the fabric shapes on the marked seam allowance.

2 Pin the shapes to the background fabric, making sure that the pins will not get caught in the machine foot, and use a straight stitch to sew along the marked line.

3 Using small, sharp scissors, trim away the seam allowance, cutting as close to the line of stitches as possible without cutting the thread.

4 Zigzag or satin stitch along the trimmed edge to finish the raw edge and hide the straight stitches.

# Fused appliqué

Fusible bonding web is a nonwoven fabric impregnated with glue that is activated by heat. One side is anchored to paper on which shapes can be drawn. When ironed to the wrong side of a shape and then to the background fabric, it forms a firm bond that is almost impossible to remove. It is most suitable for machine appliqué because it creates a stiffness that is difficult to sew by hand.

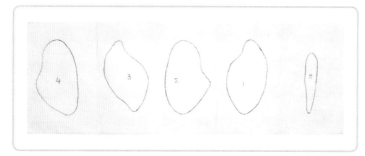

1 Transfer the shapes, in reverse, to the paper side of the web and cut them out roughly. If you group pieces that are to be cut from the same fabric close together, you can cut the whole group at once, rather than cutting each individual shape separately.

2 Following the manufacturer's instructions, place the rough, non-paper side on the wrong side of the appliqué fabric and press in place.

3 Cut out the shapes, cutting carefully along the drawn line, and peel off the backing papers. Position the shapes on the background fabric and iron in place.

4 Finish by sewing around the edges of each appliquéd piece with machine zigzag or satin stitch.

# Stained-glass appliqué

Stained glass appliqué gets its name from the bias strips that separate the elements in the design, which resemble leading in church windows. You can make bias strips yourself (see pp.48–49) or purchase bias strips with fusible bonding web on the back, which can be ironed in place to secure the strip while you sew it in place. If your design features straight lines, you can use strips cut on the straight grain.

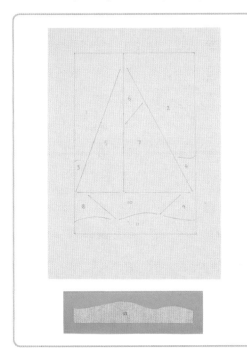

**1** Transfer the pattern onto the background fabric. If the design is complicated, number the shapes on the background.

**2** Following the manufacturer's instructions, place the rough, non-paper side of the bonding web on the wrong side of the fabric and press in place.

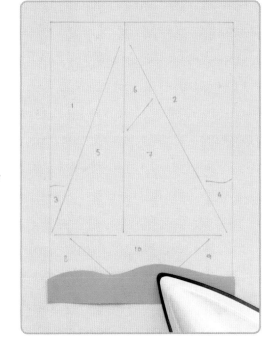

**3** Cut out the appliqué shapes without adding any seam allowances. Iron them in place on the background.

**4** Butt each piece up tightly against its neighbor, so that it will be easier to catch the raw edges under the bias strips.

**5** Plan the order in which you apply the bias strips so that you can cover any raw ends with another strip. Iron on the strips and sew them in place, using a blind stitch.

**6** The bias strips cover the raw edges of the pieces over which they are placed. Continue until all of the raw edges are covered.

**For the best results,** pair fabrics that have a strong contrast so that the appliqué shapes stand out on the background fabrics.

# Soft blocks

Baby wins again with these easy-to-make patchwork blocks decorated with delightful appliquéd designs and filled with a soft stuffing. Once you've made one block, you're sure to want to make more—which just adds to Baby's fun!

## Essential Information

**DIFFICULTY** Easy

**SIZE** 4½in (12cm) square

**TOOLS AND MATERIALS**
Pencil or marker pen
Tracing paper
Scissors
Tailor's chalk or water-soluble pen
Pins
Sewing needle
Basting thread
Threads to match your fabrics
Seam ripper (optional)
Dark embroidery thread
Darning needle
Ruler or quilter's ruler
Sewing machine
Toy filling

**FABRICS**
One 5in (13cm) Charm Pack™, containing a
   minimum of 36 fabrics, in the fabrics of your
   choice (12 charm squares are needed to
   make 1 block)
Small scraps of white fabric for the owl's eyes
Small scraps of the fabric of your choice for
   the owl's beak

**SKILLS**
Set-in seams (see p.101)
Needle-turned appliqué (see p.172)

**SEAM ALLOWANCE**
¼in (6mm) throughout, unless otherwise stated

1 Using a pencil or marker pen, trace the templates (see p.295) onto tracing paper and cut them out.

2 With the tailor's chalk or a water-soluble pen, trace each template onto the fabric of your choice. (We have used a pencil so that readers can see the lines easily.)

Clip into the curves

Trim off the point

3 Cut out the shapes, leaving a ¼in (6mm) seam allowance around each one. Clip any curves and trim off all points (see p.169). You will need one set of each of the six shapes for each block you're making.

**4** Center the pattern piece on a contrasting square of fabric and pin it in place.

Pin the pattern piece on a contrasting square

**5** Baste the pattern piece in place around the edge, about ³⁄₈in (1cm) inside the marked line.

Fold under the seam allowance as you sew

**6** Turning the seam allowance under as you work (see p.172), and, using matching thread, appliqué the pattern piece to the fabric square, using blind stitch (see p.168).

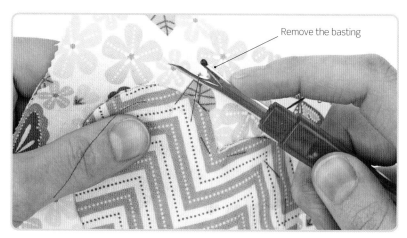

Remove the basting

**7** Remove the basting stitches. Repeat Steps 4–6 to appliqué each shape to a contrasting fabric square. Repeat Steps 4–5 to attach the owl's eyes and beak to its head. Following the guides on the templates and using embroidery thread and a darning needle, embroider a face on the bunny and the owl and the antennae on the butterfly.

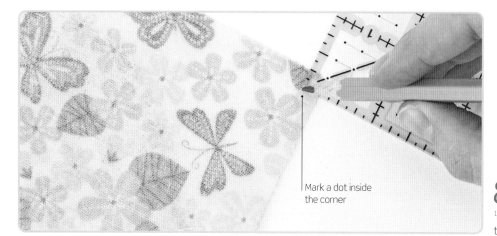

Mark a dot inside the corner

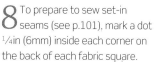

**8** To prepare to sew set-in seams (see p.101), mark a dot ¹⁄₄in (6mm) inside each corner on the back of each fabric square.

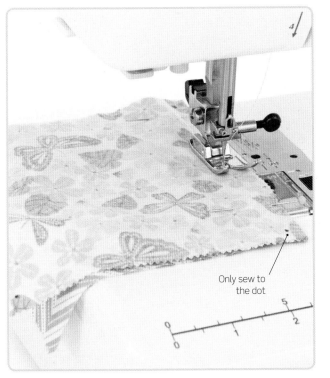

**9** Pin two squares, right sides together, along one edge. Sew the squares together between the two marked dots, making sure not to sew beyond the dots.

Only sew to the dot

**10** Continue to sew the squares together, sewing between the dots until they form the shape of a cross, as above. Six squares form one block.

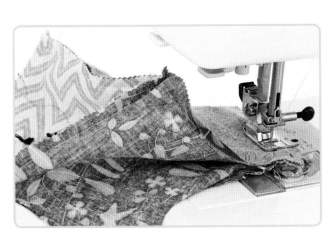

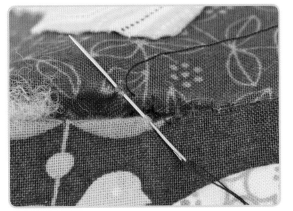

**11** Following the arrows indicated in Step 10, join the sides of the squares together as in Step 9 to form the block. Leave the final seam unsewn for turning through.

**12** Turn the block to the right side and stuff firmly with toy filling. Slip stitch (see p.43) the final seam closed.

# Reverse appliqué

This technique uses two or more layers of fabric, cutting away the top layers to reveal the fabric beneath. The raw edges are turned under to finish the shape. Floral, pictorial, and geometric designs work well.

## Reverse appliqué by hand

1 Choose two fabrics and pin or baste them together, right-sides up, around the outside edge. Trace the motif onto a template and cut it out. Place the template right-side up on top of the fabric and with a water-soluble pen, trace around the template. (We have used a pencil so that readers can see the lines easily.)

2 Remove the template and baste around the outline approximately ³⁄₈in (1cm) from the outside edge.

3 Using small, sharp scissors, begin cutting away the shape ¹⁄₄in (6mm) inside the marked line, being careful to cut only the top layer of fabric. Cut one section at a time, clipping or cutting small notches into any curves, peaks, or valleys (see p.169).

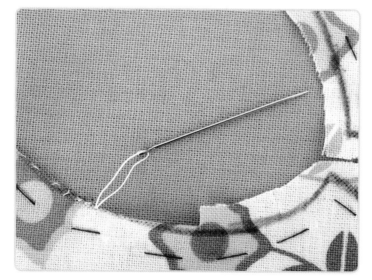

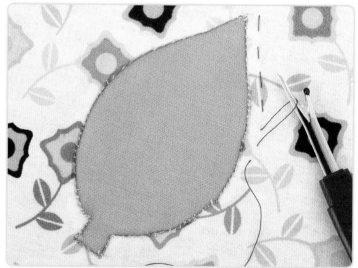

4 Turn under the seam allowance along the marked line. Using thread to match the top fabric, slip stitch the edge in place.

5 Remove all of the basting stitches.

# Reverse appliqué by machine

1 With your paper or freezer paper template in place on the top fabric, trace around the outside edge with a water-soluble pen. (We have used a pencil so that readers can see the lines easily.) Place the marked fabric on top of the bottom fabric, both right-side up.

2 Using a needle and thread, baste around the traced shape approximately ³⁄₈in (1cm) from the edge to hold both layers in place. Pin before basting, if needed.

3 Using the traced line as a cutting guide, carefully cut through the top layer of fabric only revealing the fabric below.

4 Using your sewing machine with a tight zigzag stitch or satin stitch, encase the raw edges of the top fabric with the bottom fabric. Carefully remove the basting stitches.

# Turned reverse appliqué

This method uses an extra piece of fabric sewn to the main fabric and then turned through to create a window for your desired shape to show through. It is a quicker method of traditional reverse appliqué (see pp.184–185) and can give a cleaner, neater edge. This method works best on simple shapes. You may see the edges of the turned-through piece of fabric, so either use a fabric to complement your design, or the same fabric as your main fabric.

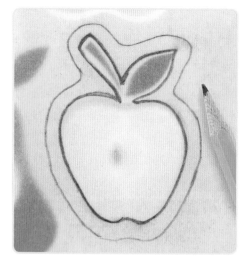

**1** Choose a fabric with a motif suitable for appliqué. Using a sheet of tracing paper, trace around the object with a pencil. Add your desired space around the object.

**2** Cut out the traced shape along the outside line. Place the template on the wrong side of the lining fabric to be turned through. Trace around the template.

**3** Position the lining fabric on the main fabric, right sides together, where you'd like the shape to appear. Pin the lining fabric in place.

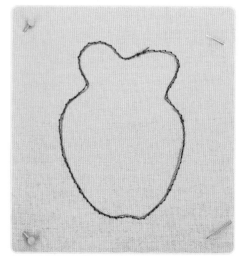

**4** Using a sewing machine, sew along the motif outline through both the layers of fabric.

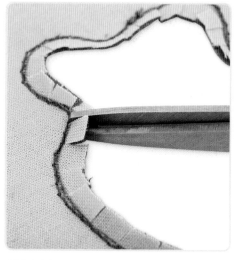

**5** Using sharp scissors, cut inside of the sewn shape, leaving approximately a ⅛–¼in (3-6mm) seam allowance.

Leave a seam allowance

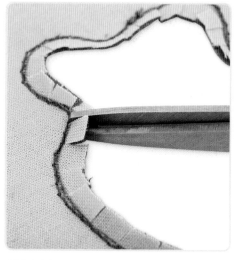

**6** Snip into any curves and trim any points without cutting through the stitches.

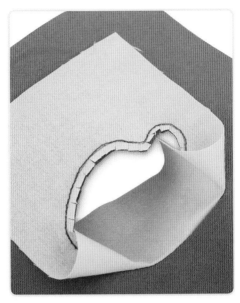

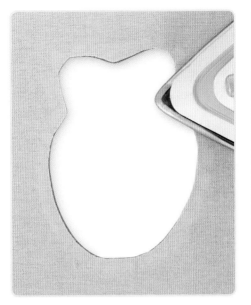

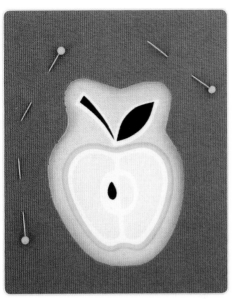

7 Push the lining fabric through the hole to the wrong side of the main fabric and out the other side.

8 Press the edges flat on the lining side to get a neat finished look.

9 With the main fabric facing up, position the fabric with the motif underneath, making sure that the motif is centered inside the cutout shape. Pin in place.

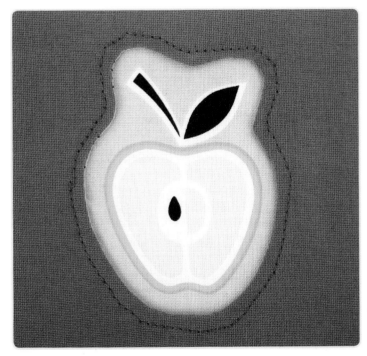

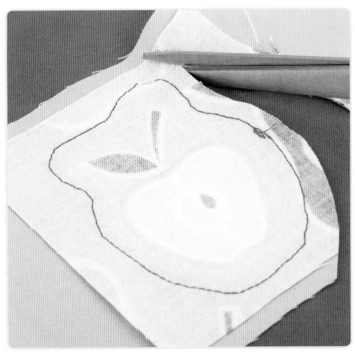

10 Using a matching or complementary thread, topstitch about ⅛in (3mm) from the edge to secure all the layers together.

11 Trim off the excess fabric from around the stitched shape on the back side of the piece. Be careful not to cut the main fabric or the stitches.

**Thread a matching ribbon** through the eye of the zipper pull to add an extra touch to the toiletry bag.

# Appliqué zipper pouch

This bag is so quick and easy that once you've mastered how to make one, you'll want to make many more, and in all shapes and sizes. Use a cotton fabric so that it can easily be thrown in the wash. These bags also make fantastic gifts.

## Essential Information

**DIFFICULTY** Easy

**SIZE** 8⅝ x 7⅝ x 3⅛in (22 x 19.5 x 8cm)

**TOOLS AND MATERIALS**
Quilter's ruler
Rotary cutter
Cutting mat
Pencil
Tracing paper
Scissors
Pins
Sewing machine
Thread to match main fabric
Iron and ironing board
1 standard zipper 12in (30cm) long (minimum) in a color to match the main fabric
Thin ribbon to match (optional)

**FABRICS**
21¼ x 11in (54 x 28cm) cotton main fabric, plus 5 x 5in (12.5 x 12.5cm) extra
21¼ x 11in (54 x 28cm) cotton lining fabric
A scrap of fabric with a motif, maximum of 4in (10cm) square, that you'd like to feature on the front of the bag

**SKILLS**
Turned reverse appliqué (see pp.186–187)

**SEAM ALLOWANCE**
¼in (6mm) throughout, unless otherwise stated

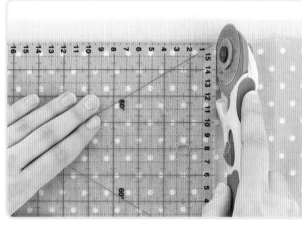

1 Cut two pieces of main fabric and two pieces of lining fabric each 10⅝ x 11in (27 x 28cm).

2 Trace around the motif that will feature in the middle of your reverse appliqué to create a template for it.

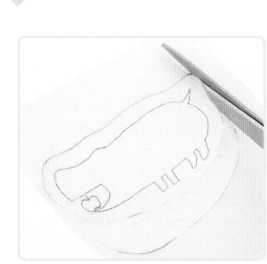

**3** Add ³⁄₈in (1cm) extra all around the shape, then cut out the template along this line.

**4** Pin the extra 5 x 5in (12.5 x 12.5cm) square of main fabric right sides together onto the front piece of the main fabric so that the top of the rectangle sits about 2in (5cm) down from the top edge of the front fabric. Center the template in the square and trace around it. This is where your motif will appear on the bag front.

**5** Using a matching thread, carefully sew along the traced line.

**6** Cut inside your stitching, leaving a ¹⁄₄in (6mm) seam allowance.

The matching thread sewn along the traced markings.

**7** Snip into the seam allowance, being careful not to cut any of the stitches (see p.186).

8 Turn the small square of fabric through the hole, to the wrong side of the main front fabric. The wrong side of the square will sit wrong side to the bag front, leaving a finished turned-edge seam.

9 Make sure that the shape of the hole forms the same shape as your paper template. Press the seam flat on both sides.

10 Center the motif under the hole with both fabrics right-side up. Pin around the edges leaving enough room to topstitch.

11 Thread your machine with a thread to match your main fabric, then topstitch around the edge of the hole approximately ⅛in (3mm) from the edge using a straight stitch, or a decorative stitch, if you choose to. Remove the pins as you work.

12 Turn the bag front over, then trim the excess fabric from around the motif and the turned-through square to ¼in (6mm). Be careful not to cut the main fabric of the bag front.

Pin the lining, zipper, and front together, aligning all three

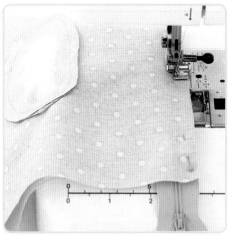

**13** Lay a piece of the lining fabric right-side up, then lay the zipper right-side up, aligning the top edge with the top edge of the lining. Lay the bag front wrong-side up on top of this, aligning the top edge with the top edges of the zipper and lining. Pin through all three.

**14** Put a zipper foot on your machine and sew through all three layers. Fold the front and lining down on either side of the zipper so they both face right-side out.

**15** Lay the second lining piece right-side up, then lay the free edge of the zipper—right-side up—to align with the top of the lining fabric; lay the main back fabric right-side down on top. Pin through all three layers, aligning the edges as in Step 13.

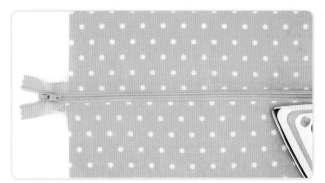

**16** Sew along the edge to attach the zipper. Fold the back and back lining down so that the zipper is visible between the front and back bags on both the main and lining fabrics. Press as shown. Topstitch at this point if you want. Open up the zipper by about an inch (a few centimeters) so that the pull sits within the main fabric.

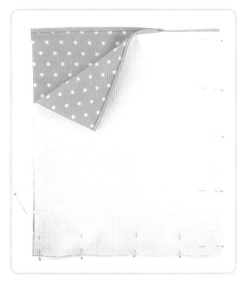

**17** Using a long quilter's ruler and a rotary cutter and cutting mat, trim all the edges and the ends of the zipper even with one another so that the entire width is 9in (23cm). Make sure all the layers are flat and straight before cutting. Trim the bottom edges of the bag front and back so that they sit 9½in (24cm) away from the zipper.

**18** Fold the bag in half at the zipper so the front and back of the main fabrics sit right sides together. Align all the edges and pin around the three raw edges, through all four layers. Leave the zipper open.

**19** Sew around the three pinned raw edges using a ¼in (6mm) seam allowance. Remove the pins as you sew.

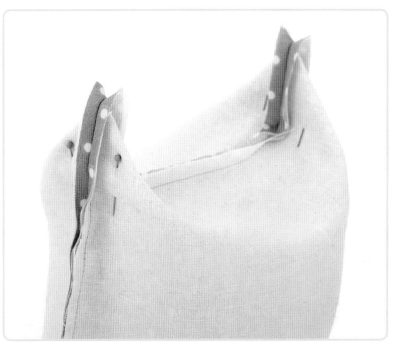

**20** Press the seam open. Take the two bottom corners of the bag and pinch them in as shown, so that the bottom seam of the bag aligns with the corresponding side seam on the bag. This will create the boxed corners. Pin either side of the matched seam.

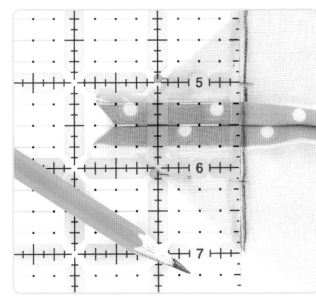

**21** Mark a line 1½in (3.8cm) from each corner of the bag, perpendicular to the seams.

**22** Sew along the marked lines, then trim the corner off leaving a ¼in (6mm) seam allowance. Zigzag stitch back and forth over the raw edges to prevent them from fraying and to extend the life of your bag. Carefully turn the bag right-side out and press all the seams flat.

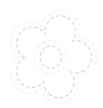

# Frayed-edge appliqué

The edges of appliquéd pieces need not always be neatly finished. Leaving the edges frayed gives a casual and worn look to an appliqué piece. This technique works well on items for kids. You can add interfacing to the back of the appliqué piece, just inside the seam allowance, to give it more stability and to keep the edges from fraying back too far and the shape from becoming detached.

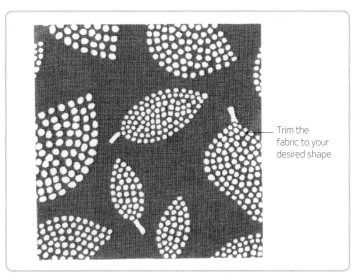

Trim the fabric to your desired shape

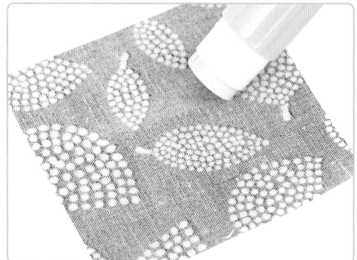

**1** Cut out the shape you want to attach to your main fabric, adding a ³⁄₈in (1cm) seam allowance all around. If you'd like to interface the shape to give it more stability, cut a piece of interfacing the same size as the shape, without the seam allowance and apply it to the wrong side of the shape.

**2** Using a fabric glue stick designed for appliqué, lightly apply glue to the wrong side of the shape. If you are not using a fabric glue stick, skip to Step 3.

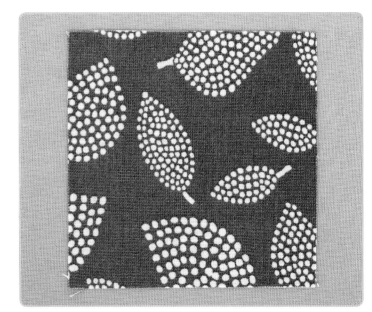

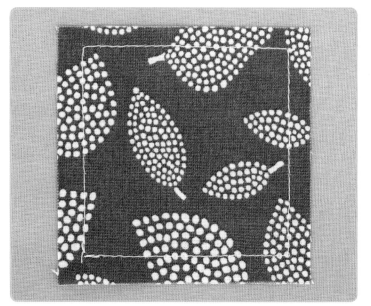

**3** Position the shape in place on the right side of the background fabric. If you used glue, go to Step 4. If not, pin or baste the shape in place.

**4** Using your sewing machine or a needle and thread, sew through both layers inside the edge of the appliqué shape leaving a ³⁄₈in (1cm) seam allowance. Remove any pins or baste stitches. The edges will fray over time, but to speed up the process you can put the finished item through a normal wash and dry cycle to roughen up the free edges.

# Free-motion appliqué

Free-motion appliqué uses the same idea as frayed-edge appliqué, but the shapes are sewn on using a free-motion, or darning, foot. Sew around each shape as many times as you like. Often, the piece looks best when you've sewn around it a few times, slightly altering the seam line with each pass. See page 213 for troubleshooting information on sewing with a free-motion foot.

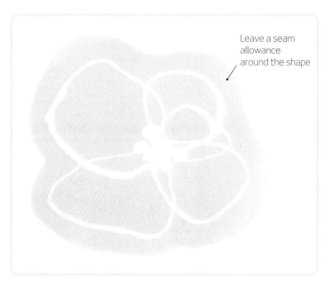

Leave a seam allowance around the shape

1 With a sharp pair of fabric scissors, cut out the desired shape from your fabric of choice leaving approximately a ³⁄₈in (1cm) seam allowance.

2 Using a fabric glue stick, pins, or basting stitches, position the shape in place on the right side of the background fabric.

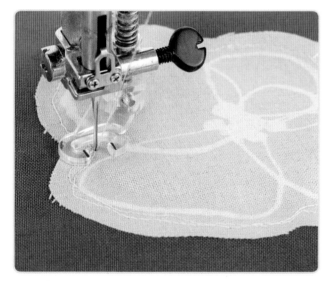

3 Using your sewing machine and a free-motion sewing foot, sew inside the edge of the appliqué fabric. The free-motion foot will make it easy for you to sew the free-form shape of your choice.

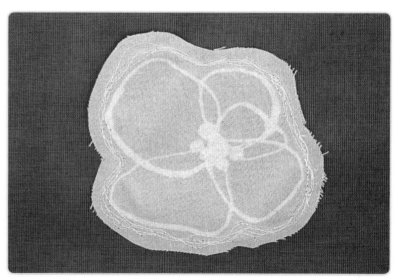

4 Sew around the shape as many times as you want, then remove the pins or basting stitches, if used. Over time, the edges will fray, but you can speed up this process by putting the finished item through a normal wash and dry cycle.

# Essential Information

**DIFFICULTY** Easy

**SIZE** Approximately 12⅝ x 15¾in (32 x 40cm)

**TOOLS AND MATERIALS**

Tailor's chalk
Quilter's ruler
Cutting mat
Rotary cutter
Tracing paper
Pencil
Pins
Measuring tape
Sewing machine
Iron and ironing board
Quilter's fabric adhesive (optional)
Free-style (or darning) foot for your
    sewing machine
Threads to match your fabrics

**FABRICS**

26¾ x 16½in (68 x 42cm) main fabric
26¾ x 16½in (68 x 42cm) lining fabric
Scraps of fabric in colors of your choice,
    to fit the template pieces
47in (120cm) length of 2in (5cm) wide
    cotton webbing (or straps of your choice)

**SKILLS**

Free-motion appliqué (see p.195)

**SEAM ALLOWANCE**

⅜in (1cm) throughout, unless otherwise
    stated

# Boat tote

Free-motion appliqué is a little like drawing, but you use a needle and thread instead of a pencil. Sew around each appliqué piece as many times as you like: multiple lines of stitching plus the frayed edges of the appliquéd shapes produce a casual look.

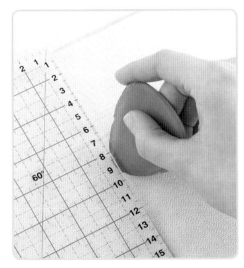

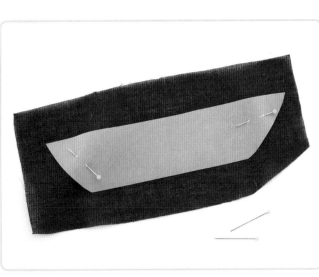

**1** Cut two pieces—the bag front and back—from the main fabric and two pieces from the lining fabric, each 13³⁄₈ x 16¹⁄₂in (34 x 42cm).

**2** Trace the templates (see p.296) onto the tracing paper and cut them out. Pin the pattern pieces to the scraps of fabric and cut them out—one hull, one cabin, two portholes, one front sail, and one flag.

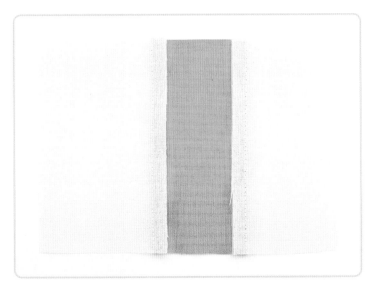

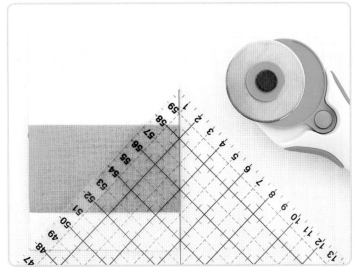

**3** To create the stripe on the main sail, cut two strips of white and one strip of colored fabric, each 2¹⁄₂ x 4in (6.5 x 10cm). With right sides together, sew them together to make a 6¹⁄₂ x 4in (16.5 x 10cm) rectangle, as shown above. Press the seams toward the darker strip.

**4** Using the quilter's ruler, cut the sail 2¹⁄₂in (6.5cm) tall by 2³⁄₄in (7cm) wide, with a 45 degree angle at the top. Center the colored fabric so there is an equal depth of white fabric above and below the colored fabric along its vertical side.

**5** Center the hull right-side up about two-thirds of the way down the right side of the bag front. Pin, glue, or baste the hull in place. Using matching thread and a darning foot, sew around the edges of the hull to secure it in place. Here it has been sewn three times to give it a rough, casual look, but you can sew it as many or as few times as you wish. Continue in the same way using the appropriate threads and attaching the cabin, then the sails, then the portholes, and, finally, the flag.

**6** When all the pieces have been sewn in place, use the darning foot to sew the water, mast, and a few seagulls. Your design can be as simple or complex as you wish. Refer to the image below and the image on page 196 for guidance.

**This delightful little boat design** uses a combination of appliqué and free-motion machine stitching, both done using a darning foot.

**7** Replace the standard foot on your sewing machine. With right sides together, pin the bag front and back together. Starting at a top corner, sew along the sides and along the bottom edge, pivoting at the bottom corners and leaving a ¼in (6mm) seam allowance. Snip off the bottom corners, making sure not to cut through the stitches.

**8** To make the bag lining, pin together the two pieces of the lining fabric, right sides together. Leaving a ⅜in (1cm) seam allowance, sew along the sides and along the bottom edge as in Step 7, but leave an opening in the bottom edge about one-third the length of that edge. This is for turning through. Snip off the bottom corners of the lining, making sure not to cut through the stitches.

Snip off the corners     Leave gap here

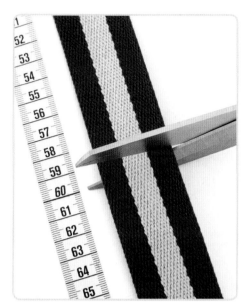

**9** For the straps, use a pair of scissors to cut two pieces of cotton webbing, each 23½in (60cm) long.

Match the seams

**10** With right sides together, insert the bag lining into the outer bag. Match the side seams and pin in place.

**11** Measure and mark the front and back of the bag 3½in (9cm) from each of the side seams (a total of four marks). Placing a strap inside the bag between the outer bag and the lining, align one end of the strap so its outer edge is aligned with one of the marks. Pin it in place. Making sure the strap is not twisted, pin its other end at the corresponding mark on the other side of the bag, as shown. Repeat to attach the second strap on the other side of the bag.

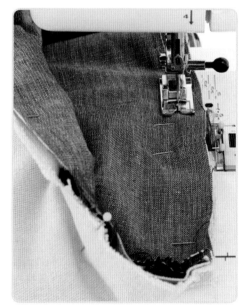

**12** Leaving a 1in (2.5cm) seam allowance, sew around the top edge of the bag, attaching the lining to the outer bag and securing the straps in place. Sew back and forth over the ends of the straps a few times to make them completely secure.

**13** Turn the bag to the right side through the opening left in the lining in Step 8. Push the lining inside the outer bag.

**14** Turn the bag inside out and slip stitch (see p.43) the opening in the lining closed. Turn the bag to the right side and press it well.

# Quilting

# Quilting

Quilting holds the layers of a quilt together, gives a quilt its texture, and should add to the overall beauty of the piece. Quilting motifs range from geometric grids and simple heart shapes to elaborate scrolls. Some appliqué motifs look best if they are outlined or echoed by quilting.

## Transferring designs

Once the quilt top is finished, you need to transfer the quilting pattern onto it. Use equipment that can be easily removed, such as water- or air-soluble pens or light pencil marks, to mark the pattern. Tailor's chalk applied lightly can usually be removed. Slivers of soap can make effective and washable marks on dark fabrics. Dressmaker's carbon paper is indelible and not recommended.

## Masking tape

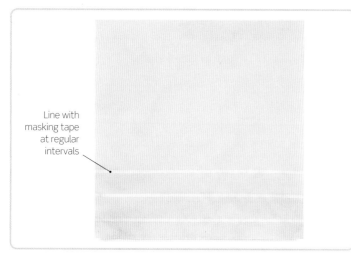

Line with masking tape at regular intervals

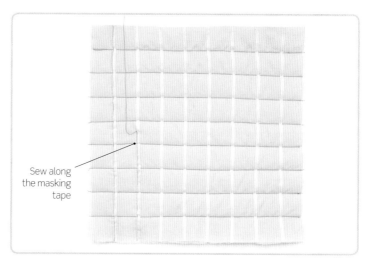

Sew along the masking tape

**1** This method only works for quilting designs in straight lines. After the quilt has been layered with batting and backing, apply ¼in (6mm) masking tape in lines as a guide.

**2** Sew along the edge of the tape by hand or machine, then remove the tape as soon as possible. When the rows are complete, repeat in the other direction.

## Tracing

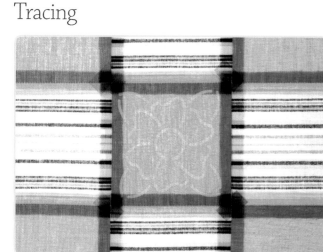

If your project is small and light in color, you can trace the pattern directly on the fabric. Place the quilt top over the pattern on a lightbox or a glass-top table with a table lamp underneath. Alternatively, tape it to a clean window. Trace the design lightly onto the fabric.

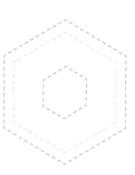

## Templates or stencils

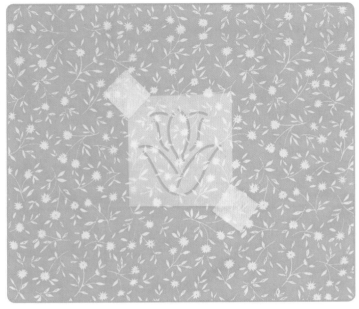
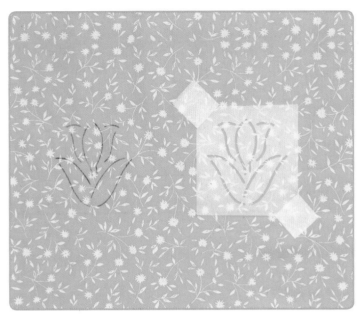

**1** Mark the design on the finished quilt top before making the quilt sandwich. Place the pattern on the quilt top and secure it with masking tape or weights. Draw around a template or in the channels of a stencil with a very sharp pencil. Keep the line as light as possible.

**2** Move the pattern as necessary and repeat until the entire top has been marked.

## Trace and baste

**1** On fabrics that are hard to mark, you can transfer the pattern to the quilt top before making the quilt sandwich. Transfer the design to tissue paper and pin in place. With the knot on top, sew along the pattern lines with a small running stitch. Secure with a double backstitch.

**2** Pull the paper away gently without disturbing the basting. If necessary, score the marked lines with a pin to break the paper.

# Hand quilting basics

Quilting by hand gives a soft look. Straight, even stitches are worked, ideally with the needle at an angle of 90 degrees, and the same stitch length on front and back. Because of the thickness of the quilt layers, the stitches are executed using a technique known as "rocking" the needle, which uses both hands. Use quilting threads and needles, and wear a thimble on your middle finger and a protective guard underneath.

## Knotting to begin

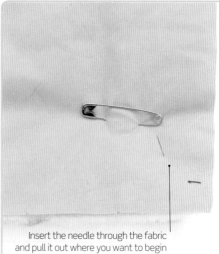

Insert the needle through the fabric and pull it out where you want to begin

**1** Knot a 20in (50cm) length of quilting thread. Take the needle down through the top layer of fabric, about 1in (2.5cm) away from where you want to start sewing.. Bring it out where you want to begin.

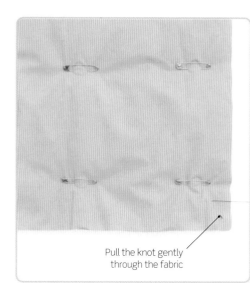

Pull the knot gently through the fabric

**2** Pull the thread gently until the knot pops through the top layer of fabric, but not hard enough to bring it out again. The knot will bury itself in the batting and be virtually undetectable.

## Finishing

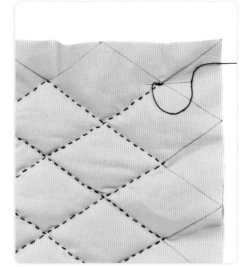

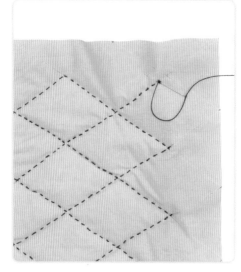

**1** To secure the thread at the end, take a small backstitch through the top layer and pull the thread through to the top. Make a French knot close to the end of the stitches. Secure the wraps with your finger and pull the knot tight.

**2** Insert the needle point into the top layer only, next to where the thread emerges and in the opposite direction from the stitches. Slide the needle within the batting and bring it out about ¾in (2cm) from the end of the stitches. Gently pull the French knot through into the batting.

**3** Carefully cut the thread close to the surface and let the tail sink into the batting.

# Quilting or rocking stitch

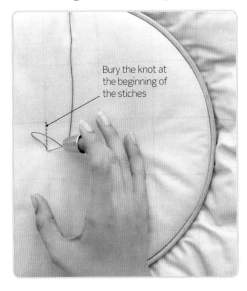

Bury the knot at the beginning of the stiches

1 Place the area to be worked inside a large embroidery hoop. Bury the knot as in Knotting to begin (see opposite). Place one hand under the quilt where the needle should emerge.

2 With the needle between thumb and forefinger of your needle hand, push the needle with your thimbled finger straight down until you feel the point with your underneath hand. Stop pushing.

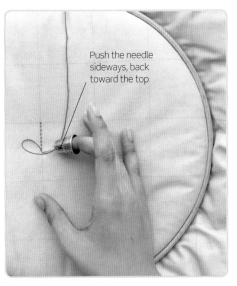

Push the needle sideways, back toward the top

3 With your underneath finger, push up gently against the side of the needle and the quilt. At the same time, push down with your top thumb and make a bump in the layers while you push the needle sideways back through to the top. Stop pushing when the length of the needle protruding on the top is the same length as the next stitch.

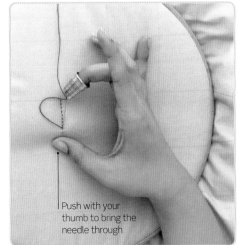

Push with your thumb to bring the needle through

4 Use the thimbled finger to bring the eye of the needle upright again, while at the same time pushing in front of it with your thumb. When the needle is upright and the point breaks through the fabric, push down as in Step 1.

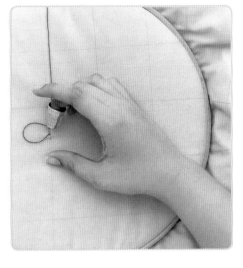

5 Continue this motion until the needle has as many stitches as it will hold. Pull the needle and thread through. Repeat.

# Stab stitch

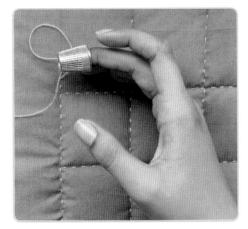

1 Place the area to be worked inside a large embroidery hoop. Stab stitch is an alternative way to work on thick quilts. Use a thimble on each middle finger. Bury the knot as in Knotting to begin (see opposite). Push the upright needle straight down through all layers. Pull the needle and thread through to the back.

2 Push the upright needle back up through all layers, working a stitch length away from the previous stitch. Pull the needle and thread through to the top. Repeat.

**A bright, complementary** backing fabric color can give your pillow a fresh, contemporary feel.

# Hand-quilted pillow

Hand quilting uses running stitch to hold the layers of the piece together. This pretty pillow cover with a slit opening at the back gives you a chance to try out this simple technique. The finished cover has authentic handmade charm.

## Essential Information

**DIFFICULTY** Easy

**SIZE** 16 x 16in (40 x 40cm)

**TOOLS AND MATERIALS**
Rotary cutter
Scissors
Cutting mat
Quilter's ruler
Pins
Safety pins
Darning needle
Threads to match your fabrics
Contrasting embroidery thread
Sewing machine
Iron and ironing board
Pillow cushion 16 x 16in (40 x 40cm)

**FABRICS**
17 x 17in (43 x 43cm) patterned front fabric
35 x 20½in (88 x 52cm) backing fabric
17¾ x 17¾in (45 x 45cm) batting

**SKILLS**
Hand quilting (see pp.204-205)

**SEAM ALLOWANCE**
⅜in (1cm) seam allowance throughout, unless otherwise stated

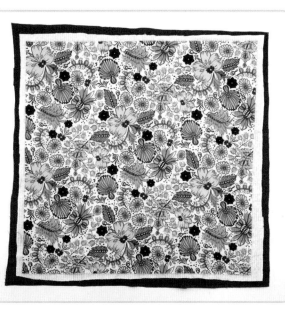

1 For the pillow front, lay an 18 x 18in (46 x 46cm) square of backing fabric on a flat surface. Center the batting on top of the backing fabric, then center the patterned front fabric on top of that.

2 Starting from the center and working outward, pin the backing, batting, and front fabric together using safety pins. Make sure that all the layers lie flat and check that the underside of the backing fabric also lies flat.

3 Starting at one corner and using a darning needle and a length of embroidery thread, use a running stitch (see p.43) to sew a line through all three layers of fabric. Make the stitches and the gap between them about ¼in (6mm) long. At the opposite edge, tie the thread off at the back.

Do not cut through the embroidery threads

Trim away excess batting and backing fabric

4 Continue sewing rows of running stitch, spacing the rows approximately ³⁄₈in (1cm) apart. Try to keep the stitches and the gaps in line from row to row, as above. Continue until you have sewn the entire top. Remove the safety pins as you work.

5 Use your quilter's ruler and rotary cutter to cut around all four edges to remove the excess batting and backing fabric, trimming the pillow front to a 16¹⁄₂in (42cm) square.

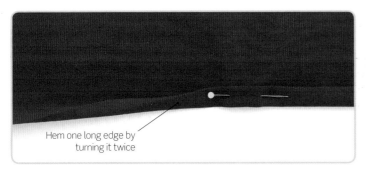

Hem one long edge by turning it twice

Align the edges and pin all the way around

The back pieces overlap and the wrong sides are faceup

6 To make the pillow back, cut two pieces of backing fabric, each 16¹⁄₂ x 10in (42 x 26cm). Fold one of the long edges of one piece to the wrong side of the fabric by ³⁄₈in (1cm). Fold it again by the same amount to create a neat hem and to enclose the raw edge. Pin the hem in place, check that it is straight, then sew along the edge of the second fold to secure the hem. Repeat on the other piece of fabric.

7 Lay the quilted pillow front right-side up. Place one of the back pieces on top, right-side down, aligning its long, unhemmed edge with the top raw edge of the pillow front. Place the second back piece right-side down on top of the first, aligning its long, unhemmed edge with the bottom raw edge of the pillow front. The two back pieces should overlap. Pin along all four edges.

If you find it easier, use tailor's chalk and a ruler to draw sewing

Do not cut
through the
stitches

8 Leaving a ³⁄₈in (1cm) seam allowance, sew around all four edges of the pillow cover to secure the back pieces to the pillow front. Remove the pins as you work.

9 Snip off all four corners, making sure not to cut through the stitches. Turn the pillow cover to the right side through the opening in the back. Iron, then insert the pillow cushion.

**Loose, casual running stitches** give this pillow its handmade charm. To add even more color and to give the pillow a very personalized touch, use more than one color of embroidery thread, changing color after every few rows.

guidelines, or use masking tape to mark straight lines.

# Machine quilting basics

Beautifully machined quilts are in no way second best to those worked by hand. Because the stitches are continuous, the finished product is usually flatter than a hand-quilted one. An even-feed, or "walking," foot, which feeds the layers through at the same speed top and bottom, is useful. Start and finish either by setting the stitch length to 0 and taking a few stitches before resetting, or leave a tail of thread to tie off.

## Preparing a quilt for machine sewing

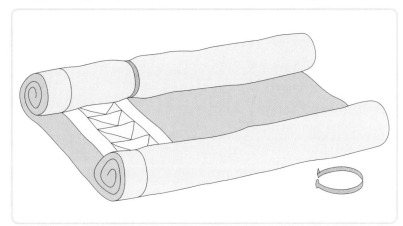

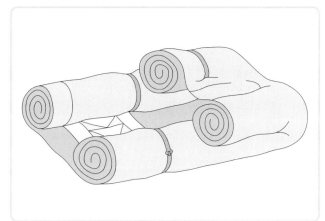

1 To work on a small area at a time, roll up both sides of the quilt toward the center, leaving 12in (30cm) open in between. Hold the edges with clips.

2 Fold or roll up the other ends of the piece and secure them using clips, leaving space to work on. Repeat the rolling and/or folding process as you work your way around the piece.

## Grid patterns

Traditional gridded quilting patterns can be square or diamond-shaped. Mark the grid by drawing the center line in each direction, or use ¼in (6mm) masking tape. If you set a quilting guide on your walking foot, you can use it to measure the distance between rows as you work.

1 Take a few short stitches. Set the quilting guide to the correct distance on one side and sew the first marked row from edge to edge. Turn the work and use the quilting guide to measure each vertical row in turn.

2 Repeat to work the horizontal rows.

# Concentric quilting

Concentric quilting lines can be worked by hand or machine. Outline quilting emphasizes a pieced or appliquéd design and requires minimal marking. Straight lines can be marked with 1/4in (6mm) masking tape; curves can be lightly drawn. Echo quilting is similar, but consists of a series of evenly spaced concentric quilted lines. It is most often used in Hawaiian appliqué (see pp.174–175).

## Outline quilting

Following the seam lines or outlines of the motif, work your quilting stitches 1/4in (6mm) inside or outside, or on both sides, of the motif's edges.

## Echo quilting

Make a row of outline quilting (see left). Then continue to add evenly spaced rows to fill the background around the motif.

## Seeding

This hand-quilting method uses small, straight stitches to fill the background. The back of the piece will have longer, stranded stitches, so this is best used on pieces where the back will not show, such as wall hangings or items with linings.

**1** Bury the knot (see p.204). Bring the needle and thread out near the motif. Take to the back and come up a short distance away from the first stitch.

**2** Take another stitch straight down and pull the thread through and come up a short distance away. Work outward from the motif. Keep the stitches small on the front and position them randomly so that they look like scattered seeds.

## Quilting in the ditch

Here, the sewing follows the piecing lines on the quilt top and is hidden in the seams. It is best to use a walking foot on your machine when quilting in the ditch. Sew along each row of piecing in turn, working from the center outward. Stop and start as little as possible.

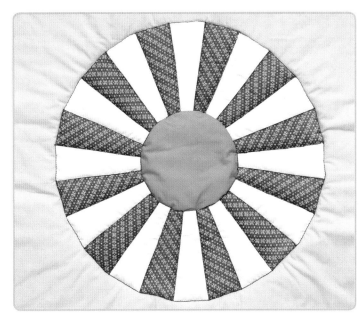

# Corded quilting and trapunto

Corded quilting, or Italian quilting, and trapunto, or stuffed quilting, are techniques that can be used separately, but they work well together. Both involve stitching a design through a top and a thin backing layer, usually of butter muslin. The motif is then filled from the back with lengths of quilting, knitting yarn or soft cord, or with stuffing material. The outline is traditionally worked by hand.

1 Cut a background fabric and transfer the design to the right side, using a water-soluble pen. Cut a piece of butter muslin or similar fabric the same size. Baste them together around the edges.

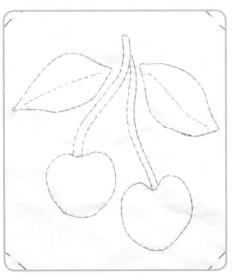

2 Outline the motif(s) with a small running stitch. Here we have used a contrasting colored thread for clarity. Where lines meet, keep stitches separate so they don't cross over. When sewing is complete, remove the marks.

3 Thread a tapestry needle with quilting or knitting yarn or soft cord. From the back, slip the needle through the first channel, leaving a short tail at each end.

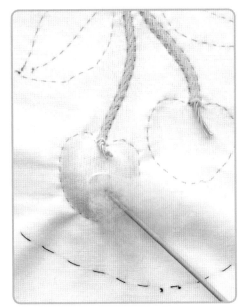

4 Make small slits in the center of each element through the backing layer only and stuff small pieces of batting between the top and the muslin.

5 Close each slit in the backing with a crossed stitch, such as herringbone. Remove the basting stitches once the design is complete.

6 The cording and trapunto gives the finished motif a three-dimensional quality on the right side.

# Tying

This involves tying lengths of cotton thread, lightweight yarn, or ribbon through the layers of a quilt to hold them together. Use a sharp-pointed needle with an eye that is large enough to hold the thread but small enough to prevent making holes in the quilt. Space the ties according to the type of batting, the block pattern, and the size of the quilt. Cotton and wool batting shift easily and should be tied more closely than polyester. A general guide is 4–6in (10–15cm) apart.

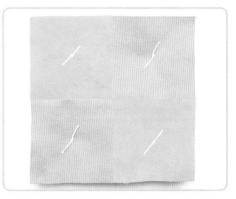

1 Working from the center out, take a stitch down and back up through all the layers and pull the needle and thread through, leaving a 4in (10cm) tail on the top.

2 Take a second stitch in the same way in the same place.

3 Tie the ends of thread in a square knot. Cut the thread from the reel and trim the ends to the same length. Repeat, double-stitching and knotting over the entire quilt.

# Freestyle or free-motion quilting

Freestyle, or free-motion, quilting gives machine quilters freedom to create their own designs. Mastering the technique requires patience and practice, but the effort can be very rewarding. You need a darning foot or a free-motion foot and to know how to lower the feed dogs. If your machine has the option to stop work with the needle always down, use it.

1 With the presser foot down where you will start, take one stitch. Hold the top thread and use it to gently pull the bobbin thread to the top. Secure with a few very short stitches. Start slowly and take a few more short stitches. Cut away the thread tails.

2 Guide the fabric with your hands, moving the work in any direction. Position your hands in an open circle around the machine foot and press the layers gently. Keep a moderate speed and make the stitches the same length. Tie off with a few short stitches, as in Step 1.

## Troubleshooting

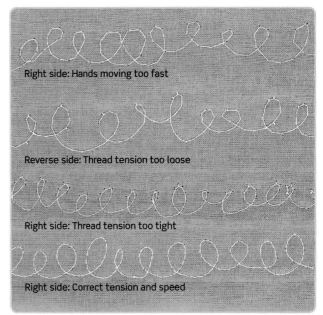

Right side: Hands moving too fast

Reverse side: Thread tension too loose

Right side: Thread tension too tight

Right side: Correct tension and speed

# Quilted pot holders

These pot holders are quick to whip up in any size. Each pot holder is like a mini-quilt with a backing, batting, and front all quilted together and bound. They're the perfect project for trying out your quilting skills, or for using up scraps of fabric.

## Essential Information

**DIFFICULTY** Easy

**SIZE** 7½in (19cm) square

**TOOLS AND MATERIALS**
Quilter's ruler
Cutting mat
Rotary cutter
Sewing machine
Pins
Threads to match the fabrics and binding tapes

**FABRICS**
8½ x 17in (21.5 x 43cm) main, patterned cotton fabric
8½ x 17in (21.5 x 43cm) insulated batting
8½ x 17in (21.5 x 43cm) cotton terry cloth fabric
40in (100cm) bias binding tape

**SKILLS**
Machine quilting (see pp.210–213)
Binding with premade bias binding (see pp.50–51)

**SEAM ALLOWANCE**
¼in (6mm) throughout, unless otherwise stated

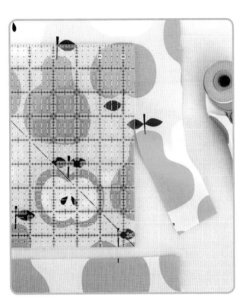

1 Cut one piece of main fabric, one piece of insulated batting, and once piece of terry cloth fabric all 8½in (21.5cm) square. Next, cut one piece of main fabric, one piece of terry cloth fabric, and one piece of insulated batting all 6½ x 8½in (16.5 x 21.5cm).

2 Pin each piece of main fabric wrong sides together with its corresponding piece of terry cloth, placing the insulated batting in the middle. Place the pins inside the motif to be quilted so that they will not be in the way of your seam lines.

3 Using a matching or complementary thread in the top of your machine and a thread to match your terry cloth in your bobbin, sew around each shape on both pinned units. Alternatively, you can quilt the units using the pattern of your choice.

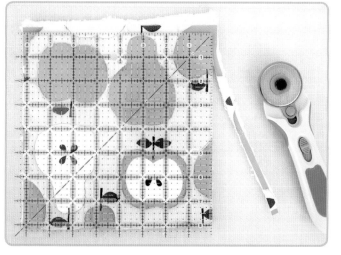

**Zigzag the edges**

4 Once you are done quilting both pieces, trim the larger unit an equal amount on all four sides so that it is 7½in (19cm) square. Trim the smaller unit so that it is 7½ x 5½in (19 x 14cm).

5 Zigzag stitch around all four raw edges of both units to keep the edges neat and tidy.

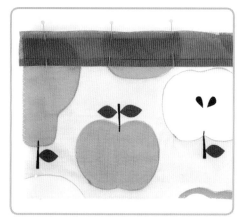

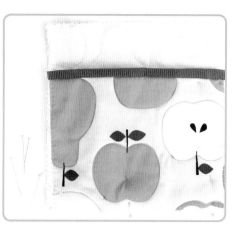

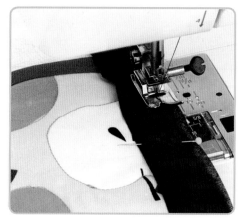

6 Cut a piece of bias binding 7½in (19cm) long. Open it up and pin it along the top edge of the smaller unit. Sew it in place, then fold it around to the back and sew it in place either by machine or by hand (see pp.50–51).

7 Lay the large unit terry cloth side up, then lay the smaller unit on top of it, terry cloth side down. Align the bottom and side edges, pinning in place. Sew the two units together, around the three unfinished edges of the small unit, leaving a ¼in (6mm) seam allowance to create the pot holder.

8 Attach a piece of bias binding to fit all the way around the pot holder, mitering the corners and finishing by hand or machine (see p.50–51).

## Pot holder variation

You can easily make variations on the pocket-style pot holder just shown. If you'd like to make one without a pocket and with fabric on both sides, cut two squares of main fabric and one square of insulated batting of the same size. Sandwich the batting between the two layers of fabric, pin, and quilt as you desire. Bind all four edges.

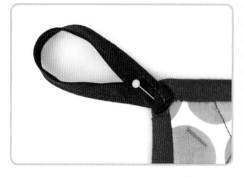

**You can attach a handy loop** to your pot holders if you'd like to be able to hang them. Fold a piece of binding tape approximately 6in (15.5cm) in half, along the length, wrong sides together. Fold in the two raw ends so that they will not be visible. Sew along the edges to create a long thin strip. Create a loop out of the strip, as shown right, and pin it to the corner of the potholder. Sew it securely in place.

# Embellishing quilts

From surface embroidery and beading to adding buttons, bows, and found objects, the ways to embellish a quilt are endless. You can use sequins, charms, or shisha mirrors, or add machine embroidery.

## Buttons

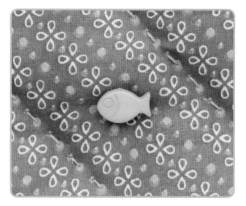

Novelty buttons make charming embellishments on theme quilts or folk-art versions. Buttons can also become "flowers" at the end of stems in a basket or accents in any number of places. Sew buttons to the quilt top and knot them if you don't want to sew through the backing. Otherwise, tie a knot at the back. They are best reserved for decorative pieces such as wall hangings and should not be used on quilts for children and babies, since they can become detached.

## Charms

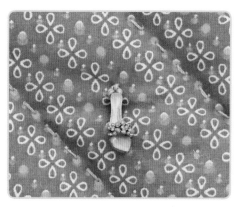

Simply tie charms in position on the quilt top, depending on the type and size. Charms are usually used to add a personal touch to a quilt—wedding motifs for a bride's quilt, for example. They are best reserved for decorative pieces such as wall hangings and should not be used on quilts for children and babies, since they can become detached.

## Bows

Tie ribbon bows to the desired size and sew them in place on the quilt top. They can be single or double bows. Make sure the knot is secure before sewing. If adding bows to a baby quilt be sure the tail ends are not long enough to present a hazard. You can sew a few small stitches through the central knot in the bow to help prevent it from unknotting.

# Cording and piping

Quilted pillow covers, home accessories, or bags often require a contrasting decorative edging of cording or piping. Cording is the easiest to apply; however, with piping your choice of color is unlimited.

## Sewing on cording

Baste the cording in place

1 Sew cording in between two layers of fabric, for example, along the seam line of a pillow cover. Align the fabric edge of the cording with the raw edge of the right side of the front piece. Baste in place along the edges.

2 Lay the back piece over the cording, with the right sides of the fabric pieces together, and machine sew along the outer edge of the cording using a zipper foot.

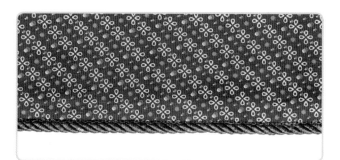

3 Remove the basting and turn the fabric pieces right-side out. Press the fabric away from the cord so that the cord sits neatly along the seam line.

# Covering and inserting piping cord

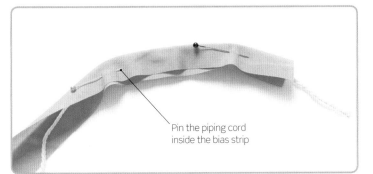

Pin the piping cord
inside the bias strip

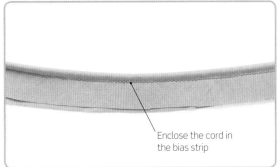

Enclose the cord in
the bias strip

1 Prepare bias strips approximately 1½in (4cm) wide (see pp.48–49). Fold the bias cut fabric strip in half, wrong side to wrong side, over the piping cord. Pin or baste in place.

2 Machine sew in place close to the cord using a zipper foot or special piping foot. If the zipper foot doesn't run smoothly against the covered cord, baste the fabric in place before sewing.

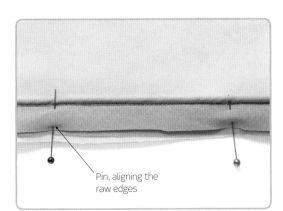

Pin, aligning the
raw edges

3 Trim the seam allowance on the piping cover so that it is the desired seam allowance width—it can be less than this width, but not more. Align the seam on the piping cover with the intended seam line on the right side of the front of the fabric and pin. Baste in place with the piping facing inward.

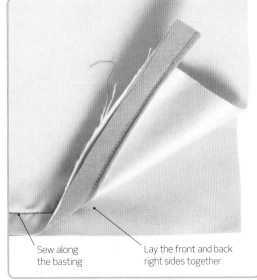

Sew along
the basting

Lay the front and back
right sides together

4 If you are sewing the piping around a corner, bend it carefully to form a 90-degree angle and continue basting.

5 Place the back fabric piece over the front piece with the right sides together and pin. Using a zipper foot, machine sew the layers together, sewing on top of the piping cord seam.

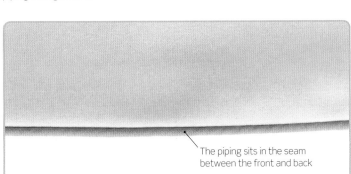

The piping sits in the seam
between the front and back

6 Turn the piece right-side out and carefully press the fabric away from the piping.

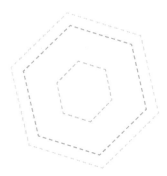

# Fastenings

Although fastenings have a practical use—securing closings on pillow covers, bags, garments, and home accessories—many of them also serve as decorative finishing details. Techniques for adding very simple fastenings are provided here, including hand-sewn buttonholes, snaps, and zippers.

## Sewing on buttons

**1** Thread your needle with a double strand of thread. Secure the thread to the fabric where the button is to be positioned. Pass the needle up through one hole of the button, down through the other hole to the back. Do not pull the thread taut yet—first insert a toothpick (or matchstick) under the stitch. Then pull the thread taut. Continue working back and forth through the holes of the button and the fabric, until at least five stitches have been worked.

**2** Remove the toothpick. Wrap the working thread several times around the thread under the button to form a shank. Secure the thread end with three small stitches at the back.

## Hand-sewn buttonholes

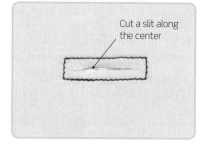

Cut a slit along the center

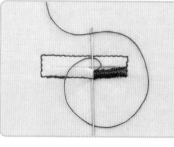

**1** Mark the desired finished length of the buttonhole on the right side of the piece, then machine stitch a rectangle ¼in (6mm) wide and as long as the required finished buttonhole length. Carefully cut a slit along the exact center of this rectangle.

**2** Using a thick, strong buttonhole thread, work tailor's buttonhole stitch (as shown) along both edges of the slit. Insert the needle through the fabric just outside the machine stitches, so that the stitches are ⅛in (3mm) long.

**3** Finish each end of the buttonhole with three or four stitches that are the same width as the total width of the buttonhole. Always work buttonholes through two layers of fabric that have an interfacing in between them.

## Sewing on snaps

Secure the snaps with several stithes

Although snaps are not visible, align them carefully when sewing them on. Use a doubled thread and work three or more stitches through each hole around the edge of the snap pieces.

# Sewing on a zipper

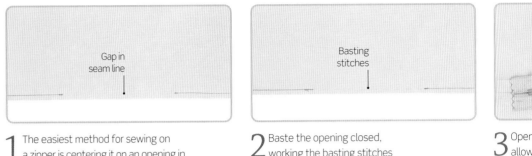

1 The easiest method for sewing on a zipper is centering it on an opening in a seam line. To begin, sew the seam line, leaving a gap in the stitches that is the length of the zipper.

2 Baste the opening closed, working the basting stitches along the seam line.

3 Open out the seam and press the seam allowance open on the wrong side. Open the zipper and place it facedown on top of the wrong side of the seam. Centering the zipper teeth carefully on top of the seam, baste one side of the zipper tape in place ⅛in (3mm) from the teeth.

4 Close the zipper and baste the other side of the zipper tape in place. Using a matching thread, machine sew the zipper in place, sewing on the right side of the fabric and forming a rectangle around the zipper just outside the basting stitches.

5 Remove the basting around the zipper tape and along the opening. Press.

# Inserting trim in a seam

If a piece is backed, trims, in addition to piping (see p.219), can be inserted between the top and the other layer, such as in the seam joining the front and back of a pillow or place mat.

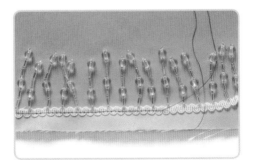

1 Measure the edge to be trimmed and add an extra 4-6in (10-15cm) to the trimming. Starting in the center of the bottom edge on the right side of the top, align the top edge of the trim on the seam line with the decorative edge pointing away from the raw edge. Pin and baste, then sew in place.

2 With the trim inside and pointing inward, position the back and top right sides facing. Sew along the same seam line that was made in Step 1.

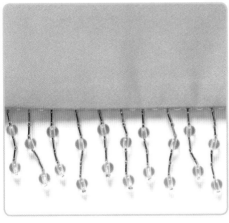

3 Turn through to the right side and press on both sides. Topstitch along the edge if desired.

# Things to make

# Needle book

Keep your needles safely stored, neat, and easily transportable in this cute little needle book. The cover protects the needles and the felt page inside makes them readily accessible. If you wish, you can add extra felt pages to hold more needles.

## Essential Information

**DIFFICULTY** Easy

**SIZE** 4 x 4in (10 x 10cm) when closed

**TOOLS AND MATERIALS**
Threads to match your fabrics
Sewing machine
Pins
3in (7.6cm) elastic cord
Scissors
Iron and ironing board
Sewing needle
Thread to match your felt
³⁄₄in (2cm) self-covered button in
    a coordinating fabric

**FABRICS**
Nine 2 x 2in (5 x 5cm) pieces of
    coordinating fabrics with different prints
4¹⁄₂ x 4¹⁄₂in (11 x 11cm) back cover fabric
4¹⁄₂ x 8¹⁄₂in (11 x 22.5cm) lining fabric
3³⁄₄ x 3³⁄₄in (9.5 x 9.5cm) felt, or aida cloth
8 x 4in (20 x 10cm) batting

**SKILLS**
Sewing intersecting seams (see p.74)

**SEAM ALLOWANCE**
¹⁄₄in (6mm) throughout, unless otherwise stated

## Make the front cover
Arrange the coordinating fabrics in a nine-patch arrangement of your choice. With the right sides together, stitch the three patches in each row together, then join the top, middle, and bottom rows. Press the seams. This forms the front cover of the needle book.

## Join the front and back
Lay the front cover on top of the back cover fabric, right sides together. Pin along the edge that is to be the spine, then sew together to join the front and back covers. Open up and press the seam open.

## Add the lining and the elastic
Lay the joined front and back covers on top of the lining fabric, right sides together. Fold the piece of elastic in half to create a loop. Place the loop between the back cover and the lining fabric, halfway along the short side. The raw ends of the elastic should stick out of the side of the book by about ¹⁄₄in (6mm) and the loop should sit between the two layers of fabric. Pin the elastic in place, then pin around all four sides of the book.

## Sew the sides and turn through
Sew around all four sides, leaving a 2in (5cm) gap along one long side. Sew back and forth over the ends of the elastic several times to make sure they are held securely in place. Snip off the four corners, making sure not to cut through the stitches. Turn the needle book to the right side through the gap. Carefully pull out all the corners with a pin, then iron.

**A neat edge** Felt does not fray, which makes it perfect for a project such as this because it does not require any hemming.

## Insert the batting
Insert the piece of batting inside the book through the gap in the stitches. Make sure it lies flat and even, then hand sew the gap closed. If you want to quilt your needle book, do it at this stage, before adding the felt page.

## Attach the felt page
Place the piece of felt so that one of its edges sits at the center fold of the book. Pin in place along this edge. Using a matching top thread and a bobbin thread that matches the back cover fabric, topstitch along the edge, leaving a ¹⁄₁₆in (2mm) seam allowance.

## Sew on the button
Position the button on the front cover so it aligns with the elastic loop. Sew it in place, only catching the front cover fabric so the stitches are not visible on the other side.

# Pentagon ball

Baby will just love this soft ball plaything. It is easily made using a pentagon-shaped template, adjusted to suit the size you want the ball to be. Made from scraps of fabric in coordinating patterns, it will withstand hours of play.

## Essential Information

**DIFFICULTY** Easy

**SIZE** Approximately 5in (13cm) in diameter

**TOOLS AND MATERIALS**
Tracing paper
Pencil or marker
Scissors
Stiff cardboard, paper, or freezer paper
Pins or paper clips
Sewing needle
Threads to match your fabrics
Toy filling
Child-safe toy bell or rattle (optional)

**FABRICS**
12 scraps of coordinating fabric, each a
    minimum of 4 x 4in (10 x 10cm)

**SKILLS**
English paper piecing (see pp.134–135)
Fussy cutting (optional, see p.40)

## Pentagon ball layout

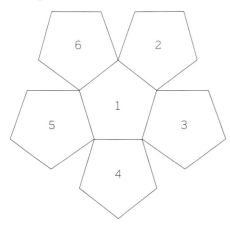

## Cut the template

Using a pencil or marker, trace the pentagon template (see p.297) onto tracing paper and cut it out. You can make the template larger or smaller if you'd like to alter the size of the ball. Copy the template onto cardboard, paper, or freezer paper to make a total of 12 pentagon pattern pieces, all the same size. Carefully cut out each pattern piece.

## Make the patches

Pin each pattern piece to the wrong side of a fabric scrap (see p.134) or use a paper clip to hold them together (see p.137). To center a specific design detail from the fabric on the finished pentagon, make sure you attach the pattern piece so it is centered over the detail (see p.40).

Cut out the fabric around each pattern piece, leaving approximately a ³⁄₈in (1cm) seam allowance. Folding the seam allowance over the edge of the pattern piece to the wrong side, baste along the edges of the fabric, making sure not to sew through the pattern piece. Fold each corner of the fabric neatly and sew through the fold to hold it securely. Repeat for all the pentagons, then remove the pins or paper clips.

## Join the patches

Lay out six of the pentagon patches in the shape of a flower, with one pentagon in the middle surrounded by five more pentagons (see diagram, left). With right sides together, whipstitch (see p.43) the patches together. The sewn patches will take on the shape of a bowl. Repeat to make another bowl using the

**For added interest,** try centering a few of the pentagon pattern pieces over some of the design details in the fabric. This playful image of bunnies now takes center stage.

remaining six patches. With the wrong sides face out, invert one bowl and place it over the other, matching the alternating edges. Whipstitch the matched edges together, leaving one pair unsewn for turning through. Remove the pattern pieces.

## Stuff the ball

Turn the ball to the right side through the unsewn edge. Stuff the ball firmly with toy filling. If you wish, insert a child-safe rattle or bell into the center of the filling. Slip stitch (see p.43) the opening closed.

## Essential Information

**DIFFICULTY** Easy

**SIZE** 63 x 44in (160 x 112cm)

**TOOLS AND MATERIALS**
Measuring tape
Quilter's ruler
Rotary cutter
Cutting mat
Scissors
Sewing machine
Threads to match your fabrics
Iron and ironing board
Safety pins (optional)
Machine quilting thread (optional)

**FABRICS**
**A:** 20 x 44in (50 x 112cm) of fabric
**B:** 14 x 44in (35 x 112cm) of fabric
**C:** 14 x 44in (35 x 112cm) of fabric
**D:** 20 x 44in (50 x 112cm) of fabric
**E:** 20 x 44in (50 x 112cm) of fabric
138 x 44in (350 x 112cm) backing fabric
20 x 44in (50 x 112cm) binding fabric
69 x 52in (175 x 130cm) batting

**SKILLS**
Joining two or more strips (see p.62)

**SEAM ALLOWANCE**
¼in (6mm) throughout

# Garden fairies strip quilt

This simple quilt is made from strips of five different fabrics. For best effect, include a couple of fabrics with a linear print and cut them so that the print runs horizontally. We finished by quilting the layers with a pattern of leaves and vines.

## Cut the fabrics

Cut all strips from selvage to selvage. Cut eight strips from fabric A, each 2in (5cm) wide. Cut four strips each from fabrics B and C, each 3in (7.5cm) wide. Cut four strips from fabric D, each 3½in (9cm) wide. Cut three strips from fabric E, each 5½in (13.5cm) wide.

## Make the quilt top

With right sides together and leaving a ¼in (6mm) seam allowance, sew the strips together in three repeating A, B, C, D, and E sequences. The fourth and last sequence is then A, B, C, D, A. The first and last fabric A strips form the top and bottom border. Join the three remaining fabric A strips together into one long strip. Measure the length of the quilt top and cut two strips to this measurement from the long fabric A strip. With right sides together, sew the strips to each of the long sides of the quilt top to complete the border.

## Assemble the layers

Join the backing fabric so it is large enough to fit the finished quilt top (see p.47). Lay the backing fabric on a flat surface, right-side down. Lay the batting on top and carefully smooth out the batting and backing fabric (see p.46). Lay the quilt top right-side up on the batting. Both the batting and the backing fabric will overhang the quilt top by about an inch (several centimeters). Join the layers together using the method of your choice (see p.46), making sure all the layers sit flat and are even with one another.

## Quilt the layers

We used free-motion quilting and variegated thread. You can machine or hand quilt with a design of your choice. After quilting, cut away the excess backing and batting so that the edges of all the layers of the quilt are aligned.

## Attach the binding

Finish the quilt by adding binding made from the binding fabric (see p.48). Attach the binding to the edges, following the instructions for Double-fold binding (see p.53).

# Diamond floor pillow

This floor pillow uses the frayed-edge appliqué technique. Here we've sewn diamonds onto the top in a pattern radiating from the center, but you can choose a different arrangement, or different shapes altogether, for your pillow cover.

## Essential Information

**DIFFICULTY** Easy

**SIZE** 28in (70cm) square by 4in (10cm) high

**MATERIALS**

Tracing paper or cardboard

Scissors

Quilter's ruler

Rotary cutter

Cutting mat

Measuring tape or ruler

Threads to match your fabrics

Pins

Basting thread or fabric glue stick (optional)

28in (70cm) square by 4in (10cm) high pillow
cushion, or batting folded to fit inside

Three 1in (2.5cm) snaps

**FABRICS**

**A:** Twenty 6 x 4in (15.5 x 10cm) scraps of
patterned fabric for the diamonds

**B:** 59 x 37½in (150 x 95cm) plain blue
main fabric

**C:** 19 x 28¾in (48 x 72cm) patterned side fabric

39½ x 12in (100 x 30cm) lightweight fuseable
interfacing

**SKILLS**

Frayed edge appliqué (see p.194)

Set-in seams (see pp.100–101)

**SEAM ALLOWANCE**

³⁄₈in (1cm) throughout, unless otherwise stated

## Cut the pieces

Cut 20 diamonds from the scraps of fabric and 20 diamonds from the interfacing using the templates on page 297. Cut one 28¾in (72cm) square pillow front and two 28¾ x 18in (72 x 46cm) rectangular back flaps from fabric B. Cut four 28¾ x 4¾in (72 x 12cm) rectangular sides from fabric C.

## Make the front

Iron one interfacing diamond to the wrong side of one fabric diamond, centering it inside. Repeat for the other 19 diamonds.

Lay the pillow front right-side up on a flat surface and arrange the diamonds right-side up on top using the diagram below for reference.

Baste, pin, or glue each diamond in place, and sew each one in place, topstitching ³⁄₈in (1cm) inside the edge of each diamond (see p.194). Remove the pins or basting stitches, if used.

### Diamond placement

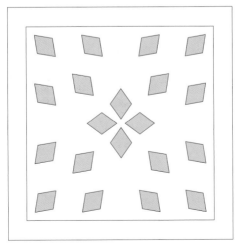

## Attach the sides

Turn the pillow front wrong-side up and mark a dot set in ³⁄₈in (1cm) from each corner (see p.101). On the wrong side of each of the four side pieces, mark a dot set in ³⁄₈in (1cm) from each corner. Pin the first side piece right sides together with one of the edges of the pillow front, matching the dots. Sew between the dots. Repeat on the other three side pieces.

Pin the short, raw ends of each side piece right sides together with the adjacent side piece, matching the dots. Sew between the dots to make each corner of the pillow.

## Make the back

Hem one of the long edges on both of the backs flaps by turning over that edge ³⁄₈in (1cm) twice, pinning, then topstitching. Mark a dot set in ³⁄₈in (1cm) from each of the two unhemmed corners on both flaps.

Lay the pillow front right-side up, with the sides folded over onto the top. Lay one of the back flaps right-side down on top, with the hemmed edge inside the pillow. Pin the raw edges to the raw edges of the sides, matching the corner dots. Lay the second flap right-side down on top of this, in the same way, but on the opposite side of the pillow. Pin the raw edges to the raw edges of the sides, matching the dots. The two hemmed edges of the flaps will overlap one another. Sew around the perimeter of the pillow, forward and reverse sewing over where the flaps overlap.

Turn the pillow right-side out and sew the snaps to the back (see p.220) where the flaps overlap. Wash and dry the finished pillow cover then insert the pillow cushion.

**Because the bowls are not rigid,** they are reversible. Simply press on the center to invert the bowl the opposite way.

## Essential Information

**DIFFICULTY** Easy

**SIZE** 9in (23cm) square

**TOOLS AND MATERIALS**
Quilter's ruler
Rotary cutter
Cutting mat
Iron and ironing board
Sewing machine
Thread to either contrast or match
   the fabrics
Scissors

**FABRICS**
Two contrasting, or coordinating, fat
   quarters, one light and one dark
9½in (24cm) square medium-weight
   interfacing
13 x 19in (33 x 48cm) fusible web

**SKILLS**
Basic patchwork and sewing skills

**SEAM ALLOWANCE**
Zigzag stitch, unless otherwise stated

# Fabric bowls

For each bowl you will need two contrasting or coordinating fabrics. Two fat quarters will make two bowls and leave you with generous scrap fabrics to use for other projects. You can adjust the depth of the bowl by changing the dart size.

## Cut the fabrics

Iron all the fabrics to ensure there are no fold lines or wrinkles. Cut one 9½in (24cm) square and one 3½in (9cm) square from each fat quarter. Cut one 9½in (24cm) square from the interfacing. Cut two 9½in (24cm) squares and two 3½in (9cm) squares from the fusible web.

## Prepare the pieces

Place a large square of fusible web on the wrong side of a large fabric square and press to fuse. Repeat for the second large square.

Following the instructions, place the fused square onto the interfacing and carefully press from the inside outward, ensuring that there are no wrinkles. Repeat, using the second fused square on the other side of the interfacing to create a sandwich.

Trim the sandwich to a 9in (23cm) square. If you'd like rounded corners, use a coin or other similar object to mark the corners evenly and carefully cut away the excess.

Place a small square of fusible web on the wrong side of a small fabric square and press to fuse. Repeat with the second square of fabric and fusible web. Trim each piece to a 3in (7.5cm) square.

## Make the bowl

You now have three pieces—a large double-sided sandwich and two small, single-sided, square base pieces.

Measure and mark a horizontal line and a vertical line in the center of the light side of the large sandwich. Place one small square on the large sandwich, matching the points of the small piece to the marked lines on the sandwich (see Figure 1). Fuse in place. Sew around the outside of the small square, but as close to its edges as possible—this will help with the placement of the second base piece. Turn the sandwich over and fuse the second base piece in place, using the square just sewn as your guide.

You now need to cut darts to shape the bowl. On either side of the horizontal and vertical marked lines, make a mark ½ in (1.2cm) from the line on outer edge of the sandwich (see Figure 2). Make a mark ¼ in (6mm) away from each corner of the small square, along the vertical and horizontal lines. Join up these marks with the marks on the edges for the darts (see Figure 2).

Cut away one dart only using sharp scissors—if you cut all the darts at this stage you may get distortion and fraying when you sew.

You will sew over each dart seam and the rim of the bowl twice, so you will need to set the first pass stitch width slightly smaller than the second pass stitch width, since the second set of stitches will need to cover the first set.

First, set your machine to a narrow zigzag stitch and medium stitch length. Practice stitches and tension on the cutaway piece before you begin sewing the bowl, to ensure the sewing is right.

Beginning at the first cut dart, sew around the small square base. When you get back to the starting point, gently pull the sandwich together, butting the cut edges of the dart against one another. Sew out toward the rim of the bowl, covering the seam and sewing the two butted edges together.

Repeat, cutting out and sewing the next dart in the same way, then the final two darts, each in turn. Finally, sew around the rim.

Set your machine to a slightly wider zigzag stitch and short stitch length to create satin stitch. Practice on a scrap to check that the tension and stitch size are correct and will cover the first set of stitches. Neatly sew over all the seams again, first sewing the darts, then around the small square, and finally around the rim. Secure all the thread ends.

**Figure 1**

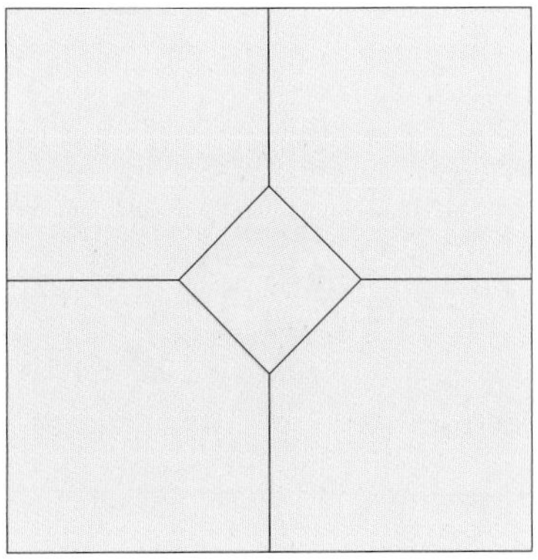

**Figure 2**

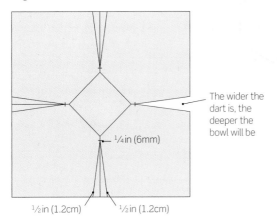

The wider the dart is, the deeper the bowl will be

¼in (6mm)

½in (1.2cm)     ½in (1.2cm)

# Chicken and egg quilt

Images on fabrics are often printed in rows that can be cut apart, which works well for blocks made of strips, and sashings and borders. Here we have used fabrics featuring hens, chicks, and eggs, but you can choose fabrics to suit your personal taste.

## Essential Information

**DIFFICULTY** Easy

**SIZE** 41 x 53¼in (104 x 135cm)

**TOOLS AND MATERIALS**
Measuring tape
Water-soluble pen
Rotary cutter
Scissors
Quilter's ruler
Cutting mat
Iron and ironing board
Pins
Sewing machine
Threads to match your fabrics
Contrast thread for tacking, or safety pins
Machine quilting thread (optional)
Sewing needle

**FABRICS**
**A:** 39 x 44in (100 x 112cm) cotton fabric with
  a pattern printed in rows (or of your choice)
**B:** 6 cotton fat eighths in different patterns
**C:** 39 x 44in (100 x 112cm) of cotton sashing
  fabric
79 x 44in (200 x 112cm) of cotton backing and
  binding fabric
47 x 59in (120 x 150cm) batting of your choice

**SKILLS**
Sashings and borders (see pp.108–113)

**SEAM ALLOWANCE**
¼in (6mm) throughout

## Make the blocks

For block A, cut a 6½ x 5in (16 x 12.5cm) strip from fabric A, another from fabric B, and one 3½ x 9½in (9 x 24cm) strip from one of the fabric B fat eights. With right sides together and leaving a ¼in (6mm) seam allowance, sew together the two 6½ x 5in (16 x 12.5cm) strips along their long edges to form a rectangle. Using the block A diagram as a guide, sew fabric B to this rectangle. Repeat to make another block.

For block B, cut two 2½ x 9½in (6.5 x 24cm) strips and one 5½ x 9½in (13 x 24cm) strip each from different fat eight pieces. Using the block B diagram as a guide, leaving a ¼in (6mm) seam allowance, and with right sides together, sew together the three strips to form a square. Repeat, using different fabrics, to make two more blocks.

For block C, cut three 3½ x 9½in (8.5 x 24cm) strips from fabric B. Using the block C diagram as a guide, leaving a ¼in (6mm) seam allowance, and with right sides together, sew together the fabric B strips to form a square. Repeat, using different fabric combinations, to make six more blocks.

Check to make sure that each finished block measures 9½ x 9½in (24 x 24cm).

### Block A (make 2)

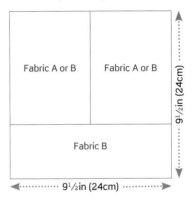

Fabric A or B | Fabric A or B
Fabric B
9½in (24cm)
9½in (24cm)

### Block B (make 3)

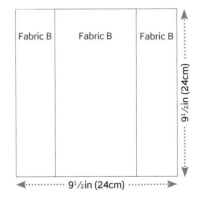

Fabric B | Fabric B | Fabric B
9½in (24cm)
9½in (24cm)

### Block C (make 7)

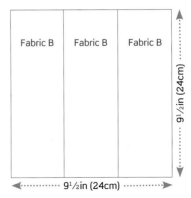

Fabric B | Fabric B | Fabric B
9½in (24cm)
9½in (24cm)

## Cut the sashings

From fabric C, cut eight short sashings, each measuring 2 x 9½in (5 x 24cm), five medium sashings, each measuring 2 x 30½in (5 x 77.5cm), and two long sashings, each measuring 2 x 44in (5 x 113cm).

## Cut the borders

From fabric A, cut two borders, each measuring 5 x 40in (12 x 101.5cm), and two more borders, each measuring 3¾ x 44in (9.5 x 113cm).

## Sew the quilt top

Using the quilt top diagram as a guide, lay out the three blocks for the first row, then place two short sashings between the blocks. Note that some blocks are rotated 90 degrees. With right sides together, sew the first row together. Repeat, following the quilt top diagram, to make the remaining three rows. Lay out the four completed rows in order and place three

**When you cut the borders,** center the pattern in the middle of the strip, so the pattern is evenly aligned all around the quilt top. If you wish, you can try mitering the border fabric so that the pattern carries on around the corners (see p.113).

Quilt top

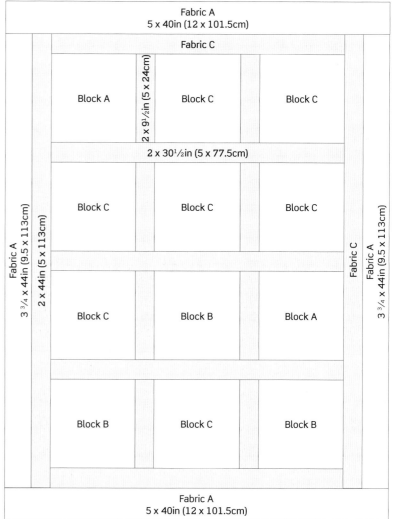

**Use this chart** as a guide when assembling the blocks, sashings, and borders for the quilt top. Make sure that the orientation of the chicken prints is correct. Refer to the finished quilt image on the opposite page.

medium sashings between the rows. Place the two remaining medium sashings at the top and the bottom. With right sides facing, sew the sashings and rows together in order. Next, with right sides together, sew the two long sashings to the long sides of the quilt top, then the 3³/₄ x 44in (9.5 x 113cm) borders to the long sides, followed by the 5 x 41in (12 x 104cm) sashings to the top and bottom of the quilt. Refer to pages 108–113 for information on sashings and borders.

## Assemble the layers

Lay the backing fabric on a flat surface, right-side down. Lay the batting on top and carefully smooth out the batting and backing fabric (see p.46). Lay the quilt top right-side up on the batting. Both the batting and the backing fabric will overhang the quilt top by an inch or so (several centimeters). Starting from the center and working outward, pin or tack the layers together (see p.46), making sure all the layers sit flat and are even with one another. Machine or hand quilt with the design of your choice. After quilting, cut away the excess backing and batting so that the edges of all the layers of the quilt are aligned.

## Attach the binding

Attach the binding to the edges, following the instructions for Double-fold binding (see p.53), or attach the binding using the method of your choice.

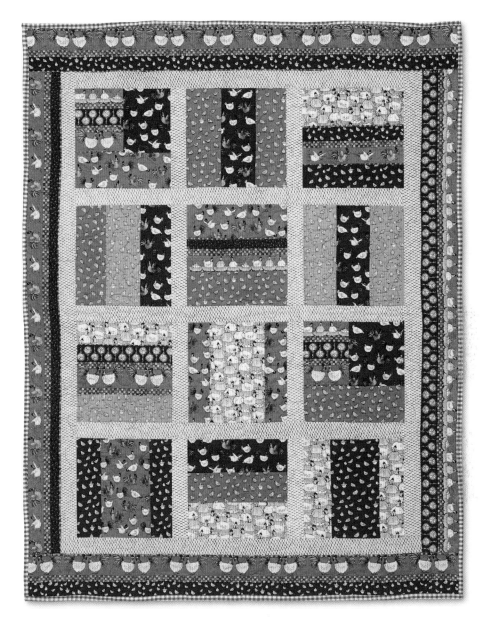

*Refer regularly to the diagram of the quilt top to be sure of success.*

# Secret garden pin cushion

This little pin cushion is made by creating a Secret garden patch (see p.151) and turning it into a small cushion by adding a back and stuffing it firmly. A covered button adds the finishing touch and, with the back button, joins front to back.

## Essential Information

**DIFFICULTY** Easy

**SIZE** 4in (10cm) square

**TOOLS AND MATERIALS**

One 9 x 9in (22 x 22cm) thin cardboard template
Iron and ironing board
Threads to match your fabrics
Sewing needle
Pins
Sewing machine
One 1in (2.5cm) button with shank, covered in fabric C
One $^5/_8$in (1.5cm) plain flat button for the back, used as a washer

**FABRICS**

**A:** One 10$^1/_2$ x 10$^1/_2$in (26.5 x 26.5cm) square of solid teal-colored fabric

**B:** One 4$^1/_2$ x 4$^1/_2$in (11 x 11cm) square of red fabric

**C:** One 4 x 8in (10 x 20cm) piece of patterned teal-colored fabric, cut and made into four half-square triangles (see p.82)

**D:** Two 3 x 6in (7.5 x 15cm) rectangles of the same patterned teal-colored fabric, for the back

Toy filling or batting

**SKILLS**

Secret garden (see p.151)

**SEAM ALLOWANCE**

$^1/_4$in (6mm) throughout, unless otherwise stated

## Make the front

With fabric A right side down, center the cardboard template on top of the fabric. Either finger press or use an iron to press the sides of the fabric over the template, starting by folding over the corners. Continue folding over and pressing the fabric over the cardboard. Remove the cardboard and press again. Find the center of the fabric by folding the square in half and pressing the fold. Repeat again in the opposite direction and press lightly. With the fabric still right-side down, fold up and press each corner of the square to the center mark on the fabric. Press all sides. Catch stitch the four corner points in place. Repeat the folding process again on the four sides, pressing the creases but not sewing them in place.

Open up the four triangular flaps and place fabric B, right side up, on the solid-colored fabric, using the creases as a guide. Fold the triangular flaps in so the points meet in the center. Pin all four outside corners and pin the four points in the center, then anchor the points in the center through all the layers with a few cross-stitches.

Pin the four half-square fabric C triangles right-side up to each of the triangular flaps, $^1/_8$in (3mm) inside the edge of fabric A. Roll the edge of fabric A over fabric C, curving fabric A so the rolled edge is wider in the middle and narrower at each end, forming a "petal" shape (see p.151). Pin as required. Repeat on the remaining seven edges. Increase the stitch size on your machine slightly, then topstitch along the rolled edge, beginning in the center. Repeat for the seven remaining curves.

## Make the back

On the reverse of one fabric D rectangle, measure 1$^1/_2$in (4cm) down along one long edge. Rotate the rectangle 180 degrees and repeat on the other side. Place the second rectangle under the first, right sides together and, leaving a $^1/_4$in (6mm) seam allowance, sew to the mark, backstitching to finish. Rotate and sew to the mark again, leaving a gap of approximately 1$^1/_2$in (4cm). Finger press the seam open.

Place the front and back of the cushion right sides together. Align and pin the edges in place. Sew around the four sides, then trim off the excess fabric so the raw edges are neat. Gently turn the cushion through the opening in the back seam, pushing out the corners.

## Stuff and button the cushion

Stuff the cushion and whipstitch the gap in the back by hand (see p.43). Sew the shanked button to the front of the pin cushion with double thread, passing the needle through to the back and through the washer button. Pull the thread to compress the pin cushion and tie the thread off securely.

**Sew the snaps** to the inside hemmed edges of the comforter cover to keep them hidden. A colorful strip of fabric inset into the comforter cover back adds a special detail.

# Large-patch comforter cover

A colorful addition to any bedroom, this comforter cover can be made from scraps of fabric, or a few lengths of fabrics of your choosing. The large patches mean it comes together quickly and gives the look of a quilt without the quilting process.

## Essential Information

**DIFFICULTY** Easy

**SIZE** 78 x 80in (200 x 203cm)

**TOOLS AND MATERIALS**
Rotary cutter
Cutting mat
Quilter's ruler
Sewing machine
Thread to match your fabrics
Pins
Iron and ironing board
Seam guide or ruler
165in (420cm) of wide trim (such as ribbon)
   for the two sides (optional)
Five 1in (2.5cm) snaps
Needle

**FABRICS**
100 scraps of patterned cotton, each 9in
   (23cm) square
44 x 160in (112 x 406cm) of white cotton
   backing fabric
10 scraps of patterned cotton fabric, each
   2 x 9in (5 x 23cm), for the back inset strip detail

**SKILLS**
Intersecting seams (see p.74)
Inserting trim in a seam (optional, see p.221)

**SEAM ALLOWANCE**
$\frac{1}{2}$in (1.2cm) throughout, unless otherwise stated

## Make the front

Lay out the 100 blocks on a large flat surface, arranging them in a 10 x 10 pattern, until you are happy with the overall effect.

Pin and sew the top row of blocks together into a strip, sewing with right sides together. Repeat to form all 10 rows. Press the seams in opposite directions on each row—odd rows to the left and even rows to the right. This will help with the alignment of the blocks.

Pin and sew the 10 rows together, in order, matching the intersecting seams as you work (see p.74), to make the comforter cover front. Press these horizontal seams open.

## Make the back

To make the inset strip on the comforter cover back, sew the 10 small strips together to create a 2 x 80in (5 x 203cm) strip.

Cut the white backing fabric into one 44 x 80in (112 x 203cm) piece and one 36 x 80in (91.5 x 203cm) piece. Lay the long colorful strip right sides together with one of the pieces of white backing fabric, matching one of the 80in (203cm) raw edges from each piece to the other, and pin. Sew to attach the strip, then open up and press the seam allowance toward the strip.

Lay this piece right sides together with the second piece of white backing fabric matching the opposite raw edge of the colorful strip to one of the 80in (203cm) edges of the white backing fabric piece. Pin, sew, and press the seam allowance toward the colorful strip. This creates the comforter cover back.

## Sew together

Using a seam guide, turn the bottom edge on both the front and back pieces up by $\frac{1}{2}$in (1.2cm) to the wrong side of the fabric, then by $1\frac{1}{2}$in (3.5cm) to create a neat hem. Pin in place. Sew along the inner folded edge to secure each hem in place.

Lay the front and back pieces right sides together and pin around all four edges. If you'd like to add a piece of trim to the side edges of the comforter cover for decoration, insert it as you pin (see p.221). If needed, hem any of the raw edges on the trim first, to neaten them and prevent them from unraveling.

Starting in one of the bottom corners, sew around the sides and top of the comforter leaving the bottom, hemmed edges unsewn.

Turn the comforter cover right side out. Pin the bottom edges together and using a 1in (2.5cm) seam allowance topstitch across the first and second squares and the ninth and tenth squares of the bottom row, backstitching at both ends of the stitches, to create the bottom corners of the comforter cover.

Evenly space the five snaps along the inside of the bottom opening and sew in place (see p.220).

# Pentagon bean bag

Sometimes kids need a space of their own. With this quick and easy bean bag chair they can sit and read a book in comfort. Made from fabrics with large, printed patterns, it can be made to suit any room in the house.

## Essential Information

**DIFFICULTY** Easy

**SIZE** Approximately 27in (68.5cm) diameter

**MATERIALS**
Rotary cutter
Cutting mat
Quilter's ruler
Iron and ironing board
One 12in (30cm) minimum long zipper
Approximately 4 cubic feet (0.12 cubic meter) of
    polystyrene beads for filling, available online
Bean bag liner, available online (recommended)
Sewing machine with zipper foot
Thread to match the fabrics

**FABRICS**
12 fat quarters of coordinating cotton fabrics
Approximately 118in (300cm) of heavy
    interfacing, or enough to cover your fat quarters

**SKILLS**
Set-in seams (see pp.100-101)

**SEAM ALLOWANCE**
1/4in (6mm) throughout

## Make the template

Make a template for the pentagon pieces by enlarging the pentagon template on page 298 so that each side of the pentagon is 11in (28cm) long. If you'd like a larger bean bag, make the template larger, but don't forget to adjust your fabric requirements.

## Cut and line the patches

Iron interfacing onto the back of each of the 12 pieces of fabric. Using the template, cut out 12 pentagons, one from each of the lined fabric pieces. On the back of each pentagon, mark a dot 1/4in (6mm) set in from each corner for your set-in seams (see p.101).

## Add the zipper

Lay the zipper along one edge of one of the pentagons, right sides together. Put a zipper foot on your machine and sew along the edge. Open up the zipper and topstitch along the zipper seam for added strength. Take a second pentagon and pin it right sides together with the opposite side of the zipper, making sure the two pentagons are even on each side of the zipper. Topstitch along the seam.

## Make the bean bag

Using the regular sewing machine foot, sew four more pentagons around the free edges of one of the two joined pentagons, sewing between the dots on each piece, to create a flower shape (see diagram, right).

Sew the petals of the flower together, sewing between the dots, to join the flower into a bowl shape. Sew the remaining six pentagons in the same way, without the zipper, to create a second bowl.

Open the zipper. With right sides together, invert one bowl to sit in the other bowl. Pin the raw edges of one pentagon to the raw edges of a pentagon on the other bowl so that the point of one pentagon fits into the valley between two pentagons on the opposite bowl. Sew between the two dots on the pinned edges. Pin and sew the next pair of free edges, working your way around the entire perimeter.

Turn the bean bag right-side out through the open zipper. Insert the bean bag liner, if you're using one. Fill with polystyrene beads.

### Pentagon bean bag layout

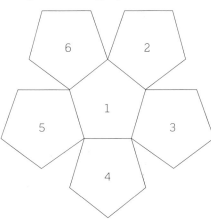

**Choosing a group of fabrics** with a theme makes the bean bag fun for children. Pick fabrics to match their room, or their unique personality and interests.

# Essential Information

**DIFFICULTY** Medium

**SIZE** 5½ x 5½ x 4in (14 x 14 x 10cm)

**TOOLS AND MATERIALS**

Pencil

Tracing paper

Scissors

Rotary cutter

Cutting mat

Quilter's ruler

Thread to match the fabrics

Long, thin, blunt object, such as a
chopstick, for turning

Embroidery needle

Dark embroidery thread

One ½in (1.2cm) button, for the nose

Dried beans or lentils, for weight

Toy filling

**FABRICS**

**A:** 8 x 8in (20.5 x 20.5cm) light-colored
belly and inner ear fabric

**B:** 8 x 23in (20.3 x 58.5cm) body fabric

**C:** 3½ x 6in (9 x 15cm) outer ear fabric

**D:** 1 x 5½in (2.5 x 14cm) tail fabric

**E:** 6½in (6½in) square bottom fabric

**SKILLS**

Curves (see pp.118–119)

Set-in seams (see pp.100–101)

**SEAM ALLOWANCE**

¼in (6mm) throughout

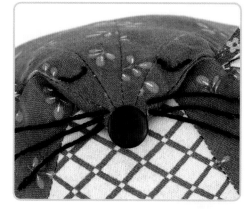

**Embroider a face on** your mouse and give it
whiskers using the same thread. You should
sew down the nose and add the button first.

# Door mouse

This little mouse will keep your door from blowing shut, and, because it's soft, there's no need to worry about stubbed toes. If you use younger-looking fabrics, it's just perfect for a nursery. Be sure to keep the button nose away from babies though.

## Cut the pieces

Trace and cut out the templates from page 299. Using the templates, cut one belly piece and two ear pieces from fabric A, three body 1 pieces and three body 2 pieces from fabric B, and two ear pieces from fabric C. The body 1 and body 2 pieces are the same, just use the template in reverse.

## Make the mouse

### Make the ears

Place one inner ear right sides together with one outer ear. Following the sewing guidelines marked on the template, sew around the ears, leaving the bottom edge unsewn. Trim the seam allowance to $1/8$in (3mm), snip into the curves, turn the ear right-side out, and press. Repeat to form the second ear.

Lay the ears faceup on a flat surface, inner fabric faceup, and turn them so they are mirror images of one another, as they will appear on the mouse's head. Fold down the top edge of each ear by approximately $1/4$in (6mm) to create the folded top to the ear. Pin the fold and press.

### Make the tail

Take the long strip of tail fabric and fold it in half lengthwise, right sides together. Sew along one short end and along the long raw edges, leaving the second short end unsewn. Trim the seam allowance to $1/8$in (3mm). Snip the corners off the sewn, short end, being careful not to cut through the seam, to reduce the bulk. Using a long, thin object, carefully turn the tail right-side out.

### Make the body

Take one body 1 piece and one body 2 piece and lay them right sides together. Insert one ear between the two pieces, where it is marked on the template, with the unsewn edge sticking out by $1/8$in (3mm) and the folded edge toward the top of the head. Pin along that edge, then sew. Forward and reverse stitch over the ends of the ear to secure it. Remove the pins, open the pieces flat, and press the seam allowance open.

Repeat for the second ear, but this time placing the ear the other way down, to create the opposite side of the body. Repeat the process with the last two body pieces, this time sandwiching the tail where indicated on the template.

Take the belly piece and place it right sides together with one of the body pieces with an ear sewn in the seam. Pin along the long edge so that when the two pieces are opened up, the inner part of the ear will face forward, toward the belly. Sew along the edge, stopping $1/4$in (6mm) from the bottom edge. Take the second body piece with an ear and pin it to the opposite side of the belly piece. Sew along the edge, stopping $1/4$in (6mm) from the

bottom edge. Take the body piece with the tail and pin it right sides together with one of the body ear pieces and sew along the edge, stopping $1/4$in (6mm) from the bottom edge. Take the two remaining free edges and sew them right sides together in the same way. This creates a pyramid shape. Trim the seams along the point of the pyramid to $1/8$in (3mm) to reduce the bulk.

Mark dots set in $1/4$in (6mm) from each corner on the wrong side of the bottom piece of fabric, fabric E (see p.100). Pin the bottom square into the bottom of the pyramid, right sides together. Sew around all four edges, leaving a gap of approximately 2in (5cm) in the back, under the tail. Turn the sewn mouse right-side out through the gap.

### Sew the face

Turn the tip of the pyramid down toward the belly approximately 1in (2.5cm) so that the top of the fold aligns with the top of the ears. Sew the point to the belly. Place the button on top of the point and sew it in place.

Using embroidery thread and a needle, sew two eyes onto the face, using the detail photo, upper left, as your guide. Cut three 4in (10cm) pieces of embroidery thread and thread them through the nose to create whiskers. Tie a knot in each end of the thread to keep them from being pulled out.

### Stuff the mouse and finish

Lightly stuff the top of the mouse with toy filling, then fill the bottom with dried beans or lentils to give it weight. Slip stitch the opening closed (see p.43).

## Essential Information

**DIFFICULTY** Easy

**SIZE** 35½ x 35½in (90 x 90cm)

**TOOLS AND MATERIALS**
Measuring tape
Rotary cutter
Scissors
Quilter's ruler
Cutting mat
Iron and ironing board
Pins
Sewing machine
Threads to match your fabrics
Safety pins or contrast thread for basting
Off-white machine quilting thread
Sewing needle

**FABRICS**
**A:** 47½ x 44in (120 x 112cm)
   patterned cotton backing fabric
**B:** 16in (40cm) of 44in (112cm) wide
   coordinating cotton binding fabric
**C, D, E:** Three 16 x 10in (40 x 25cm)
   rectangles of coordinating patterned
   cotton fabric
**F:** 28 x 44in (70 x 112cm)
   off-white plain cotton fabric
38 x 38in (95 x 95cm) batting of
   your choice

**SKILLS**
Piecing blocks (see pp.60–63)

**SEAM ALLOWANCE**
³⁄₈in (1cm) throughout

# Irish chain quilt

Traditional Irish chain patterns use a combination of patchwork and plain blocks to create a chain effect across a quilt. This simple version makes an adorable baby quilt that will be cherished for years. Choose fabrics to suit the special recipient.

## Cut the fabric

Measure and cut out the following pieces of fabric:

One 38in (95cm) square from fabric A for the backing.

Four 38 x 2³/₄in (95 x 7cm) strips for the binding from fabric B.

Five 4³/₄in (12cm) squares from each of fabrics A, B, C, D, and E.

Twenty 4³/₄in (12cm) squares from fabric F.

Four 12³/₄in (32cm) squares from fabric F.

## Make the blocks

Using one of each of the 4³/₄in (12cm) fabric A, B, C, D, and E squares, and four of the 4³/₄in (12cm) fabric F squares, arrange and then sew the squares into a nine-patch block, as follows: for row 1, piece together a fabric A square, followed by a fabric F square, followed by a fabric B square; for row 2, piece together a fabric F square, followed by a fabric C square, followed by a fabric F square; and for row 3, piece together a fabric D square, followed by a fabric F square, followed by a fabric E square. Repeat to make another four nine-patch blocks, arranging the printed fabric squares (A, B, C, D, and E) so each is in a different location on the five finished blocks. Press all the seams toward the patterned squares.

## Join the blocks

With wrong sides faceup, lay out the nine-patch blocks and the four 12³/₄in (32cm) fabric F squares in three rows, as follows: for the first and third rows, one nine-patch block, followed by one 12³/₄in (32cm) fabric F square, followed by one nine-patch block; for the middle row, one 12³/₄in (32cm) fabric F square, followed by one nine-patch block, followed by one 12³/₄in (32cm) fabric F square. With wrong sides together and matching the seams, join the first and second rows, then join the third row to the second row. Press the seams toward the 12³/₄in (32cm) fabric F squares. The quilt top is now complete.

## Assemble the layers

Lay the fabric A backing on a flat surface, right-side down. Lay the batting on top and carefully smooth out the batting and backing fabric. Lay the quilt top right-side up on the batting (see p.46). Both the batting and the backing fabric will overhang the quilt top by an inch or so (several centimeters). Starting from the center and working outward, pin or baste the layers together (see p.46), making sure all the layers sit flat and are even with one another. Machine or hand quilt with the design of your choice, then trim all four edges even.

## Attach the binding

Join the four fabric B binding strips into one long strip (see pp.48–49). With wrong sides together, press the binding strip in half lengthwise. Attach the binding strip to the edges of the quilt, following the instructions for Double-fold binding (see p.53) and mitering the corners as you work. Or, attach using the method of your choice.

# Essential Information

**DIFFICULTY** Easy

**SIZE** 41 x 36in (104 x 92cm)

**TOOLS AND MATERIALS**

Measuring tape
Water-soluble pen
Rotary cutter
Scissors
Quilter's ruler
Cutting mat
Iron and ironing board
Pins
Sewing machine
Threads to match your fabrics
Contrasting thread for basting, or
    safety pins
Machine quilting thread (optional)
Sewing needle

**FABRICS**

**A:** 40 x 44in (100 x 112cm) of printed
    fabric
**B:** 32 x 44in (80 x 112cm) of solid-colored
    fabric in a coordinating color
**C:** 6 x 44in (15 x 112cm) of contrasting
    printed fabric for inner border
16 x 44in (40 x 112cm) binding fabric
43 x 39in (110 x 100cm) backing fabric
43 x 39in (110  x 100cm) batting

**SKILLS**

Sewing triangle corners (see p.86)

**SEAM ALLOWANCE**

¼in (6mm) throughout

# Sweet as honey quilt

This pattern uses some bright, fun fabrics. The block is a traditional elongated hexagon, but the use of modern prints adds extra pizzazz. The way the quilt is constructed means there is no waste, since the cutoffs are used to form the border.

## Cut the fabrics

Cut 30 squares from fabric A, each measuring 6 x 6in (15 x 15cm). Cut 60 squares from fabric B for the corners, each measuring 3 x 3in (7.5 x 7.5cm).

For the inner border, cut two strips, each measuring 1 x 35in (2.5 x 89cm), and another two strips, each measuring 1 x 30½in (2.5 x 77cm), from fabric C.

## Piece the blocks

To make a main block, lightly draw a diagonal line across the wrong side of all the fabric B squares. Place two of these squares on a fabric A square, right sides together and on diagonally opposite corners (see below). Sew along the drawn lines, then sew another line ½in (1.3cm) from the first seam line. Carefully cut between the two seam lines to separate the half-square triangles. Repeat on the opposite corner (see p.86). Continue in this manner until you have

30 main blocks, each measuring 6 x 6in (15 x 15cm). The 60 cutoff half-square triangles (see below), each measuring 2¼ x 2¼in (5.7 x 5.7cm), will be used for the outer border.

## Sew the quilt top

With right sides together, sew five blocks to make a row. Make sure all the blocks are the same way up. Continue until you have six rows, each of five blocks, then, with right sides together, sew the rows together.

With right sides together, sew the inner border all around the quilt, placing the shorter strips along the top and bottom, and the longer strips along the sides.

With right sides together, sew the half-square triangles to form two strips, each the length of the long sides. Attach the strips to the quilt, then sew the remaining half-square triangles to make two strips that fit along the top and bottom. Attach these.

## Assemble the layers

Lay the backing fabric on a flat surface, right-side down. Lay the batting on top and carefully smooth out the batting and backing fabric (see p.46). Lay the quilt top right-side up on the batting. Both the batting and the backing fabric will overhang by about an inch (several centimeters). Starting from the center and working outward, pin or tack the layers together (see p.46), making sure all the layers sit flat and are even with one another.

Machine or hand quilt with the design of your choice. After quilting, cut away the excess backing and batting so that the edges of all the layers of the quilt are aligned.

## Attach the binding

Attach the binding to the edges, following the instructions for Double-fold binding (see p.53), or attach the binding using the method of your choice.

### Main block

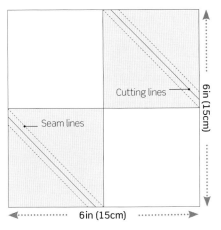

Cutting lines

Seam lines

6in (15cm)

6in (15cm)

### Half-square triangles

2¼in (5.7cm)

2¼in (5.7cm)

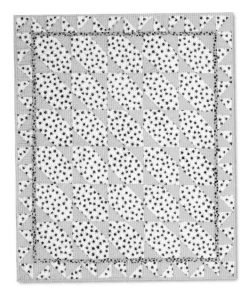

## Essential Information

**DIFFICULTY** Medium

**SIZE** 85 x 93in (216 x 236cm)

**TOOLS AND MATERIALS**
Measuring tape
Quilter's ruler
Rotary cutter
Cutting mat
Scissors
Sewing machine
Threads to match your fabrics
Iron and ironing board
Safety pins
Quilting thread

**FABRICS**
A large selection of scrap fabrics, fat
    quarters, and fat eights
16 x 44in (40 x 112cm) inner border fabric
28 x 44in (70 x 112cm) middle
    border fabric
33 x 44in (84 x 112cm) outer
    border farbic
217 x 44in (550 x 112cm) backing fabric
91 x 100in (230 x 255cm) batting
30 x 44in (75 x 112cm) binding fabric

**SKILLS**
Courthouse steps (see p.142)

**SEAM ALLOWANCE**
1/4in (6mm) throughout

# Courthouse steps quilt

This quilt uses the traditional Courthouse steps block on page 142 made in a variety of fabric scraps. This project is perfect if you have a large amount of coordinating scraps you'd like to use up. The more variety you have, the better the overall effect.

## Cut the fabrics

For each block:

Cut one 3$^{1}/_{2}$ x 3$^{1}/_{2}$in (9 x 9cm) square (piece A).

Cut two 2 x 3$^{1}/_{2}$in (5 x 9cm) strips (pieces B).

Cut two 2 x 6$^{1}/_{2}$in (5 x 16.5cm) strips (pieces C).

Cut two 2 x 6$^{1}/_{2}$in (5 x 16.5cm) strips (pieces D).

Cut two 2 x 9$^{1}/_{2}$in (5 x 24cm) strips (pieces E).

Cut enough pieces to make a total of 72 blocks.

## Make the blocks

To create each block, follow the instructions on page 142 for Courthouse steps, attaching pieces B to piece A, then pieces C, pieces D and finally pieces E. After sewing each pair of strips, press the seam allowances toward the new strips.

## Make the quilt top

Arrange all of your blocks into a nine by eight block arrangement of your choice. Rotate every other block 90 degrees so that every other block sits the opposite direction to the ones around it; see the image, right, for reference.

Once you are happy with the layout of the blocks, sew each row together. Press the seams for each row in opposite directions from one another. Then sew all of the rows together to form the top.

### Add the borders

This quilt has three borders. For the inner border, cut eight strips of fabric A 1$^{3}/_{4}$ x 44in (4.5 x 112cm). Join the strips together so you have two 76$^{1}/_{2}$in (195cm) long strips and two 71$^{1}/_{2}$in (182cm) long strips. Join the first two longer strips along the left and right sides, then add the other two to the top and bottom sides. (See p. 111)

Repeat the process for the next border, cutting eight strips of fabric B 3$^{1}/_{4}$ x 44in (8.25 x 112cm). Join the strips together so you have two 79$^{1}/_{2}$in (202cm) long strips and two 77in (196cm) long strips. Join the first two long strips to the left and right sides, then add the other two to the top and bottom.

Repeat for the third border cutting eight strips of fabric C 4 x 44in (10.5 x 112cm).

Join the strips together so you have four 85$^{1}/_{2}$in (218cm) long strips. Join the first two strips along the left and right sides, then add the other two to the top and bottom sides.

## Finish the quilt

Create a quilt sandwich (see p.46), then quilt using the pattern of your choice (see pp.204–205, 210–213). Bind the quilt using the Double-fold binding method (see p.53), or the method of your choice.

**Keep the stitches the same size** as you work, so that every shape is uniform in appearance. Bury the knots in the fabric, always at the back of the quilt.

# Kantha stitch throw

Made from snuggly flannel, this throw is perfect for chilly evenings. You can design and sew any pattern you wish. Here we've quilted a geometric pattern with borders around it. Be sure to mark the whole design before you begin sewing.

## Essential Information

**DIFFICULTY** Easy

**SIZE** 46½ x 64in (118 x 163cm)

**TOOLS AND MATERIALS**
Scissors
Curved safety pins
Cardboard
Pencil
Spray bottle or sponge
Rotary cutter
Cutting mat
Quilter's ruler
Water-soluble pen
Roll of 1in (2.5cm) masking tape
Darning needle
Five different-colored embroidery,
    or quilting, threads
Sewing machine (optional)
Thread to match the main fabric
Sewing needle

**FABRIC**
78 x 108in (200 x 275cm) of flannel for
    the main fabric front, back, and binding
48 x 65in (123 x 165cm) batting

**SKILLS**
Hand quilting (see pp.204-205)

**SEAM ALLOWANCE**
Hand quilt following the pattern

## Make the quilt sandwich

Cut two pieces of main fabric both 47 x 65in (120 x 165cm). Lay one piece right-side down, then lay the batting to fit on top of it. Lay the other main fabric piece right-side up on top so all the edges are even. Smooth all the layers from the center outward and once smooth, use curved safety pins to pin the layers together (see p.46).

## Mark the design

Measure and mark the center of the quilt sandwich. Using the templates on page 298 and a water-soluble pen, mark the pattern on the front of the quilt sandwich. Use the masking tape to mark the borders and your quilter's ruler to make sure everything is sitting even and square with one another. If you are unhappy with the design at any point, use water to remove the pen and begin again.

## Quilt the pattern

Working from the center outward and readjusting the safety pins as needed, begin to quilt the pattern using stab stitch (see p.43) and the colors indicated on the diagram. Bury the knots in the fabric at the back to hide them (see p.204). Cut a piece of embroidery thread long enough to sew each shape.

## Pattern layout

Remove any safety pins that fall within the quilted sections as you work, but leave the pins around the edges. Remove the masking tape when you are done.

## Attach the binding

Trim the edges of the quilt square with each other and the stitches. Cut and piece together a binding strip 2½ x 230in (6.5 x 585cm), (see pp.48–49). Attach the strip using the Double-fold binding method (see p.53).

# Pear quilt

This eye-catching, double-bed-sized quilt is based on a simple log cabin block using five different fabrics. Here, a pretty multicolored pear-printed cotton is the dominant fabric and the other fabrics have been chosen to complement it.

## Essential Information

**DIFFICULTY** Easy

**SIZE** 85 x 85in (216 x 216cm)

**TOOLS AND MATERIALS**
Measuring tape
Quilter's ruler
Rotary cutter
Cutting mat
Scissors
Sewing machine
Threads to match your fabrics
Iron and ironing board
Curved safety pins

**FABRICS**
**A:** 39 x 39in (1 x 1m) cotton fabric
**B:** 39 x 39in (1 x 1m) cotton fabric
**C:** 79 x 79in (2 x 2m) cotton fabric
**D:** 79 x 79in (2 x 2m) cotton fabric
**E:** 98 x 98in (2.5 x 2.5m) cotton fabric
177 x 177in (4.5 x 4.5m) backing fabric
32in (80cm) of fabric of 44in (112cm) width
   for binding
88 x 88in (2.25 x 2.25m) batting

**SKILLS**
Log cabin (see p.142–143)

**SEAM ALLOWANCE**
$\frac{1}{2}$in (1.2cm) throughout

## Guide to cutting fabric pieces

| Fabrics | Cut size | Finished size |
|---------|----------|---------------|
| A | $4\frac{1}{2}$ x $4\frac{1}{2}$in (11 x 11cm) | $3\frac{1}{2}$ x $3\frac{1}{2}$in (9 x 9cm) |
| B | $4\frac{1}{2}$ x $4\frac{1}{2}$in (11 x 11cm) | $3\frac{1}{2}$ x $3\frac{1}{2}$in (9 x 9cm) |
| C | 8 x $4\frac{1}{2}$in (20 x 11cm) | 7 x $3\frac{1}{2}$in (18 x 9cm) |
| D | 8 x $4\frac{1}{2}$in (20 x 11cm) | 7 x $3\frac{1}{2}$in (18 x 9cm) |
| E | $11\frac{1}{2}$ x $4\frac{1}{2}$in (29 x 11cm) | $10\frac{1}{2}$ x $3\frac{1}{2}$in (27 x 9cm) |

## Cut the fabric pieces

The size of the quilt depends on the size of the block; however, this log cabin design (see pp.142–143) works best with an even number of blocks, such as six, eight, or 10. This double-bed-sized quilt requires eight rows of eight blocks, so cut 64 pieces from each of fabrics A, B, C, D, and E, following the measurements given in the table above. Before cutting all the fabrics, check that the color and print combination look good. For example, fabric E is used for the biggest pieces, so this will be the dominant fabric in your quilt.

## Piece the blocks

With right sides together and leaving a $\frac{1}{2}$in (1.2cm) seam allowance, sew A and B together along one side to form a rectangle. Using chart A on page 256 as a guide, sew C to the bottom of this rectangle. A, B, and C together will now form a square. Attach D to the left of this square and E along the top. After each step, press the seam allowance to one side. Make the remaining 63 blocks in the same way. Make sure each completed block measures $10\frac{1}{2}$ x $10\frac{1}{2}$in (27 x 27cm) and is a combination of five different fabrics.

## Chart A

## Chart B

## Chart C

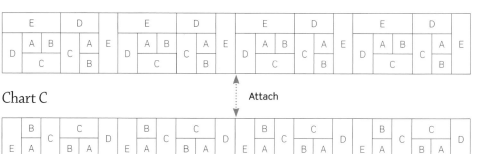

Attach

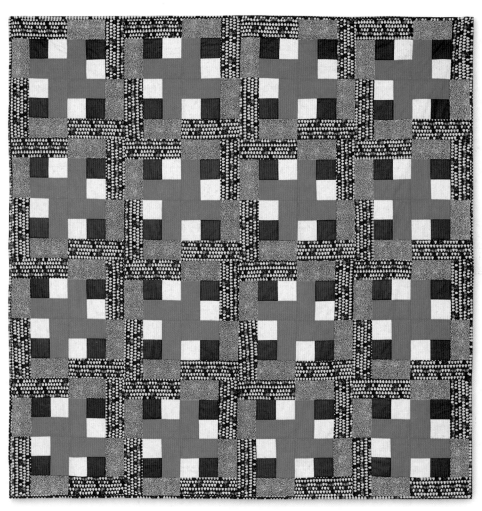

**Bold blocks** This quilt is in a traditional, simplified log cabin design. Choosing bright, modern, graphic fabrics will make the quilt look very eye-catching, while fabrics with less contrast will create a gentler effect.

## Join the rows

To make a row of blocks, with right sides together, sew eight blocks together, as shown in chart B, above. Note that the pattern of the quilt is created by rotating each pair of adjacent blocks 90 degrees.

Follow chart C to sew together the next row. Continue in this way, alternating between chart B and chart C until you have eight separate rows, each made up of eight blocks.

Press the seams in the first row in one direction and the seams in the second row in the opposite direction. Repeat for the rest of the rows so that the seams in each alternate row face in the same direction. If you have a very light fabric joined to a dark fabric, press the seam toward the darker fabric. With right sides together, join the B and C rows, alternating between them and pinning through the seams wherever necessary to ensure that all the seams line up. You have now completed the quilt top.

## Assemble the layers

Lay the backing fabric on a flat surface, right side down. Lay the batting on top and carefully smooth out the batting and backing fabric (see p.46). Lay the quilt top right-side up on the batting. Both the batting and the backing fabric will overhang the quilt top by an inch or so (several centimeters). Starting from the center and working outward, pin the layers together (see p.46) with curved safety pins at intervals of 6in (15cm) or so, or baste the layers together. Try not to lift the quilt top too much as you pin and regularly check that all the layers sit flat and are even with one another.

## Quilt the layers

For this design, we quilted through the layers by stitching in the ditch (see p.211) around each complete block, and then around the center square (square A) of each block. When quilting, it is important to consider what the stitches will look like on the back of the quilt, so use threads that will complement the fabric. We used a green top thread and white thread in the bobbin to give a subtle effect on the back of the quilt, which, in this case, is the lightly patterned white fabric that was also used on the top.

## Attach the binding

Once the quilting is complete, cut away the excess backing fabric and batting, so that all three layers of the quilt line up with each other along the sides. To finish the quilt with binding, make a long, continuous piece of binding to go around all four sides. The binding can be made either from one fabric or by joining together several pieces of fabric of varying lengths. If doing this, lay the fabric strips around the edge of the quilt before sewing, to gauge the finished effect. Attach the binding to the edges of the quilt following the instructions for Double-fold binding (see p.53).

**Subtle binding** Here one of the fabrics from the quilt top has been used to bind the edges, giving a subtly understated effect. If you prefer to make more of a statement, you can choose a complementary fabric that will stand out more.

# Flying geese quilt

The instructions for piecing this quilt are fast and simple, leaving no waste. The flying geese blocks are created in pairs. Here, we've kept the pairs together in our final layout, but you may wish to separate the pairs throughout the quilt top.

## Essential Information

**DIFFICULTY** Medium

**SIZE** 40 x 45in (100 x 115cm)

**TOOLS AND MATERIALS**

Measuring tape
Quilter's ruler
Rotary cutter
Cutting mat
Scissors
Sewing machine
Threads to match your fabrics
Iron and ironing board
Safety pins
Quilting thread

**FABRICS**

**A:** 32 x 44in (80 x 112cm) dark fabric for the geese, or three fat quarters

**B:** 32 x 44in (80 x 112cm) light fabric, or five fat eighths, for the backgrounds

**C:** 8 x 44in (20 x 112cm) fabric for the narrow inner border

**D:** 23½ x 44in (60 x 112cm) fabric for the wide outer border

20 x 44in (50 x 112cm) fabric for ½in (1.2cm) double fold binding

51 x 44in (130 x 112cm) backing fabric

46 x 51in (115 x 130cm) batting

**SKILLS**

Flying geese (see p.85)

**SEAM ALLOWANCE**

¼in (6mm) throughout

## Cut the fabrics

Cut 21 square pieces from fabric A, each measuring 6¼in (16cm). Cut 84 square pieces from fabric B, each measuring 3⅜in (9.5cm). Cut four strips from fabric C, selvage to selvage, each measuring 1½in (4cm). Cut four strips from fabric D, selvage to selvage, each measuring 5in (12cm).

## Make the blocks

Lightly draw a diagonal line across the squares from fabric B (see Chart 1, next page). Place two of these squares on a square from fabric A, right sides together and on diagonally opposite corners. The fabric B squares will overlap slightly in the middle (see Chart 2, next page). Sew a ¼in (6mm) seam on either side of the drawn lines (see Chart 3, next page). Cut along the drawn line and press the pieces open (see Charts 4 and 5, next page). Place another square from fabric B on the corner of the sewn piece (see Chart 6, next page). Sew a ¼in (6mm) seam on either side of the drawn line (see Chart 7, next page). Cut along the drawn line and press open the pieces (see Chart 8, next page). This completes the block (see Chart 9, next page). Repeat with the remaining squares from fabric A and B until you have 84 blocks, each measuring 5¾ x 3in (14.6 x 7.5cm).

### Chart 1

Fabric B

### Chart 2

Fabric B

Fabric A

Fabric B

### Chart 3

Cutting line

Seam line

### Chart 4

### Chart 5

### Chart 6

Fabric B

### Chart 7

### Chart 8

### Chart 9

3 in (7.5cm)

5¾ in (14.6cm)

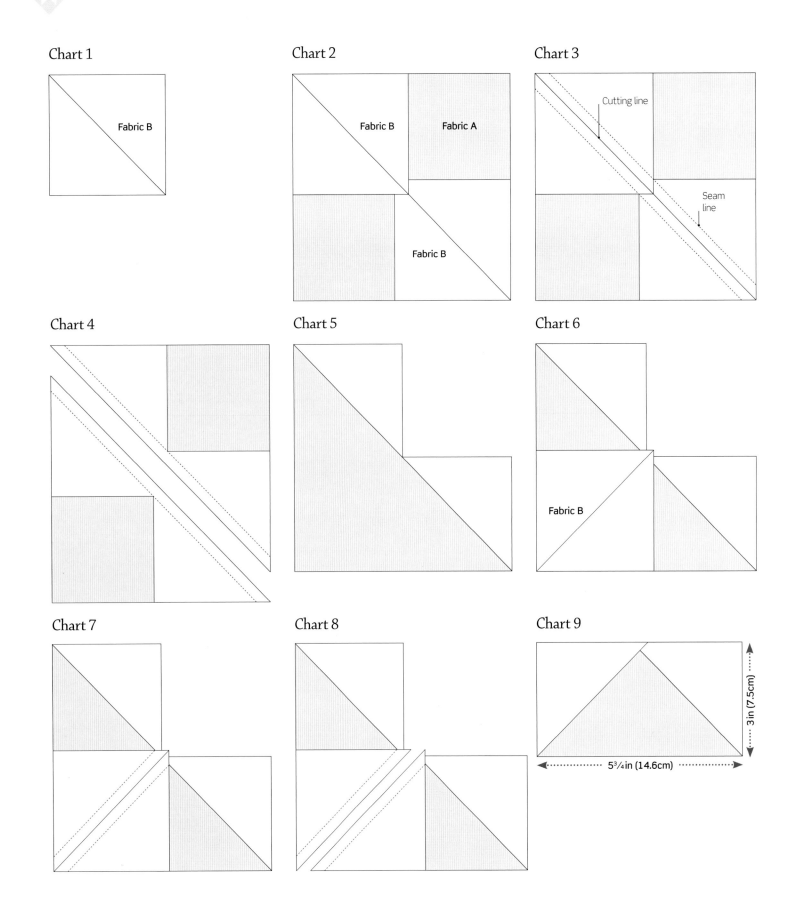

## Sew the quilt top

Lay the blocks out in 14 rows, in the pattern of your choice, with six blocks in each row. Sew the blocks in each row together. Sew the rows together, matching the corners of the Flying Geese blocks (see pp.74–75).

Sew the narrow border to both the left and right sides of the quilt top, squaring off the excess border strips. Then attach the border to the top and bottom of the quilt. Sew the larger outer border in the same left, right, top, and bottom sequence.

## Assemble the layers

Lay the backing fabric on a flat surface, right-side down. Carefully lay the batting on top. Smooth out the two to make sure there are no folds. Then lay the quilt top on the batting. The batting and the backing fabric will overhang the quilt top by an inch or so (several centimeters) each. Starting from the center and working outward, pin the layers together using safety pins, making sure all the layers sit flat and even with one another. Check the back of the quilt as well.

Machine or hand quilt with the design of your choice.

## Attach the binding

Lay the quilt, right-side up, on a flat surface. Follow the instructions for Double-fold binding, as shown on page 53, or bind the quilt using the method of your choice.

**Using a variegated quilting thread** makes more of a feature of the quilting stitches. You can use a quilting thread that either blends in, or stands out, depending on your personal preference.

*Use the same fabrics A and B for all the pieces in one chart sequence, opposite.*

# Tilted log cabin quilt

This quilt uses a traditional log cabin block set on a tilt. It features contrasting black, white, and red fabrics. The block centers were fussy cut to feature a flower. If you'd like to do the same, make sure you buy enough fabric so you have enough motifs.

## Essential Information

**DIFFICULTY** Medium

**SIZE** 43½ x 51in (110 x 130cm)

**TOOLS AND MATERIALS**
Rotary cutter
Cutting mat
Quilter's ruler
Scissors
Pins
Thread to match the fabrics
Sewing machine
Tracing paper
Pencil
Curved safety pins
Quilting thread

**FABRICS**
7 fat quarters in various white prints
7 fat quarters in various black prints
**A:** 20 x 44in (50 x 112cm) red fabric for the
   block centers and inner border, more if fussy
   cutting
**B:** 20 x 44in (50 x 112cm) bold black print for
   the outer border
**C:** 79 x 44in (200 x 112cm) backing fabric
**D:** 20 x 44in (50 x 112cm) fabric for ½in
   (1.2cm) double-fold binding
47 x 57in (120 x 145cm) batting

**SKILLS**
Log cabin (see p.142)
Tilted blocks (see p.109)

**SEAM ALLOWANCE**
¼in (6mm) throughout

## Cut the pieces

Cut twenty 2in (5cm) center squares from fabric A, fussy cutting if desired (see p.40).

From each of the fat quarters, cut strips in varying widths between 1–2½in (2.5–6.5cm). The width of the strips used in the blocks vary to add to the random look of the quilt.

Cut four strips, each 1in (2.5cm) wide, from fabric A.

Cut five strips, each 4½in (12cm) wide, from fabric B.

## Make the blocks

As each block will be trimmed at an angle for the tilt, the initial construction of each block does not need to be the same finished size.

Following the instructions for creating a log cabin block on page 142, begin piecing starting with a fabric A central square and a black print fabric strip. Sew the two together and press the seam allowance toward the darker piece. Trim the strip to fit.

Working clockwise, continue piecing, pressing and trimming, using two black printed strips then two white printed strips until the block measures approximately 11in (28cm) square. Create another 19 blocks in the same way.

Make a template 8¾in (22.2cm) square out of a clear material, such as tracing paper. Place the template on top of a finished block and rotate it until you are satisfied with the angle. Mark the angle on the template, using the central fabric A square as your reference point. Cut each block to the same size keeping the template at the same orientation (see p.109).

## Make the quilt top

Lay out the blocks in five rows of four blocks. Sew the blocks together in each row, then sew the rows together. Add the narrow, fabric A borders to the sides, then to the top and bottom of the quilt. Add the outer, fabric B borders to the sides of the quilt, then to the top and bottom. If your border pieces are not long enough, piece two strips by sewing the short sides together (see p.111).

## Finish the quilt

Create the quilt sandwich, making sure all of the layers sit flat with one another (see p.46) Hand- or machine-quilt as desired (see pp.204–205, 210–213), trim the edges square. Cut and piece fabric D into one long strip (see pp.48–49), then attach to the quilt using the Double-fold binding method (see p.53).

# Zigzag circus quilt

This quilt uses the foundation piecing technique of reverse piecing. To create the zigzag pattern, blocks are pieced as mirror images of one another, then sewn into a row. Remember to shorten your stitch length when using a paper foundation.

## Essential Information

**DIFFICULTY** Difficult

**SIZE** 50 x 57in (127 x 145cm)

**TOOLS AND MATERIALS**
Copies of the block templates
Quilter's ruler
Rotary cutter
Cutting mat
Scissors
Sewing machine
Pins
Threads to match your fabrics
Iron and ironing board
Curved safety pins
Quilting thread
Needle

**FABRICS**
**A:** 32 x 44in (80 x 112cm) fabric
**B:** 23 x 44in (60 x 112cm) fabric
**C AND H:** Two 17 x 44in (45 x 112cm) fabrics
**D AND I:** Two 6 x 44in (15 x 112cm) fabrics
**E, F, AND J:** Two 14 x 44in (35 x 112cm) fabrics
**G:** 51 x 44in (130 x 112cm) fabric
$166\frac{1}{2}$ x 44in (423 x 112cm) backing fabric
18 x 44in (46 x 112cm) cotton binding fabric
56 x 76in (143 x 193cm) batting

**SKILLS**
Foundation piecing: Reverse pieced (see p.149)

**SEAM ALLOWANCE**
$\frac{1}{4}$in (6mm) throughout

## Make the templates

Copy the correct number of templates from pages 300–301.

## Understanding the quilt

The quilt is pieced using the Foundation piecing: Reverse pieced method (see p.149). It uses three separate blocks and their mirror images, for a total of six different blocks, see Figure 1, page 267.

The quilt is made up of eight strips consisting of 10 blocks each; five of the same blocks facing one way and five of the mirror image blocks facing the other way. See Figure 2, page 267.

Each strip uses just one of the blocks throughout, but the strips are repeated in a sequence, so each block is used more than once within the quilt, see Figure 3, page 267.

You will use one paper pattern for each block you produce. The block is sewn directly onto the paper (see p.149), following the pattern lines, then the paper is removed afterward. This allows the block to be pieced accurately and allows you to match the points neatly. The pieces used are cut larger than the final size required and then trimmed down.

If you would like to piece the quilt without using the foundation piecing method, you can use the templates provided and sew the pieces together without the paper. Ensure your pieces are cut accurately to allow you to match the points of the zigzags.

The individual pieces in the blocks are cut using templates. When cutting, cut each piece of fabric larger than the template shape.

## Cut the pieces

Cut out each of the templates. Starting with block 1, take template piece A. Cut a strip of fabric $6\frac{1}{4}$in (16cm) wide across the width of the fabric. Fold the strip in half, wrong sides together, so that the short edges meet, lining up the raw edges.

Place the template piece right-side up on top. Cut diagonally across the strip approximately $\frac{1}{4}$in (6mm) from the template (see Figure 4, p.267). You will be left with two pieces approximately $\frac{1}{4}$in (6mm) larger than the template piece. One will be a mirror image of the other, to use for blocks 1A and 1B.

Turn, don't flip, the template and cut again to get the next two pieces (see Figure 5, p.267). Continue a further three cuts until you have 10 pieces, five each of 1A and 1B, for the first row of the quilt. Do the same for the other two template pieces in block 1.

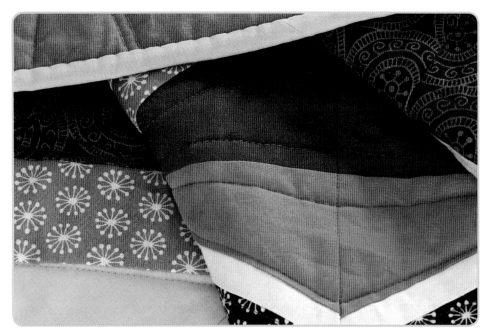

**Quilt the finished quilt** echoing the zigzag pattern of the blocks, or in the pattern of your choice.

Cut the pieces for blocks 2A and 2B and 3A and 3B in the same way. To work out the size of your starting strip each time, measure the width of the template and add at least $^1/_2$in (1.2cm). Block 2 has three pieces, but block 3 uses five pieces, two of which are the same shape. Refer to Figure 3 to establish which fabrics to use for which pieces.

## Make the blocks

Working with block 1A to start, take your paper block pattern and hold it with the printed side facing you.

Take a fabric A piece and hold it in the correct position: on the back of the paper, with the wrong side of the fabric facing the paper. The fabric will extend beyond the lines of the template pattern piece. Be aware that you have mirror image shapes, too, so check that you have selected the correct version of the shape.

Take a fabric B piece and place it in the same way in position next to the A piece. Flip it over, onto the A piece so the right sides of the fabrics are now together, being careful not to alter its position as you do so.

Shorten your stitch length on your sewing machine to 1.5. Holding, or pinning, both the pieces in position on the paper, hold the paper, printed side up and sew along the line between pieces A and B. You will be sewing through both pieces of fabric and the paper.

Fold the fabric B piece back over and press into position with the iron. It should extend beyond the lines of its position according to the paper template. You should now have both fabric pieces sewn in place, wrong sides to the paper, on the back of the paper template.

Now place the paper right side up and fold, to the right side, exactly on the line between pieces B and C. It may help to use a ruler to help you keep the line straight as you fold.

Holding this fold back over the B section on the right side, trim the B fabric piece to $^1/_4$in (6mm) from this fold. This will give you the correct seam allowance for sewing the next piece and help you to position it correctly.

Unfold the paper and flatten. Take the correct fabric C piece and place it in position. As you fold it back right sides together with the B piece, line it up with the cut edge.

Sew in the same way as before and press the block. Trim the excess fabric in line with the edges of the paper template to finish the block. Repeat this process for all of the blocks in the quilt.

## Finish the quilt top

Once you have sewn all the blocks, carefully remove the paper by folding the paper along the sewn lines and applying pressure with your fingers. You should be able to tear the paper away easily as the shorter stitch length you used perforated the paper.

Starting with the first row of blocks, sew the blocks together into a strip, referring to Figures 2 and 3 to ensure the correct placement. Pin the blocks together before sewing, matching the seams, to ensure the points of the zigzags match up as accurately as possible. Press the finished seams in the same direction.

Sew the next strip in the same way, but pressing the finished seams in the opposite direction to the first strip. Repeat to make all eight strips, alternating the direction the seams are pressed in each row.

When the strips are complete, sew them together to form the quilt top. Refer to Figure 3 throughout for correct placement of the pieces.

Once the quilt top is complete, lay the backing right-side down on a large, flat surface. Lay the batting on top of the backing, and the quilt top on top of this. Smooth the layers so they all sit flat and even with one another. Use curved safety pins or basting stitches to hold the layers together, working from the center outward to create the quilt sandwich (see p.46).

When the sandwich is complete, quilt it using the pattern and method of your choice (see pp.204–205, 210–213). We've used a pattern that echoes the zigzags of the patches.

When you are done quilting, cut the binding fabric into strips and join them together to create one long strip (see pp.48–49). Attach the strip to the quilt using the Double-fold binding method (see p.53), or the method of your choice.

## Figure 1

Block 1A    Block 1B    Block 2A    Block 2B    Block 3A    Block 3B

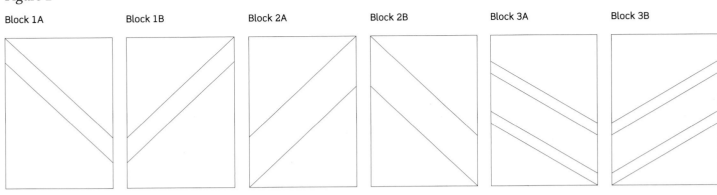

## Figure 2

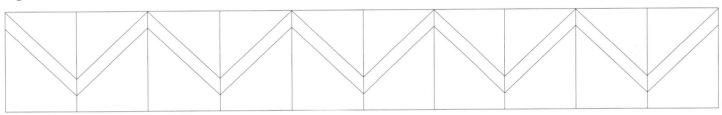

## Figure 3

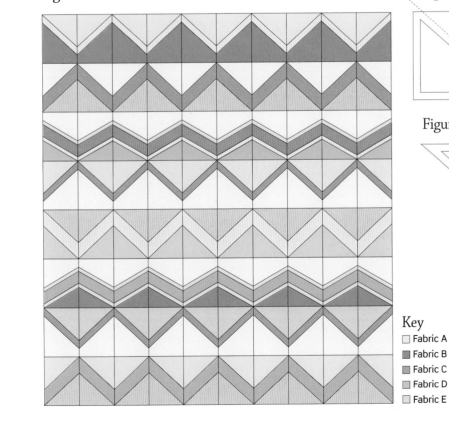

## Figure 4

Cutting line

## Figure 5

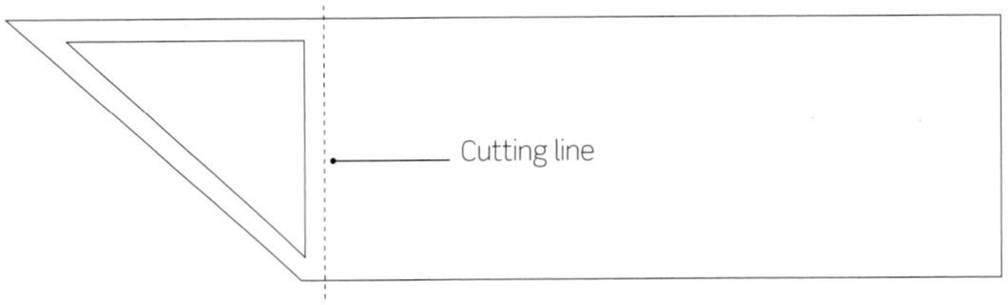

Cutting line

### Key

| | |
|---|---|
| ☐ Fabric A | ☐ Fabric F |
| ■ Fabric B | ☐ Fabric G |
| ■ Fabric C | ☐ Fabric H |
| ■ Fabric D | ■ Fabric I |
| ☐ Fabric E | ■ Fabric J |

# Hearts and flowers quilt

This quilt is a lovely assortment of patchwork blocks and appliqué hearts, flowers, and butterflies. It's perfect for a little girl, but you can create your own appliqué shapes and use a different color palette to create a less feminine quilt.

## Essential Information

**DIFFICULTY** Medium

**SIZE** 56 x 78in (142 x 198cm)

**TOOLS AND MATERIALS**

Quilter's ruler
Measuring tape
Rotary cutter and scissors
Cutting mat
Pins
Sewing machine
Threads to match your fabrics
Iron and ironing board
Curved safety pins
Quilting thread
Needle

**FABRICS**

**A:** 59 x 44in (150 x 112cm) white cotton fabric

**B:** Forty-four 4$^{1}/_2$in (11.5cm) squares from scraps
(44 Charm Pack™ squares can also be used, but
they will need to be trimmed down)

**C:** 29$^{1}/_2$ x 44in (75 x 112cm) sashing and
binding fabric

**D:** Eighteen 10 x 5in (26 x 13cm) prints in
different colors

**E:** Six different 10 x 44in (25 x 112cm) fabrics for
the appliqué backgrounds

Scraps of varying sizes for appliqué shapes
Enough fusible web for all of the appliqué shapes
180 x 44in (457 x 112cm) backing fabric
62 x 84in (157 x 215cm) batting

**SKILLS**

Appliqué (see pp.168–179, 184–187, 194–195)

**SEAM ALLOWANCE**

$^{1}/_4$in (6mm) throughout, unless otherwise stated

## Cut the fabric

With the white fabric (fabric A) folded in half, selvage to selvage, square off one side and cut five 4$^{1}/_2$in (11.5cm) strips. From these strips cut forty-four 4$^{1}/_2$in (11.5cm) squares. With the fabric still folded in half, cut three 8$^{1}/_2$in (21.5cm) strips. Cut the strips into a total of ten 8$^{1}/_2$in (21.5cm) squares.

Cut forty-four 4$^{1}/_2$in (11.5cm) squares from your fabric B scraps. Or if you are using a Charm Pack™, trim each square down to an 4$^{1}/_2$in (11.5cm) square. From the fabric C cut four 2$^{1}/_2$ x 44in (6.3 x 112cm) strips for the sashing. Attach two strips together at the short ends and press the seam open. Repeat for the second two strips. From the remaining fabric cut seven strips of fabric in the width of your choice for the binding (see pp.48–49). Join the strips to form one long strip.

Cut each fabric E piece into two parts; a 15$^{1}/_2$ x 7$^{1}/_4$in (39.4 x 18.4cm) piece and a 23$^{1}/_2$ x 7$^{1}/_4$in (59.7 x 18.4cm) piece. You will have six of the larger pieces and six of the smaller pieces. These pieces will be the background for the large appliqué flowers, butterflies, and hearts. Also cut two 3$^{3}/_4$ x 8$^{1}/_2$in (9.5 x 21.6cm) rectangles.

To create the pinwheel blocks, cut 16 of the fabric D rectangles into 5in (13cm) squares.

## Make the pinwheel blocks

Choose two contrasting prints from the 16 pairs of fabric D squares and place them rights sides together. Pin the pair together around the edges. Draw a diagonal line on the wrong side of one of the squares and carefully sew a line $^{1}/_4$in (6mm) on either side of the line.

With a rotary cutter and ruler, cut on the line creating two separate half-square triangles (see p.82). Using the same fabrics, repeat the process for the second set of half-square triangles for the block.

Lay out the four half-square triangles in a pinwheel pattern (see the image, p.271, for reference). Join the top two units together and press the seam to the right. Join the

**Blanket stitch and satin stitch** were used to add a decorative edge to the appliqué shapes on the quilt top. The quilt was then hand-quilted using outline quilting.

bottom two units together and press the seam to the left. Match the central seams (see p.75) and join the top two units to the bottom two units to form an 8$^{1}/_{2}$in (21.6cm) square pinwheel block. Repeat using the remaining twenty-eight 5in (13cm) fabric D squares to make another seven pinwheel blocks.

## Make the four-patch strips

To create the two long four-patch strips, chain piece the forty-four white 4$^{1}/_{2}$in (11.5cm) squares to the forty-four 4$^{1}/_{2}$in (11.5cm) scrap or Charm Pack™ squares. Snip the pairs apart and press all the seams toward the printed fabric.

Arrange 20 pairs in an alternating white and printed layout so that similar colors are evenly spaced throughout the arrangement. Repeat using another 20 pairs.

With right sides together and matching seams, sew the first 20 pairs into one long four-patch strip. Repeat for the second set of 20 pairs. Press the horizontal seams open.

With the remaining four pairs, create two four-patch blocks for the borders.

## Appliqué the shapes

### Make the appliqué panel strips

Using the templates on pages 302–304, trace out all of the shapes onto the paper side of the fusible web. Roughly cut $^{1}/_{4}$in (6mm) extra around the shape before pressing and fusing to the scrap fabrics of your choice.

Carefully trim along the line with a sharp pair of fabric scissors.

Using the photo, right, as a reference, peal away the paper backing and fuse each piece in place on the 15$^{1}/_{2}$ x 7$^{1}/_{4}$in (39.4 x 18.4cm) or 23$^{1}/_{2}$ x 7$^{1}/_{4}$in (59.7 x 18.4cm) fabric E background pieces. Sew around each piece, either using a sewing machine or by hand, adding a decorative stitch around the raw edges of each shape (see p.173).

Complete each of the 12 appliqué panels before attaching them into three long strips. Sew the short sides together in the following sequence: Strips one and three—long, short, long, short. Strip two—short, long, short, long.

### Make the border flowers

Using the 8$^{1}/_{2}$in (21.5cm) white background squares that were set aside, fuse and appliqué the petals and then the flower center in the same manner as the previous appliqué pieces.

## Make the borders

Following the layout of the quilt, carefully sew together the eight pinwheel blocks, two four-patch blocks, and 10 appliqué flower blocks into two border strips, pressing the seams open. Finish each of the two rows with the final 3$^{3}/_{4}$ x 8$^{1}/_{2}$in (9.5 x 21.6cm) fabric E rectangles.

## Make the quilt top

Starting with the left border, carefully pin in place one of the long fabric C sashing strips to the right edge of the border strip, right sides together, matching and pinning the centers first (the sashing strip will be longer than the border strip).

Sew the two together and press open the seam. Using the quilter's ruler and rotary cutter, square off the top and bottom of the sashing strip to match the edges of the border.

Next, pin and sew the first appliqué panel strip to the free edge of the sashing strip just sewn. Again, press open.

Pin and sew the remaining four-patch, appliqué panels, and sashing strips in the same way following the layout, above. Using the quilter's ruler and rotary cutter, square

off the top and bottom of the sashing strip to match the edges of the appliqué panel strip next to it. Finally, pin and sew the final border in place.

## Finish the quilt

Once the quilt top is complete, lay the backing right-side down on a large, flat surface. Lay the batting on top of the backing, and the quilt top on top of this. Smooth the layers so they all sit flat and even with one another.

Use curved safety pins or tacking stitches to hold the layers together, working from the center outward to create the quilt sandwich (see p.46).

When the sandwich is complete, quilt it using the pattern and method of your choice (see pp.204–205, 210–213). We've hand-quilted the top, outline quilting around some of the shape and patches.

When you are done quilting, attach the fabric C binding strip to the quilt using the Double-fold binding method (see p.53), or the method of your choice.

# Chisholm trail quilt

While this quilt might look complicated, each individual unit within the block is simple to make. If you are careful to cut and sew all of the pieces accurately and match the seams, your quilt will come together perfectly.

## Essential Information

**DIFFICULTY** Medium

**SIZE** 82½ x 82½in (210 x 210cm)

**TOOLS AND MATERIALS**

Quilter's ruler
Rotary cutter
Cutting mat
Scissors
Sewing machine
Pins
Threads to match your fabrics
Iron and ironing board
Curved safety pins
Quilting thread
Needle

**FABRICS**

**A:** 138 x 44in (350 x 112cm) solid cream fabric
for the background and borders

**B:** 59 x 44in (150 x 112cm) red gingham fabric
for the star points

**C:** 39½ x 44in (100 x 112cm) cream floral fabric
for the block corners and the star centers

**D:** 39½ x 44in (50 x 112cm) blue floral fabric for
the star centers

**E:** One fat quarter of beige floral fabric for the
star centers

29½ x 44in (75 x 112cm) fabric for ½in (1.2cm)
double-fold binding

177 x 44in (450 x 112cm) backing fabric

90 x 90in (225 x 225cm) batting

**SKILLS**

Triangles (see pp.82–91)

**SEAM ALLOWANCE**

¼in (6mm) throughout, unless otherwise stated

## Cut the fabrics

From fabric A: Cut twenty-five 7¼in (18.5cm) squares for the star background. Cut seventy-five 3⅞in (9.8cm) squares (50 for the block corners and 25 for the star centers). Cut twenty 2½ x 12½in (6.5 x 31.8cm) strips for the vertical sashings. Cut eight 2½ x 44in (6.5 x 112cm) strips for the horizontal sashings. (Sew two sashing strips together, to create four sashing strips). Cut eight 7 x 44in (17.8 x 112cm) wide strips for the borders.

(Sew two strips together, to create four border strips).

From fabric B: Cut one hundred 3⅞in (9.8cm) squares for the star points.

From fabric C: Cut fifty 3⅞in (9.8cm) squares for the block corners and cut fifty 3½in (8.9cm) squares for the star centers.

From fabric D: Cut twenty 3⅞in (9.8cm) squares D for the star centers.

From fabric E: Cut five 3⅞in (9.8cm) squares for the star centers.

# Make the star points

Place two 3⁷/₈in (9.8cm) fabric C squares onto a 7¼in (18.5cm) fabric A square, right sides together (see Figure 1) and pin. Draw a diagonal line on the wrong side of the fabric C squares, then stitch a ¼in (6mm) seam on either side of the line (see Figure 1). Cut along the drawn line. You will have two pieces. Open up and press the points out. Place another 3⁷/₈in (9.8cm) fabric C square right side down on top of one of the pieces, in the fabric A corner, see Figure 2. Draw a diagonal line on the wrong side of fabric C square. Stitch a ¼in (6mm) seam on either side of the line (see Figure 2). Cut along the drawn line. You now have a pair of star points (see Figure 3).

Repeat with the remaining piece to create another pair of star points. You need two pairs of star points (four star points in total) for each block. Repeat for the other 24 blocks.

# Make the half-square triangle block corners

Place one 3⁷/₈in (9.8cm) fabric C square right sides together with one 3⁷/₈in (9.8cm) fabric A square. Draw a diagonal line on the wrong side of the fabric (see Figure 4) and pin. Sew a ¼in (6mm) seam on either side of the line then cut along the drawn line to create two half-square triangles (see Figure 5). Repeat to create four half-square triangles for each block (one hundred total) (see p.82).

# Make the half-square triangle centers

Place one 3⁷/₈in (9.8cm) fabric D square right sides together with one 3⁷/₈in (9.8cm) fabric A square. Follow the instructions above (see Figure 4) to make a pair of half-square triangles. Make 20 pairs using fabric D and make five pairs using fabric E.

# Make the blocks

Lay out the pieces in order following the diagram below (see Figure 6). Create the center unit by sewing one 3½in (8.9cm) fabric C square to one half-square triangle center. Repeat. Sew the two pairs together, matching the seams, (see pp.74–75) to make the center unit.

Continuing to refer to Figure 6 below and sewing one row at a time, stitch one half-square triangle block corner to the left, short side of a star point. Add another half-square triangle block corner to the other short side of the star point to complete the row. Repeat this row for the bottom row of the block.

For the middle row sew one star point to the center unit, then add the last star point to the opposite side of the center unit. Once all rows have been joined, press the seams open and combine the rows to complete the block. Repeat to make a total of 25 blocks.

## Figure 1

## Figure 2

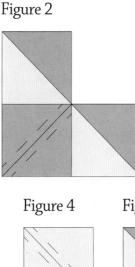

## Figure 6

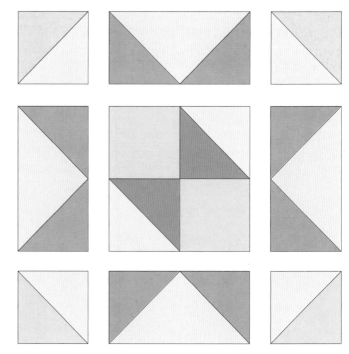

## Figure 3

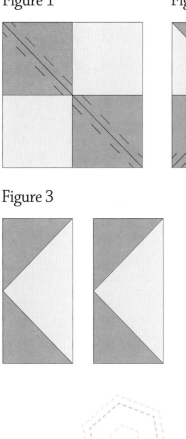

## Figure 4

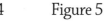

## Figure 5

# Make the quilt top

## Attach the sashings

Lay out the blocks in order, five rows of five blocks. Sew a $2^1/_2$ x $12^1/_2$in (6.5 x 31.8cm) sashing strip to the right-hand side of each block, except the last block in each row. Sew the block in each row together, row by row. Sew the four $2^1/_2$in (6.5cm) wide sashing strips to the bottom of each row, except the last row, trimming the overhanging edges even with the quilt top. Sew all five rows together.

## Attach the borders

Measure the quilt top from top to bottom down the center to obtain the length. Cut two of the 7in (17.8cm) wide border strips to fit. Sew these borders strips to the left and right sides of the quilt top. Square up the edges, then sew the remaining two border strips to the top and bottom of the quilt top. Trim the edges even with the quilt top.

# Finish the quilt

Finish the quilt by assembling the quilt sandwich (see p.46), and quilt using the design and method of your choice. We've quilted using the free-motion quilting technique (see p.213).

Square off the raw edges and attach the binding using the Double-fold binding method (see p.53), or the method of your choice (see pp.50-53).

*It is important to match the seams carefully when piecing the star blocks.*

# Pinwheel quilt

This quilt is made by foundation piecing using the reverse pieced method. For the quilt shown we've used two shades of the same color for each pinwheel, giving a contrast in the pinwheels to make them look as if they are spinning.

## Essential Information

**DIFFICULTY** Medium

**SIZE** 80 x 95in (203 x 241cm)

**MATERIALS**
Rotary cutter
Cutting mat
Quilter's ruler
Iron and ironing board
Scissors
Pins
Thread to match fabrics
121 copies of the block template (see p.305)
   for foundation piecing
Sewing machine
Quilting thread
Needle

**FABRICS**
Twenty 10 x 44in (25 x 112cm) patterned fabrics
   in varying colors and prints for the pinwheels
   (or twenty fat quarters)
**A:** 157$^{1}/_{2}$ x 44in (400 x 112cm) of a solid
   off-white background and sashing fabric
**B:** 236$^{1}/_{4}$ x 44in (600 x 112cm) backing fabric
**C:** 29$^{1}/_{2}$ x 44in (75 x 112cm) binding fabric
86 x 101in (220 x 255cm) batting

**SKILLS**
Foundation piecing: Reverse pieced (see p.149)
Sashings and borders (see pp.108–113)

**SEAM ALLOWANCE**
$^{1}/_{4}$in (6mm) throughout, unless otherwise stated

## Before you begin

Foundation piecing using the reverse pieced method on a paper foundation is a method of patchwork where you use a printed paper template as your reference when creating the blocks (see p.149). This method allows challenging block configurations to be made more easily, without having to align different angles. It does mean you have a bit more waste than with traditional piecing, but it ensures all of the blocks are identical.

Remember to adjust the stitch length on your machine to a shorter 1.25–1.5 length when using a paper foundation. This will allow the paper to be perforated and torn away with ease. Try different lengths to see what works best on your machine before you begin. The paper should be able to be torn away without distorting the stitches or patchwork.

## Cut the blocks

Using one of the paper block templates, carefully trim out all four template pieces, individually, from the main template.

Choose two different-pattered pinwheel fabrics for the first pinwheel block. Place template piece 2 on the wrong side of the first patterned fabric and trim around it adding $^{1}/_{2}$–$^{3}/_{4}$in (1.2–2cm) extra all around. Cut

another three pieces using the same template piece and fabric.

Repeat the process using template piece 4 and the second patterned fabric, cutting a total of four fabric pieces.

Repeat the process using template pieces 1 and 3 and fabric B, the solid off-white background fabric. You should now have a total of 16 fabric pieces. These will make one complete pinwheel block.

## Assemble the block

Place one of the patterned fabric 2 pieces in front of you, right-side up. Place one of the patterned fabric 1 pieces on top of the fabric 2 piece, right side down (see Figure 1).

Take one of the paper block templates and score the line between pieces 1 and 2. Fold on the scored line.

Place the paper block template on top of the fabrics, printed side up, centering the outline of paper piece 1 over fabric piece 1. Use the fold as your guide for positioning, making sure the edge of the fabric extends above the fold by approximately $^3/_8$in (1cm). Once positioned, unfold the paper (see Figure 2).

Pin through the three layers (fabric pieces 1 and 2 and the paper). Hold the paper up to a light source, if needed, to check the position of the fabrics under the block template.

Carefully place the three layers under the foot of your sewing machine. Starting at the top edge of the scored line slowly begin sewing over the line, ending at the bottom edge of the block template.

Remove from the sewing machine and remove all of the pins.

Fold the paper back on the seam line so you can see the raw seam allowance of the fabric pieces. Using a quilter's ruler and rotary cutter trim the excess seam allowance to a neat ¼in (6mm).

Unfold the paper and turn it over so the fabric pieces are facing you. Open up the two fabric pieces and press the seam open, so that the right sides of both pieces are facing you (see Figure 3).

Carefully score the line on the paper block template between pieces 2 and 3. Place a fabric 3 piece in front of you with the right side facing up (see Figure 4).

Fold the paper block template along the scored line. Pick up the paper block template and place it, face up, on top of the fabric 3 piece so that the fabric 2 piece and fabric 3 pieces sit right sides together. Make sure the edge of the fabric 3 piece is sticking out past the folded edge of the paper. Once it is positioned, unfold the paper, then pin and sew along the scored line being careful to stop where the line intersects the next line (see Figure 5). Remove from the sewing machine and remove all of the pins.

Fold the paper back on the seam line so you can see the raw seam allowance of the fabric piece. Using a quilter's ruler and rotary cutter trim the excess seam allowance to a neat ¼in (6mm).

### Figure 1

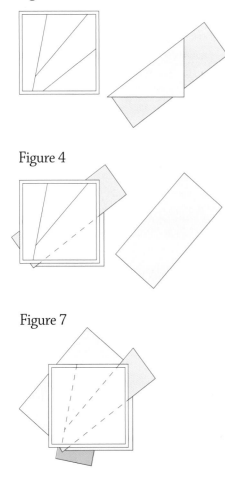

### Figure 2

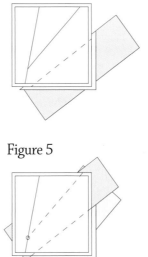

### Figure 3

### Figure 4

### Figure 5

### Figure 6

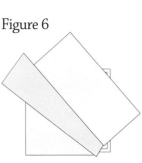

### Figure 7

### Figure 8

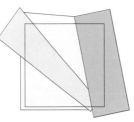

### Figure 9

Figure 10

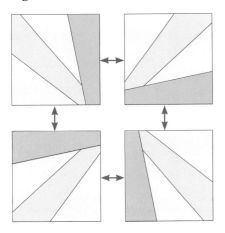

Figure 11

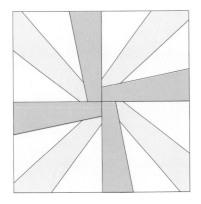

Figure 12

Unfold the paper and turn it over so the fabric pieces are facing you. Open up fabric piece 3 and press the seam open, so that the right sides of all the fabric pieces are facing you (see Figure 6).

Repeat the process for the final piece, using fabric piece 4, scoring, folding, positioning, unfolding, pinning, sewing, and trimming as before (see Figure 7). Turn over the block and press the seams flat so that the right sides of all the fabrics are facing you (see Figure 8).

Using the four square edges of the paper block template as your guides, carefully trim away the excess fabric giving you a perfectly square block (see Figure 9).

Repeat the process three more times using the remaining 12 fabric pieces. Lay out the four blocks in a pinwheel (see Figure 10).

Attach the top two blocks together, then the bottom two blocks together. Press the seams in opposite directions from one another, then pin the two rows right sides together, matching the seams. Sew the two rows together to create the final pinwheel block. (see Figure 11).

Repeat the entire process 29 more times, using two different-pattered fabrics for each block (for template pieces 2 and 4) for a total of 30 blocks.

After all 30 blocks have been completed lay them out into an arrangement of five blocks across by six blocks down. Adjust the position of the blocks to suit your preference.

## Cut and sew the sashings

Cut strips of fabric B 3½in (9cm) wide, then sub cut them to the length of the blocks to create the sashing strips. Cut a total of 24 sashing strips.

With your blocks still arranged in front of you, place a sashing strip to the right of blocks 1–4 in each row (see Figure 12). Attach all of the pieces together in each row, to create a total of six rows (see p.108).

Measure, cut, and piece five long 3½in (9cm) wide sashing strips to fit between the rows, leaving row six without a bottom sashing.

Lay the sashings between the rows. Pin and sew the sashings and rows together to create the quilt top.

## Cut and sew the borders

Measure, cut, and join strips of fabric B 7in (17.8cm) wide for the left and right borders. Pin right sides together with the quilt top and attach the borders to the left and right sides (see p.111).

Measure, cut, and join strips of fabric B 7in (17.8cm) wide for the top and bottom borders. Pin right sides together with the quilt top and attach the borders to the top and bottom sides to complete the border.

## Assemble the layers

Create a back for the quilt from fabric B. Lay the backing fabric on a flat surface, right side down. Lay the batting on top and carefully smooth out the batting and backing fabric (see p.46). Lay the finished quilt top right side up on the batting. Both the batting and the backing fabric will overhang the quilt top by an inch or so (a few centimeters). Starting from the center and working outward, pin or baste the layers together (see p.46) Try not to lift the quilt top too much as you pin and regularly check that all the layers sit flat and are even with one another.

## Quilt the layers

For this quilt, we quilted all of fabric A with a free-motion quilting pattern (see p.213), but you can quilt using the pattern and method of your choice.

## Attach the binding

Once the quilting is complete, cut away the excess backing fabric and batting. Finish the quilt with binding by making a long, continuous piece of binding from fabric C to fit around all four sides of the quilt. Attach the binding to the edges of the quilt following the instructions for Double-fold binding (see p.53), or the method of your choice.

# Sailboat quilt and pillow

Spruce up any child's room with this adorable appliqué sailboat quilt and pillow set. For the best effect, use a large selection of colorful printed and plain fabrics for the appliqué shapes in a color scheme of the child's choice.

## Essential Information

**DIFFICULTY** Medium

**SIZE** 55¼ x 78¾in (140 x 200cm)

**TOOLS AND MATERIALS**
Quilter's ruler
Rotary cutter
Cutting mat
Scissors
Pins
Tracing paper or cardboard for the templates
Sewing machine
Threads to match your fabrics
Iron and ironing board
Curved safety pins or thread for tacking
Quilting thread

**FABRICS FOR THE QUILT**
197 x 44in (500 x 112cm) of white fabric for the background, sashing, and borders
14 colorful fat quarters in both plains and prints
Two different prints of fabric for the inner top and bottom borders, each 5 x 44in (13 x 112cm)
197 x 44in (500 x 112cm) backing fabric
20 x 44in (50 x 112cm) binding fabric
Enough fusible web for all of the appliqué pieces
50 x 112in (155 x 215cm) batting

**FABRICS FOR THE PILLOW**
20 x 44in (50 x 112cm) white fabric for background, sashing, and back flaps
Scraps of colorful fabric (leftover from quilt top)
Enough fusible web for all of the appliqué pieces

**SKILLS**
Appliqué (see pp. 168-179, 184-187, 194-195)

**SEAM ALLOWANCE**
¼in (6mm) throughout, unless otherwise stated

## Sailboat quilt

### Cut the fabrics

Cut twenty 12½in (32cm) squares of white fabric for the backgrounds.

Cut fifteen 2½ x 10½in (6.5 x 26.6cm) of white fabric for the vertical sashings.

Cut fifteen 2½in (6.5cm) squares of solid-colored fabrics for the corner squares.

Cut two 2½ x 44in (6.5 x 112cm) strips from each of the printed inner top and bottom border fabric.

Cut four 7½ x 44 in (19 x 112cm) strips of white fabric for the top and bottom outer borders.

### Make the blocks

Copy the master templates on page 306 to make your own templates. Cut out the templates and trace the shapes onto the paper side of the fusible web. You will need twenty of each piece, one for each of the twenty blocks. Cut out the fusible web shapes leaving approximately ¼in (6mm) extra around all the edges.

Following the manufacturer's instructions, apply the fusible web pieces onto the back of your chosen plain and printed fabrics. Using a rotary cutter and a quilter's ruler, carefully trim the shapes to the final dimensions.

Remove the paper from the fusible web on one of the masts and center it onto one of the 12½in (32cm) squares of white background fabric. Use your iron and follow the manufacturer's instructions to fuse the mast in place. Continue adding the remaining pieces for that boat, fusing them to the background fabric.

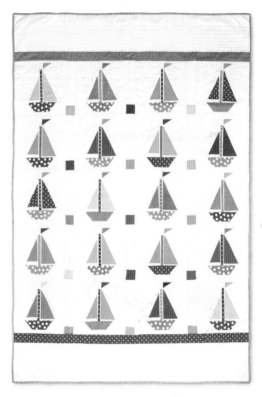

Machine or hand appliqué around each shape using blanket stitch, or another stitch of your choice. You can also add decorative stitches to any of the elements, for more visual interest, if you wish. Repeat to make all twenty blocks.

### Make the sashings

Sew each of the colored corner squares to the bottom of each vertical sashing strip, right sides together, to make fifteen 2½ x 12½in (6.5 x 32cm) vertical sashing strips.

Lay out the twenty appliqué boat blocks in five rows of four blocks. Lay the sashing strips between the rows of blocks, arranging them in the order you want them to appear on the quilt top. Sew a sashing strip to the right-hand side of each of the first three blocks in each row. Sew all of the blocks in each row together and press all of the seams in one direction, alternating the direction the seams are pressed on each row (see p.108), Match the seams and sew the five rows together to make the quilt top.

## Make the borders

Sew the two inner border strips of the same fabric together, to create two long strips that will fit across the width of the quilt top. Sew one of the inner borders to the top of the quilt top and one to the bottom of the quilt top.

Just as you did with the inner borders, sew two of the outer border strips together into one long strip, then the other two into another long strip to create the top and bottom outer borders. Sew one outer border to the top of the quilt and the other outer border to the bottom of the quilt.

## Finish the quilt

Create the quilt sandwich making sure all of the layers sit flat with one another (see p.46). Hand- or machine-quilt as desired (see pp.204–205, 210–213). We've used a free-style quilting pattern around the boats and on the outer borders to create patterns that look like clouds and water.

Trim the edges square and even with one another. Cut and piece the binding fabric into one long strip (see pp.48–49), then attach to the quilt using the Double-fold binding method (see p.53), or the method of your choice.

# Sailboat pillow

## Cut the fabrics

Cut one 19 x 14$^1$/$_4$in (48 x 36cm) piece of white fabric for the background.

Cut two 2$^3$/$_4$ x 14$^1$/$_2$in (7 x 36cm) strips of white fabric for the side sashings.

Cut four 2$^3$/$_4$in (7cm) squares of solid-colored fabric for the corner squares.

Cut two 19 x 13$^3$/$_4$in (48 x 35cm) rectangles of white fabric for the back flaps.

## Make the pillow

To create the sailboat pillow you will need to assemble an additional boat block, as you did with the quilt top, but for this block you will use the slightly larger 19 x 14$^1$/$_4$in (48 x 36cm) piece of white fabric for the background.

Using the same templates you made for the quilt, trace the shapes onto the fusible web. Trim the pieces leaving $^1$/$_4$in (6mm) on all sides. Fuse the pieces to the plain and printed fabrics of your choice, cut around each shape, and fuse in the same order as before onto the background fabrics. Sew around each shape by hand or machine, as before.

Sew a corner square to each end of both side sashing pieces. Then sew each complete side sashing piece to the sailboat block. This finished pillow front should measure 19in (48cm) square. To create the envelope flap for the back of the pillow cover, take both back flap pieces and hem one of the long sides on each: simply fold over and press $^1$/$_2$in (1.2cm), then fold over again 1in (2.5cm). Topstitch the edge to secure the hem.

With the front of the pillow faceup in front of you, place one of the back flaps right side down aligning the long raw edge with the top of the pillow front. The hem should be in the middle of the block. Place the second back flap right side down aligning to the bottom of the block. Again, the hem should be in the middle. Pin around all four edges.

Using a $^1$/$_2$in (1.2cm) seam allowance, sew around all four edges of the pillow. On both side edges reverse stitch over the hemmed edges of the back flaps to add more strength. Snip off the corner to reduce the bulk, being careful not to cut through the seam. Turn the pillow right-side out and insert the pillow cushion.

# Hive quilt

This quilt is an offset medallion design, but rather than piecing it layer by layer around the center in the traditional way, it is pieced in blocks. There are only seven pattern pieces used and each block uses a combination of all or some of these pieces.

## Essential Information

**DIFFICULTY** Difficult

**SIZE** 52 x 65in (132 x 165cm)

**TOOLS AND MATERIALS**
Measuring tape
Quilter's ruler
Rotary cutter
Cutting mat
Scissors
Pins
Sewing machine
Threads to match your fabrics
Seam roller (optional)
Iron and ironing board
Safety pins
Quilting threads to match your fabrics
Sewing needle

**FABRICS**
**A:** 22½ x 44in (58 x 112cm) printed fabric
**B:** 18 x 44in (46 x 112cm) printed fabric
**C:** 9 x 44in (23 x 112cm) printed fabric
**D:** 9 x 44in (23 x 112cm) printed fabric
**E:** 22½ x 44in (58 x 112cm) for the pattern pieces, plus 126 x 44in (320 x 112cm) printed fabric for the backing and binding
**F:** 108 x 44in (275 x 112cm) light, creamy gray fabric for the background
58 x 71in (147 x 180cm) batting

**SEAM ALLOWANCE**
¼in (6mm) throughout, unless otherwise stated

## Cut the fabric

For piece 1, cut 3in (7.5cm) squares from the fabrics, then cut them diagonally to create half-square triangles (see p.82). You will need 34 squares of fabric A, 35 squares of fabric B, seven squares each of fabrics C and D, 19 squares of fabric E, and 74 squares of fabric F.

Create the rest of the pieces by cutting the fabrics into 2in (5cm) wide strips and using the templates on page 307 to cut the required number of individual shapes from the strips. You can place the strips on top of each other when cutting. This will allow you to cut multiple pieces at once and considerably speed up the cutting process.

Pieces 4 and 5 and pieces 6 and 7 are the same shape, but mirror images of each other. You can place piece 4 on top of piece 5, right sides together, to cut. This will give you both the pieces in one cut. Repeat for pieces 6 and 7.

### Quilt top: Number of fabric pieces needed for each pattern piece

| Fabrics | Piece 1 | Piece 2 | Piece 3 | Piece 4 | Piece 5 | Piece 6 | Piece 7 |
|---------|---------|---------|---------|---------|---------|---------|---------|
| A | 68 | 4 | 5 | 13 | 12 | 3 | 2 |
| B | 69 | 1 | 6 | – | 2 | 2 | 2 |
| C | 13 | 10 | – | 1 | 2 | – | – |
| D | 13 | 4 | 2 | 2 | – | 1 | – |
| E | 37 | 34 | – | 4 | 2 | – | – |
| F | 148 | 102 | 69 | 38 | – | 6 | – |

### Pattern piece reference

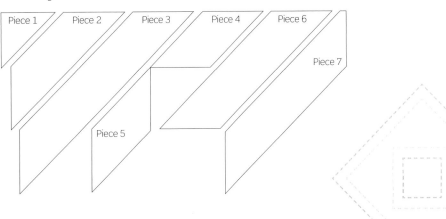

# Piece the blocks

Make each block using a combination of all or some of the pieces. An example of a block formation is shown below.

Sew the pieces together using a 1/4in (6mm) seam allowance. Create the six strips for each block, then sew the strips together to create the block.

To make it easier to match points, finger press the edges, or use a seam roller, as you are piecing the blocks. Using an iron can distort the edges, particularly as the pieces are cut diagonally. Easing the edges gently avoids stretching and is more precise.

Once the block is complete, press with an iron from the top, being careful not to affect the line of the edges. Then press the seams open or to the side, in whichever direction the bulk gets reduced. Piece the rest of the blocks for the quilt top, using the Quilt top diagram, right, as your reference.

## Quilt top

### Key

| | |
|---|---|
| ▨ Fabric A | ▨ Fabric D |
| ▧ Fabric B | ▨ Fabric E |
| ▧ Fabric C | ▢ Fabric F |

## Example block

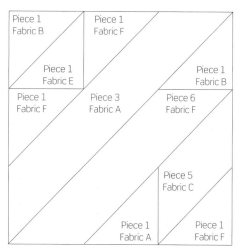

| Piece 1 Fabric B | Piece 1 Fabric F | |
| --- | --- | --- |
| | | Piece 1 Fabric B |
| Piece 1 Fabric F | Piece 3 Fabric A | Piece 6 Fabric F |
| | | Piece 5 Fabric C |
| | Piece 1 Fabric A | Piece 1 Fabric F |

## Join the blocks

Once you have pieced all the individual blocks, sew the blocks together in rows, then sew the rows together to complete the quilt top. Follow the Quit top diagram, left, throughout.

## Assemble the layers

To make the quilt sandwich (see p.46), lay the backing fabric on a flat surface. Place the batting on top of this. Smooth out the two to make sure there are no folds or creases. Then lay the quilt top on the batting. The batting and the backing fabric should overhang the quilt top by approximately an inch or so (a few centimeters) each.

Starting from the center and working outward, pin the layers together using safety pins, making sure all the layers sit flat and even with one another. Check the back of the quilt is sitting flat, too.

## Quilt the top

The quilt has simple filler lines in the background (light gray) areas and zigzag quilting around all the colored rings of the medallion. We've used a baby pink thread on the front of the quilt and a darker fuchsia pink thread in the bobbin. Starting with the first cream ring after the center square, quilt a line all the way around, $^1\!/_4$in (6mm) from the center square. Quilt a second line on the other side of the cream ring, $^1\!/_4$in (6mm) from the edge. Now, quilt directly in between these two lines. You will have three lines, $^1\!/_8$in (3mm) apart and $^1\!/_4$in (6mm) from the edges. Repeat this for all the cream rings in the medallion area of the quilt.

Continue into the light gray background area. The seams in the blocks will help you continue with the quilting. The background area should have consistent lines, $^1\!/_8$in (3mm) apart. In the colored rings, quilt zigzag lines following the triangles in the piecing. You can also quilt using the design of your choice, if you wish.

## Sew the binding

Lay the quilt, right side up, on a flat surface. Create a long binding strip from fabric E to fit around your quilt top. Then follow the instructions for Double-fold binding as shown on page 53, or bind using the method of your choice.

**You can add a detail** to the back of the quilt by creating a simple block, turning under the final raw edges, and topstitching around the edges to hold it in place on the backing fabric before creating the final quilt sandwich.

# Heirloom star quilt

The photographed quilt is an heirloom quilt that grew organically, so it is not completely symmetrical. The pattern below will give you a very close representation of the original quilt, but will not match exactly.

## Essential Information

**DIFFICULTY** Medium

**SIZE** 60 x 50in (152 x 127cm)

**TOOLS AND MATERIALS**

Rotary cutter and scissors
Cutting mat
Quilter's ruler
Measuring tape
Iron and ironing board
Pins
Threads to match the fabrics
Sewing machine
Safety pins or tacking thread
Quilting thread
Needle

**FABRICS**

Five dark and five medium-shade fat quarters in
   light and dark browns
Five dark and five medium-shade fat quarters in
   reds and greens
20 x 44in (50 x 112cm) each of six different
   cream fabrics
20 x 44in (50 x 112cm) each of six different
   green fabrics
20 x 44in (50 x 112cm) each of six different red
   fabrics
126 x 44in (320 x 112cm) backing fabric
18 x 44in (46 x 112cm) binding fabric

**SKILLS**

Triangles (see pp.82–91)
Seminole patchwork (see pp.153–155)

**SEAM ALLOWANCE**

$1/4$in (6mm) throughout, unless otherwise stated

## Cut the fabric

Finished block size is $11^{1}/_{2}$ x $11^{1}/_{2}$in (29.2 x 29.2cm), including seam allowances.

Cut twelve 6in (15.2cm) squares for star centers from the brown and blue fat quarters.

Cut ninety-six $3^{1}/_{4}$in (8.3cm) squares for the star points from the red and green fabrics. (You will need eight for each block, so be sure to cut eight of the same color for each block).

Cut forty-eight 6 x $3^{1}/_{4}$in (15.2 x 8.3cm) rectangles for the star backgrounds from mixed cream fabrics. (For each block be sure to cut four rectangles from the same cream fabric.)

Cut forty-eight $3^{1}/_{4}$in (8.3cm) squares for star block corners from mixed cream fabrics. (For each block be sure to cut four squares from the same cream fabric to match the four star background rectangles.)

## Make the star points

On each of the small red and green squares draw a diagonal line from one corner to the opposite corner. This will be your seam line (see p.85, Flying geese).

Place one marked $3^{1}/_{4}$in (8.3cm) square on a rectangle piece, making sure that the line lands in the corner. Carefully pin in place and sew along the line. Trim away the excess to leave a $1/4$in (6mm) seam allowance. Press the piece open. Place the matching square fabric on the other side of the rectangle with the line facing the other direction. Pin and sew along the diagonal line. This creates one of the four star points for each block. Repeat the process three more times with the same fabrics to complete this block. Repeat to make the other 11 blocks.

## Figure 1

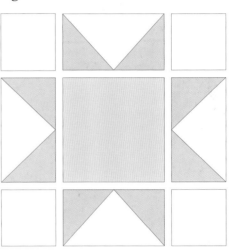

## Make the blocks

Sew a star point block to one side of a central square with the points facing away from the sqaure (see Figure 1). Sew another star point block to the opposite side of the square. This will be the middle row. Sew a $3^{1}/_{4}$in (8.3cm) square background fabric to each end of the remaining two star blocks. These will be the top and bottom rows. Sew the top and middle rows together. Press the seams open and then attach the bottom row to complete the block. Press the seams open. Repeat the process for the remaining 11 blocks.

## Make the quilt top

Lay out the blocks in three rows of four blocks. Sew the blocks in one row together and press the seams in one direction. Repeat sewing the rows together but pressing the seams of each row in the opposite direction to the previous row. Match the seams and sew the rows together. Press the horizontal seams open.

## Make the sawtooth border

Cut forty-seven $3^{1}/_{8}$in (8cm) squares from light fabrics. Cut forty-seven $3^{1}/_{8}$in (8cm) squares from green and red fabrics. On the light squares, draw a diagonal line on the wrong side of the fabric. Place a marked light square right sides together with a green or red square. Pin and sew a $^{1}/_{4}$in (6mm) seam on either side of the drawn line. (A faster method is to sew in one direction, $^{1}/_{4}$in/6mm

from the drawn line and then without breaking the thread, turn at the end of the seam and sew back on the opposite side of the line.)

Cut the block apart on the drawn line and press the seam allowance toward the dark fabric. You will have made 94 half-square triangle units.

Sew together three strips of 20 units and two strips of 17 units following the sawtooth pattern—all the light fabrics oriented to one side and all the dark fabrics oriented to the other side. Refer to the image below.

## Make the Seminole border

From a dark brown fabric cut three strips, each 1½in (3.8cm) wide. From a cream fabric and a medium brown fabric cut three strips, each 2½in (6.5cm) wide.

Sew a cream strip and a medium-brown strip to either side of the dark brown strip (see p.154, Steps 1 and 2). Use a short stitch length when sewing the Seminole border. Press the seam allowances toward the dark fabric; press the right side of the strip carefully, making sure that the seams are straight.

Cut pieces $1^{1}/_{2}$in (3.8cm) wide from the strips, using a quilter's ruler to ensure they are cut at 90 degrees (see p.154, Step 3). Lay out all the cut pieces into an angled band (see p.154, Step 4) and sew together with a $^{1}/_{4}$in (6mm) seam allowance. Press carefully on the right side of the band ensuring that there is no distortion. Trim the points off the patchwork band making sure that the long edges are parallel to each other (see p.154, Step 5).

## Make the four-patch border

From a variety of red and green fabrics cut five strips each $1^{1}/_{2}$ x 14in (3.8 x 35.5cm). Also cut five cream strips each $1^{1}/_{2}$ x 14in (3.8 x 35.5cm).

Sew a cream strip to a colored strip and press the seam allowance toward the darker fabric. Using a rotary cutter and quilter's ruler, cut the strips into $2^{1}/_{2}$in (6.5cm) wide units. You will need 45 units. Lay out the units in a four-patch checkerboard pattern strip and sew together, matching the seams.

## Make the striped border

From a selection of cream and green fabrics, cut a variety of strips between $1^{1}/_{2}$–$2^{1}/_{2}$in (3.8 x 6.5cm) wide and between 4–5in (10–12cm) long. Sew the strips together, alternating light and dark colors. Once your strip is $50^{1}/_{2}$in (128.3cm) long, use your quilter's ruler to cut the strip to the final $3^{1}/_{2}$in (9cm) width.

## Make the solid borders

For both the first and second inner borders, cut strips 1in (2.5cm) wide from dark fabrics. Measure the quilt top and if needed, piece the strips together to get the required length. The second inner border needs to be several inches longer than the inner border.

For the outer border, cut strips 2in (5cm) wide from dark fabrics. Piece the strips until you have the required lengths (measure after attaching all of the other borders, to get the correct length).

## Assemble the quilt

Sew the first inner border to the sides, top and bottom of the quilt top and press. To both long sides sew the 20-unit sawtooth border and press. Sew the 17-unit sawtooth border to the top and bottom of the quilt top. Sew the second narrow dark border to the sides, top, and bottom of the quilt top and press.

Centering the Seminole border along one of the long sides, pin and carefully sew in place. Press the seams. Sew the striped border to the opposite long side. Sew the squares border to the top. Sew the remaining 20-unit sawtooth border to the top. Measure and sew the final 2in (5cm) outer border around all four sides.

## Finish the quilt

Create the quilt sandwich making sure all of the layers sit flat with one another (see p.46) Hand- or machine-quilt as desired (see pp.204–205, 210–213), trim the edges square. The original quilt was hand-quilted with a combination of outline quilting and motifs sewn onto the star centers.

Cut and piece the binding fabric into one long strip (see pp.48–49), then attach to the quilt using the Double-fold binding method (see p.53), or the method of your choice.

## Simple squares tote (pp.76–81)

Enlarge by 200% on a photocopier

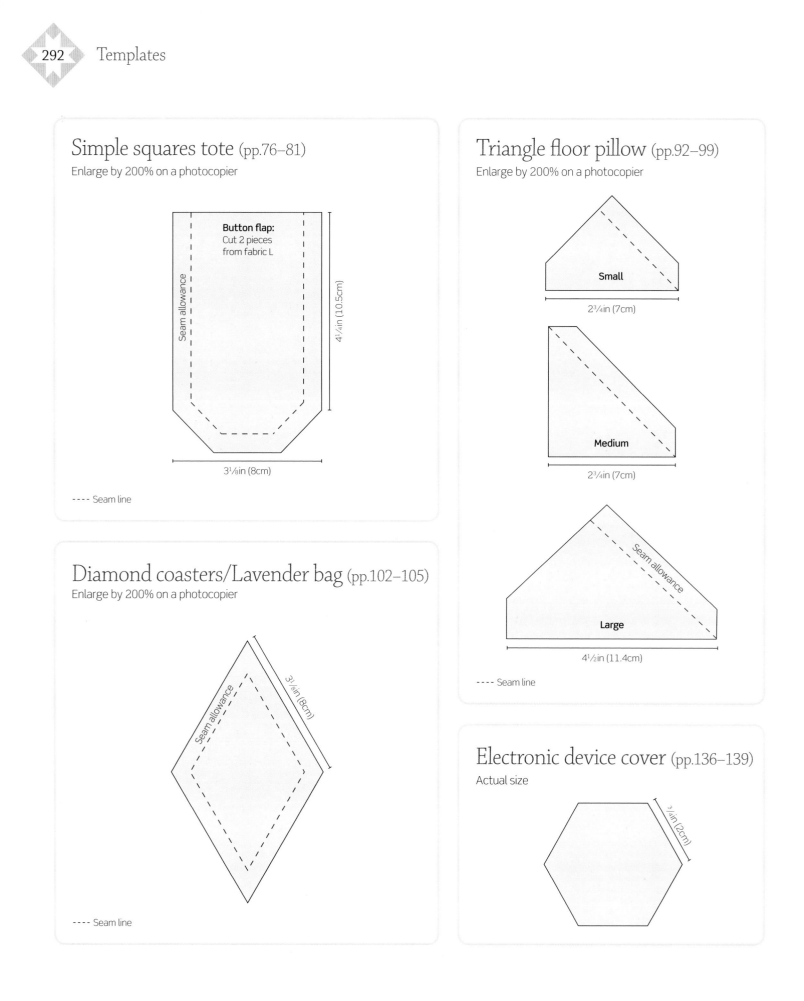

**Button flap:**
Cut 2 pieces
from fabric L

Seam allowance

4¼in (10.5cm)

3⅛in (8cm)

---- Seam line

## Diamond coasters/Lavender bag (pp.102–105)

Enlarge by 200% on a photocopier

Seam allowance

3⅛in (8cm)

---- Seam line

## Triangle floor pillow (pp.92–99)

Enlarge by 200% on a photocopier

**Small**

2¾in (7cm)

**Medium**

2¾in (7cm)

Seam allowance

**Large**

4½in (11.4cm)

---- Seam line

## Electronic device cover (pp.136–139)

Actual size

¾in (2cm)

# Dresden plate pillow (pp.122–127)

Use the measurements in the diagrams
below to make the templates

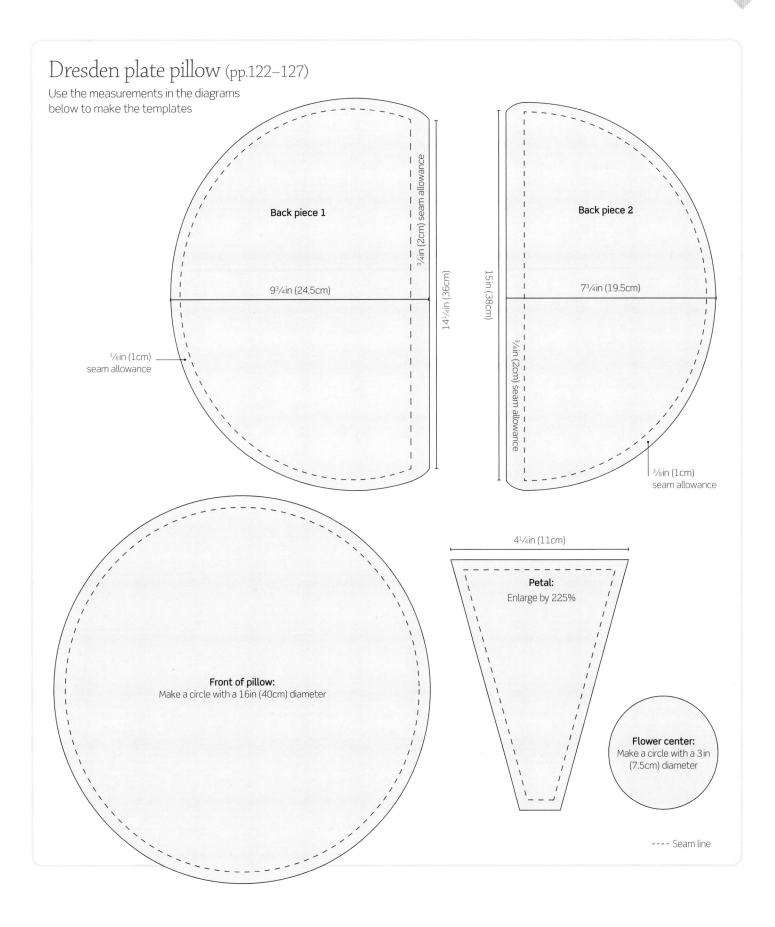

**Back piece 1**

³⁄₄in (2cm) seam allowance

9³⁄₄in (24.5cm)

14¹⁄₄in (36cm)

³⁄₈in (1cm)
seam allowance

**Back piece 2**

15in (38cm)

7³⁄₄in (19.5cm)

³⁄₄in (2cm) seam allowance

³⁄₈in (1cm)
seam allowance

**Front of pillow:**
Make a circle with a 16in (40cm) diameter

4¹⁄₄in (11cm)

**Petal:**
Enlarge by 225%

**Flower center:**
Make a circle with a 3in
(7.5cm) diameter

---- Seam line

# Bird toy (pp.128–133)

Actual size

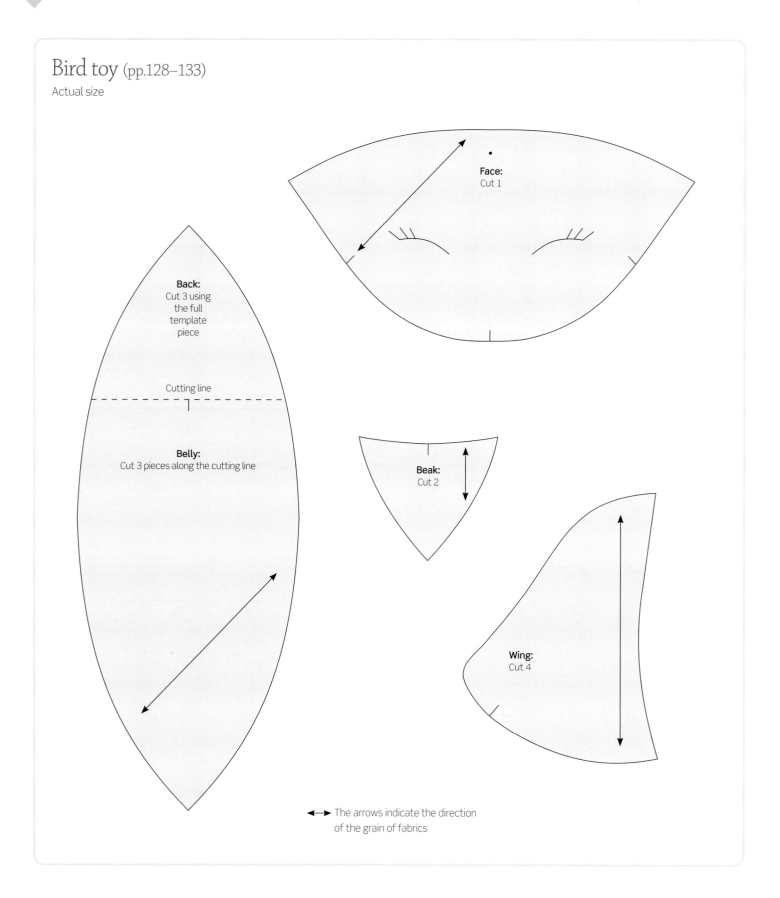

**Face:**
Cut 1

**Back:**
Cut 3 using the full template piece

Cutting line

**Belly:**
Cut 3 pieces along the cutting line

**Beak:**
Cut 2

**Wing:**
Cut 4

The arrows indicate the direction of the grain of fabrics

# Soft blocks (pp.180–183)

Enlarge by 135% on a photocopier

Moon

Heart

Rabbit

Star

Butterfly

Eyes and beak of owl

Owl

# Boat tote (pp.196–199)

Actual size

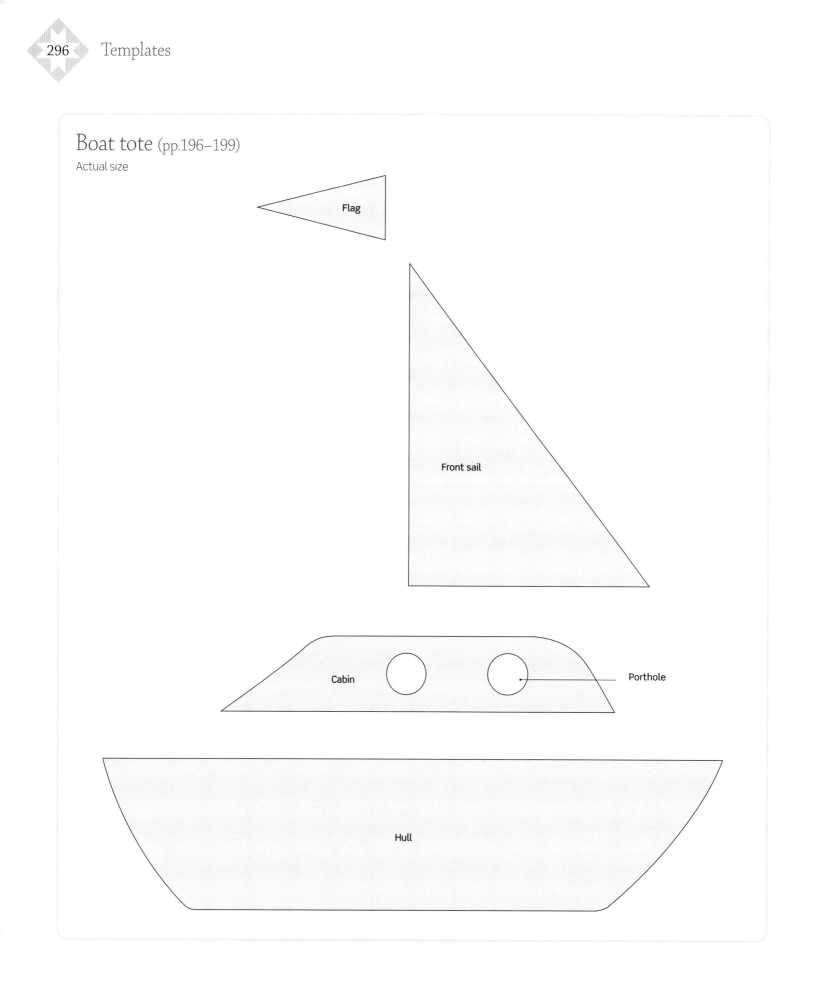

Flag

Front sail

Cabin

Porthole

Hull

# Diamond floor pillow (pp.230–231)

Actual size

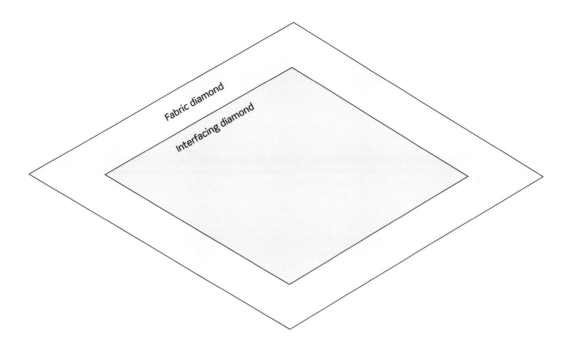

Fabric diamond

Interfacing diamond

# Pentagon ball (pp.226–227)

Actual size

# Pentagon bean bag (pp.242–243)

Enlarge by 400% on a photocopier

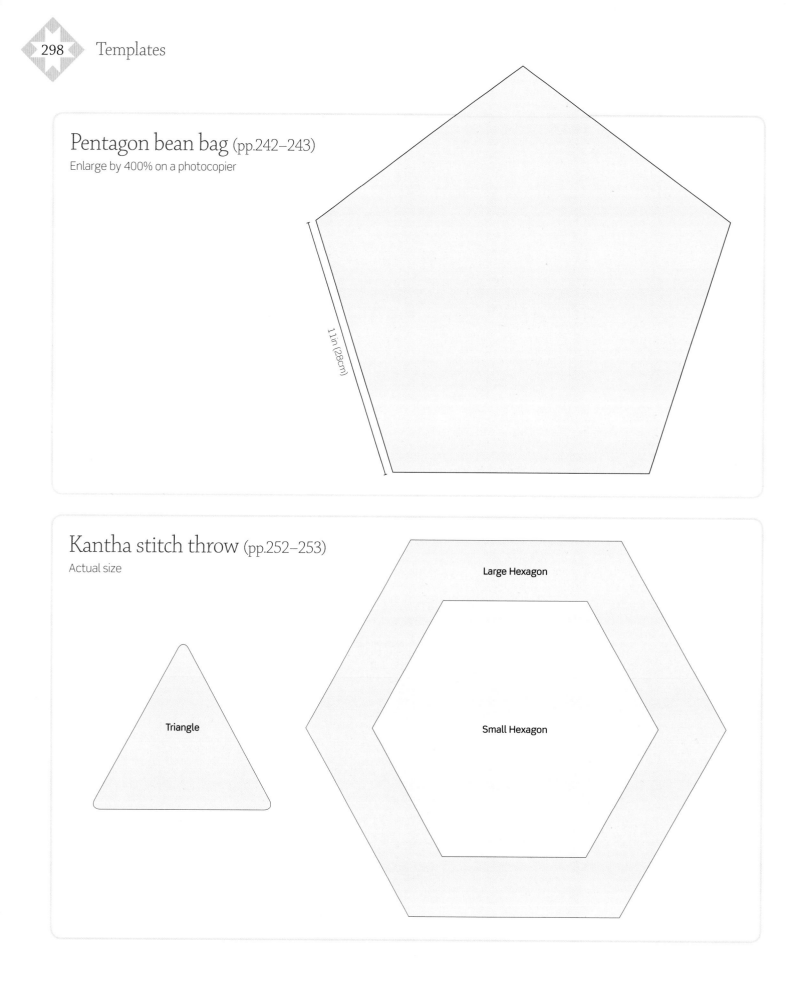

11in (28cm)

# Kantha stitch throw (pp.252–253)

Actual size

Large Hexagon

Triangle

Small Hexagon

# Door mouse (pp.244–245)

Actual size

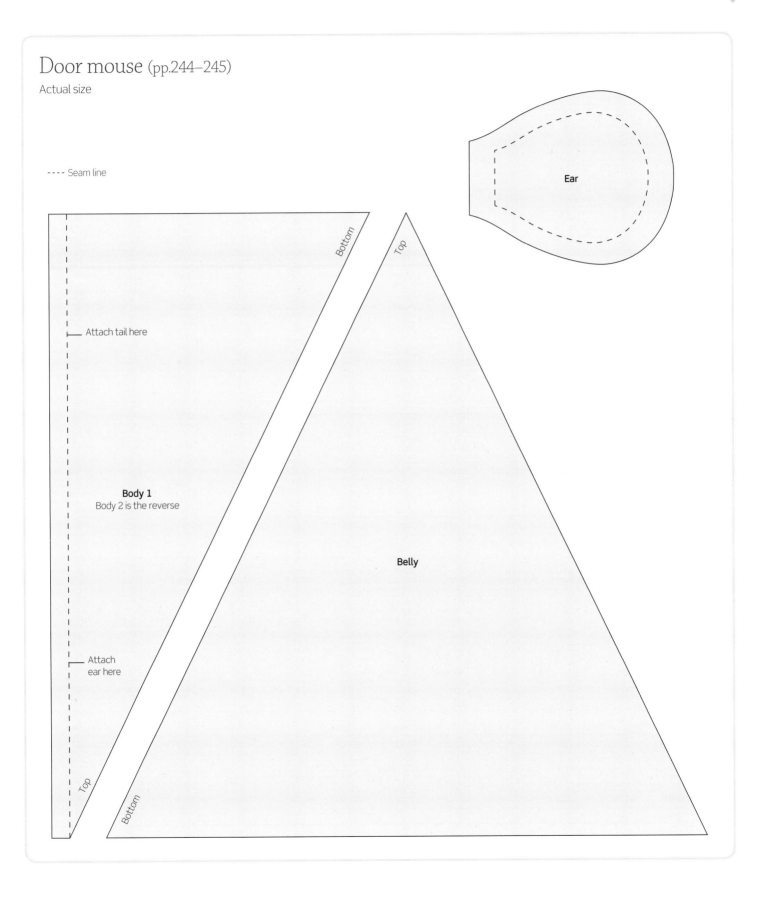

- - - - Seam line

Ear

Bottom

Top

Attach tail here

Top

**Body 1**
Body 2 is the reverse

Belly

Attach
ear here

Top

Bottom

# Zigzag circus quilt (pp.264–267)

Enlarge by 200% on a photocopier; all blocks measure 5¹⁄₂ x 7¹⁄₂in (14 x 19cm)

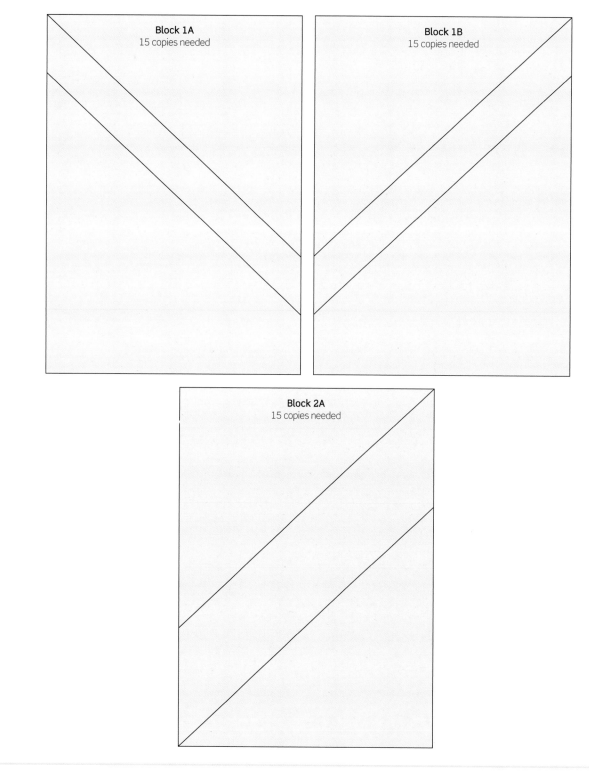

**Block 1A**
15 copies needed

**Block 1B**
15 copies needed

**Block 2A**
15 copies needed

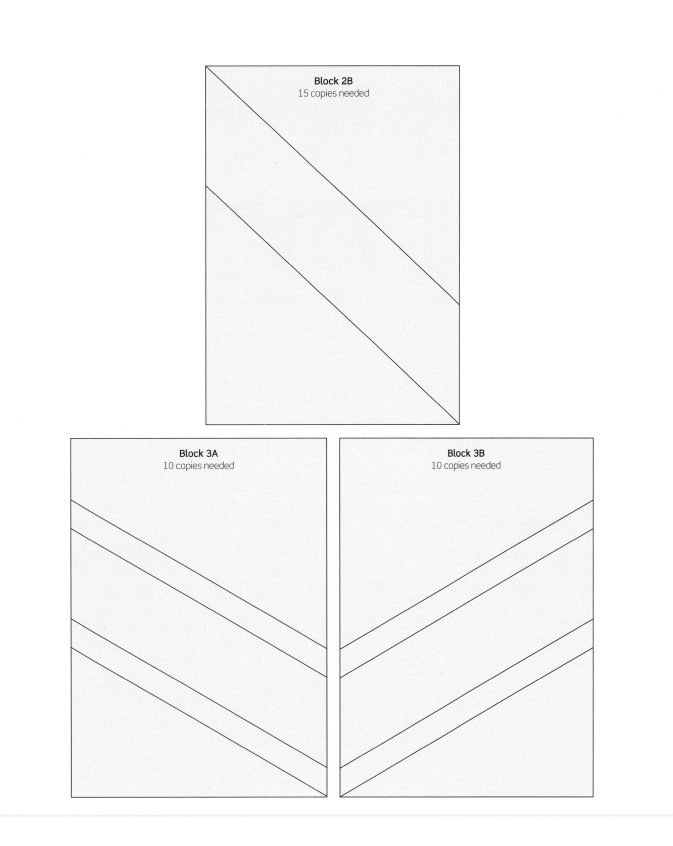

**Block 2B**
15 copies needed

**Block 3A**
10 copies needed

**Block 3B**
10 copies needed

# Hearts and flowers quilt (pp.268–271)

Enlarge by 200% on a photocopier; continued next page

Center

Petals

Flower petals and center

Leaf

Leaf

Butterfly wing

Stem

Butterfly body

Flower

Heart

Stem and leaf

Leaf

Stem

Stem and leaf

Heart

# Hearts and flowers quilt (pp.268–271) continued

Enlarge by 200% on a photocopier

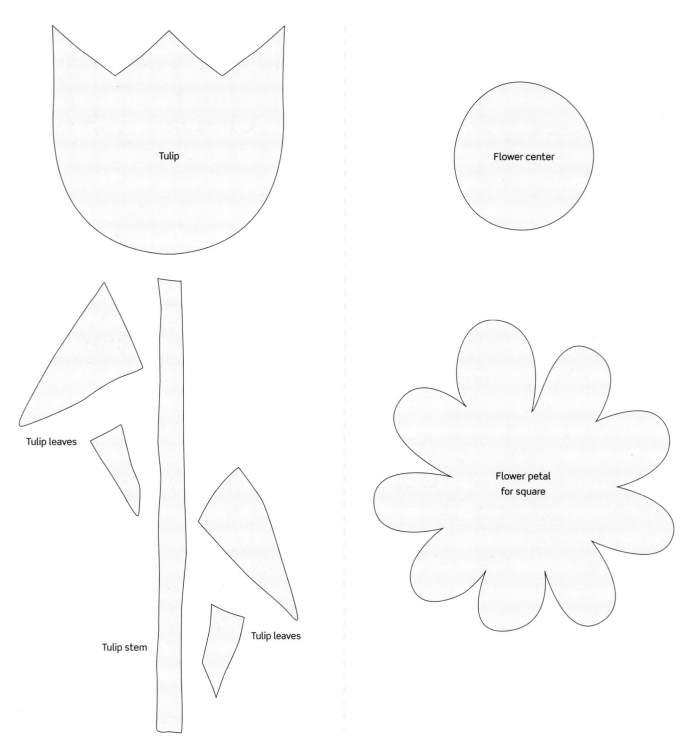

Tulip

Flower center

Tulip leaves

Tulip stem

Tulip leaves

Flower petal
for square

# Pinwheel quilt (pp.276–279)

Actual size (121 copies needed)

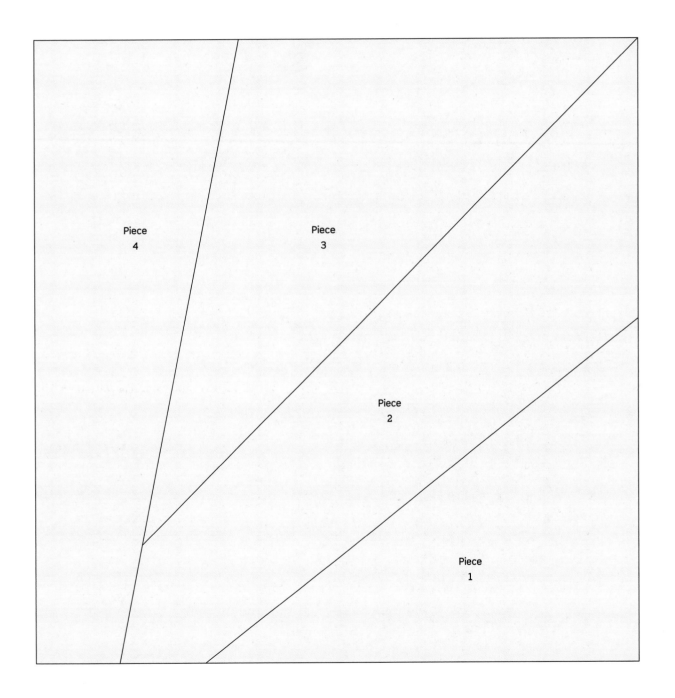

Piece
4

Piece
3

Piece
2

Piece
1

# Sailboat quilt and pillow (pp.280–283)

Actual size

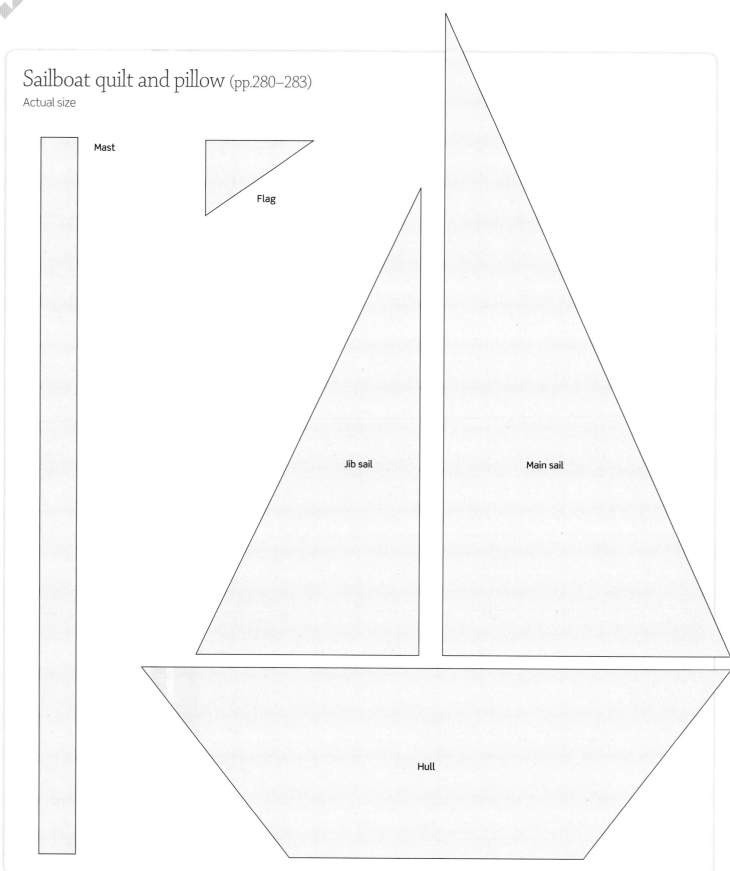

Mast

Flag

Jib sail

Main sail

Hull

# Hive quilt (pp.284–287)

Enlarge by 140% on a photocopier

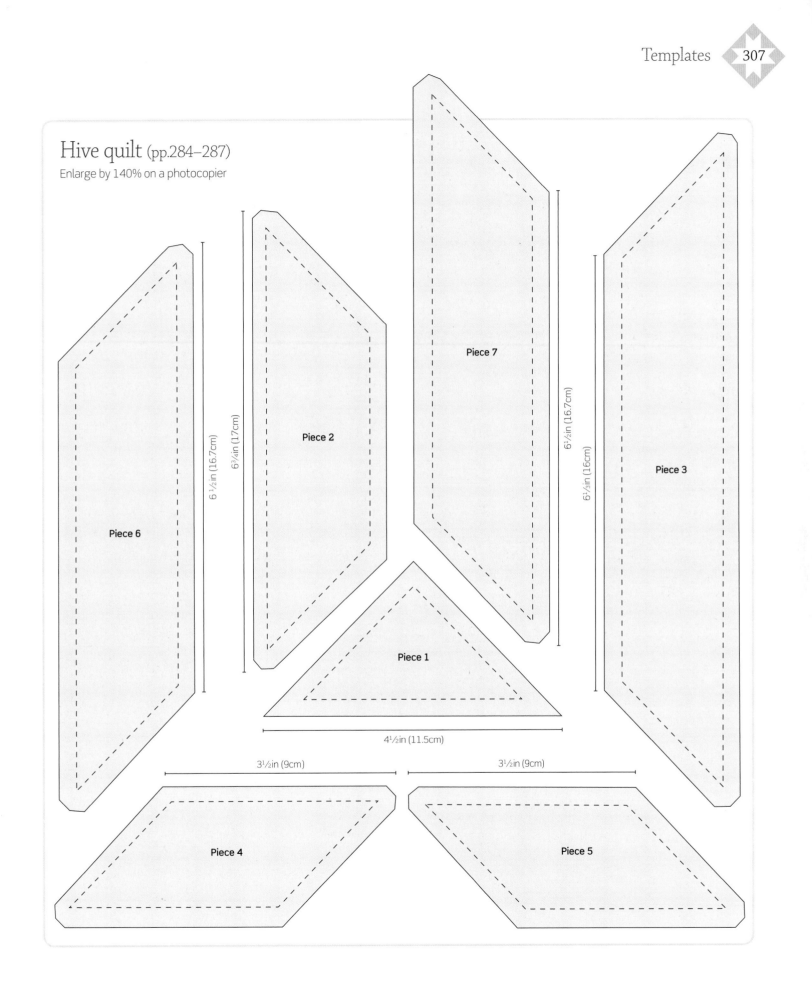

Piece 6

6 1/2in (16.7cm)

Piece 2

6 3/4in (17cm)

Piece 7

6 1/2in (16.7cm)

Piece 3

6 1/3in (16cm)

Piece 1

4 1/2in (11.5cm)

3 1/2in (9cm)

3 1/2in (9cm)

Piece 4

Piece 5

# Glossary

### Appliqué

From the French verb appliquer, meaning "to apply," a decorative technique in which shapes are cut from one fabric and applied to another, either by sewing them in place or by heat bonding with fusible bonding web.

### Backstitch

A hand stitch used to seam patchwork. A more secure alternative to running stitch.

### Basting

A temporary stitch used to hold pieces of fabric together or for transferring pattern markings to fabric. It can be worked by hand or machine and can be a straight line or individual doubled stitches.

### Batting

Also called wadding, this is a layer of filling made from polyester, cotton, wool, or even silk and used to provide warmth and give body to a quilt. Batting is available in many different lofts, or thicknesses.

### Bias

The diagonal grain of a woven fabric, at 45-degrees to the straight grain.

### Binding

A narrow strip of fabric used to cover the raw edges of a quilt to provide a neat finish and prevent it from fraying. For straight edges, the binding can be cut on the straight grain; bias-cut binding has more stretch, and should always be used for curved edges.

### Blanket stitch

Decorative hand or machine stitch worked along the raw or finished edge of fabric to neaten it. Often used in appliqué work.

### Block

A single design unit in patchwork and appliqué. Patchwork blocks traditionally fall into one of four main categories: four-patch (two rows of two patches), nine-patch (three rows of three patches), five-patch (five rows of five patches), and seven-patch (seven rows of seven patches).

### Bodkin

A large needle with a ball-point end and a large eye. Most commonly used for threading elastic or ribbon through a tube or casing, but it can also be used for turning thin tubes of fabric right-side out.

### Buttonhole

Opening through which a button is inserted to form a fastening. Buttonholes are usually machine sewn but may also be worked by hand or piped for reinforcement or decorative effect.

### Buttonhole stitch

A hand stitch that wraps over the raw edges of a buttonhole to neaten and strengthen it. Machine-sewn buttonholes are worked with a special close zigzag stitch.

### Chain piecing

A method of piecing together patchwork units by feeding them through the sewing machine in sequence without lifting the presser foot or breaking the thread so that they form a chain with a short length of thread between each one.

### Dye magnet

An untreated piece of plain, colorless fabric used to attract loose dye from other fabrics during a wash-cycle to prevent them from bleeding into other fabrics and ruining the colors. Dye magnets are available commercially, but you can also use a piece of untreated, white terry cloth. Also known as color catchers.

### Dog ears

The pieces of a seam allowance that stick out past the edges of the fabric when two pieces of fabric are sewn together on an angle.

### English paper piecing

A traditional patchwork method for making a quilt of mosaic shapes by tacking the fabric pieces (all of which have some bias edges) to precut paper templates the size of the finished element.

### Facing

A separate layer of fabric placed on the inside of an edge of fabric to finish off raw edges. A useful way to finish off shaped bindings such as scallops.

### Feed dogs

The thin, short metal bars in the needle plate of the sewing machine which move back and forth as you sew, pulling the fabric forward at an even speed.

### Finger pressing

Pressing a seam using your thumbnail. It is usually used as a temporary solution for seams within a larger piece of patchwork that will be pressed with an iron at a later stage. Make sure not to distort the fabric.

## Foundation piecing

A patchwork technique in which fabric pieces, or patches, are sewn to a foundation, either a lightweight fabric such as muslin, or to paper, which is removed once the design is completed.

## Fusible bonding web

A nonwoven material impregnated with heat-activated adhesive. Widely used in machine appliqué work.

## Fussy cutting

Isolating an individual motif on a printed fabric and cutting it out to use as a feature in a patchwork or appliqué block.

## Grain

Lengthwise and crosswise direction of threads in a fabric. Fabric grain effects how a fabric drapes.

## Hem

The edge of a piece of fabric neatened and sewn to prevent unraveling. There are several ways to hem an edge, but the most common way in soft furnishings is to fold the raw edge of the fabric over twice, then sew along the fold, closing the raw edge inside.

## Inferfacing

A fabric placed on the wrong side of another fabric to give it structure and support. Available in different thicknesses, interfacing can be fusible (bonds to the fabric when heat is applied) or non-fusible (needs to be sewn to the fabric).

## Lining

Underlaying fabric used to give a neat finish to an item.

## Medallion

A style of quilt in which a large central motif is surrounded by several borders.

## Mirrorwork

Also called shisha work, a traditional form of textile decoration from Central Asia and India that involves sewing around or over small disks of mirror, glass, or tin to hold them in place on the fabric.

## Miter

To finish a corner by sewing adjacent sides of fabric together at a 45-degree angle. Or the diagonal line made where two edges of a piece of fabric meet at a corner, produced by folding.

## Muslin

Fine, plain, open-weave cotton.

## Nap

The raised pile of fabric made during the weaving process, or a print on a fabric that runs one way. When cutting out pattern pieces, ensure the nap runs in the same direction.

## Patch

An individual piece of fabric used in making a patchwork design. Patches may be whole squares or rectangles, or subdivided into triangle units, curved units, or combinations thereof.

## Patchwork

The technique of sewing together small pieces of fabric to make a larger one.

## Pattern marks

The marks on a sewing pattern that should be transferred to the fabric when cutting out. They are often in the form of notches, with the notches on one pattern piece corresponding to the notches on other pattern pieces, acting as a guide for matching, pinning, and sewing two pattern pieces together accurately.

## Pile

Raised loops on the surface of a fabric, for example velvet.

## Plain-weave fabric

A tightly woven fabric in which the warp and weft form a simple crisscross pattern. The number of threads in each direction are not necessarily equal. Examples of plain-weave fabrics include cotton, linen, and silk.

## Presser foot

The part of a sewing machine that is lowered on to the fabric to hold it in place over the needle plate while sewing. There are many different types of feet available.

## Quilting

The process of sewing the three layers of a quilt (top, batting, and backing) together. In addition to serving a practical purpose in holding the three layers together, the quilting stitch pattern often forms an integral part of the quilt design. It is normally marked out on the quilt top in advance and may consist of a geometric grid of squares or diamond shapes, concentric lines that echo shapes within the design, intricate shapes such as hearts, feathers, and swags, or a continuous meandering pattern.

## Quilting guide

Also known as a quilting bar. An l-shaped metal bar that attaches to the back of the presser foot and allows a quilter to sew evenly spaced lines by following the previous line of quilting stitches. The bar can be adjusted to different widths.

## Quilt sandwich

The three layers of a quilt: the top, batting, and backing. The quilt top and backing form the "bread" of the sandwich and the batting forms the filling.

## Raw edge

Any cut edge of fabric. Raw edges are usually hidden in seams or turned under and hemmed or sewn in place, as in appliqué. Some techniques depend for their effect on leaving the raw edge unsewn.

## Reverse stitch

Machine stitch that sews backward over a row of stitches to secure the threads.

## Right side

The front of a piece of fabric, the side that will normally be in view when the piece is assembled.

## Rocking stitch

The ideal stitch for hand quilting in which the needle takes several stitches up and down vertically before pulling the thread through.

## Running stitch

A simple, evenly spaced, straight hand stitch separated by equal-sized spaces, used for seaming and gathering.

## Sashing

Strips of fabric interspersed between blocks when making a quilt top.

## Seam

The join formed when two pieces of fabric are sewn together.

## Seam allowance

The amount of fabric allowed for on a pattern where sections are to be joined together by a seam. The standard seam allowance in patchwork is $\frac{1}{4}$in (6mm).

## Seam edge

The cut edge of a seam allowance.

## Seam line

The line along which a seam should be sewn.

## Seam ripper

A small, pointed, hooked tool with a blade on the inside edge of the hook used for undoing seams and unpicking stitches.

## Seam roller

Tubular pressing aid for pressing seams open on fabrics that mark.

## Selvage

The rigid edge woven into each side of a length of fabric to prevent the fabric from fraying or unraveling. It occurs when the weft thread turns at the edge of the warp threads to start the next row.

## Set or setting

The way the blocks that make up a quilt top are arranged. Blocks may be straight set (sewn together edge to edge, with each block oriented the same way), or set "on point" (turned on the diagonal so that they appear as diamonds rather than squares). Pieced and appliqué blocks may be alternated with plain "spacer" blocks, or blocks may be rotated to create secondary patterns.

## Setting in

In patchwork, sewing one shape or patch into an acute angle formed when two other shapes have been joined together.

## Sewing gauge

Measuring tool with an adjustable slider for checking small measurements, such as hem depths and seam allowance.

## Slip stitch

A hidden stitch used mainly in appliqué work.

## Square knot

A type of double knot that is made symmetrically by tying a single knot with right over left, then a second single knot with left over right, or vice versa. Also known as a reef knot.

## Stab stitch

An alternative hand quilting stitch used particularly on thicker fabric layers. The needle is taken up then down to make individual stitches.

## Stitch in the ditch

A line of straight stitches sewn on the right side of the work, in the ditch created by a seam. Used as a form of hidden quilting.

## Straight grain

The parallel threads of a woven fabric running at 90-degrees to either the lengthwise (warp) or crosswise (weft) direction of the weave.

## Straight stitch

Plain machine stitch, used for most applications. The length of the stitch can be altered to suit the fabric.

## String piecing

In patchwork, similar to strip piecing, but the strips can be of uneven width.

## Strip piecing

A patchwork technique in which long strips of fabric are sewn together and then cut apart before being reassembled in a different sequence. The method is used to create many popular blocks, including log cabin and Seminole patchwork.

## Tailor's chalk

Square- or triangular-shaped pieces of chalk used to mark fabric. Available in a variety of colors, tailor's chalk can be removed easily by brushing.

## Tension

The tautness of the stitches in a seam.

## Thimble

A metal or plastic cap that fits over the top of a finger to protect it when hand sewing.

## Throat

The space on a sewing machine underneath the arm. Standard sewing machines have a throat space of less than 12in (30cm). When working on many quilts the project will have to be rolled or folded so that it fits within the throat, neatly out of the way of the needle.

## Topstitch

Machine straight sewing worked on the right side of an item, close to the finished edge, for decorative effect. Sometimes sewn in a contrasting color.

## Topstitched seam

A seam finished with a row of topstitching for decorative effect on soft furnishings and garments.

## Trimming a seam

Trimming back one of the two pieces of seam allowances in a seam, after sewing, to help a seam sit smoothly when pressed to one side.

## Turning

A finishing technique that involves placing the quilt top and backing right sides together, on top of the batting, and then sewing around the edges before turning the quilt through to the right side—thereby obviating the need for a separate binding.

## Tying

A utilitarian quilting method in which thread, string, cord, etc., is sewn through the layers and tied in a secure knot.

## Warp

The vertical threads of a woven fabric, also known as the lengthwise grain.

## Weft

The horizontal threads of a woven fabric, also known as the crosswise grain.

## Whipstitch

Also known as overcast stitch, this is a hand stitch used particularly in English paper piecing.

## Wrong side

The reverse of a piece of fabric, the side that will normally be hidden from view when the piece is made up.

## Yo-yo

A type of patchwork made from a round piece of fabric that has been gathered. Usually, many yo-yos are and joined together, but they can also be individually applied within larger patchwork pieces to add decoration.

## Zigzag stitch

A machine stitch used to neaten and secure seam edges and for decorative purposes. The width and length of the zigzag can be altered.

## Zipper foot

Narrow machine foot with a single toe that can be positioned on either side of the needle.

# Index

# Contributors

## Debi Birkin

Debi was taught to sew, knit, and crochet at a young age by her grandmothers and mother. Although she originally trained as a historical researcher, when her daughter was born she began her own line of baby and children's clothing. Her home business quickly grew to include bridal-wear and a store of its own. She eventually began freelancing her own pattern designs and craft kits, contributing to magazines.

Her focus finally turned to the toy market and today she designs and makes toys and patterns for books, magazines, manufacturers, and to sell through her website.

Website: www.debibirkin.com

Debi made the Soft blocks (see pp.180–183).

## Beth Blight

Beth received a degree in performance design at Central Saint Martins College of Arts and Design in London, UK, graduating in 2013. She has a strong interest in making costumes for theater, but loves sewing for the home and making pillows, quilts, and writing craft project instructions.

Website: bettyblight.wordpress.com

Beth made the Dresden plate pillow (see pp.122–127).

## Jennifer Campbell-Kirk

Jennifer is a British designer and quilter. She was taught the art of American patchwork by her 81-year old Texas mother-in-law and it changed her life. She is inspired by the names and stories behind old quilt patterns from the 18th and 19th centuries, which she combines with her love of English country style.

Her work has been featured on televisions and in magazines. She lives in London, UK, with her husband, who is a jazz musician.

Website: www.vintageandfloral.com

Jennifer made the Chisholm trail quilt (see pp.272–275) and the Sailboat quilt and pillow (see pp.280–283).

She would like to thank the fabric designers Minnick and Simpson for the kind use of their fabrics, manufactured by Moda Fabrics.

## Isabel de Cordova

In addition to being an experienced designer, art director, and prop stylist, Isabel is a talented crafter. Over the years she has created and conceptualized many craft and upcycling projects.

She is always on the lookout for vintage finds to reinvent. She has worked extensively for the publishing industry and is the author of *Transferred: How to Add Original Images to Everything from Fabrics to Ceramics*.

Website: www.isabeldecordova.com

Isabel made the Large-patch comforter cover (see pp.240–241).

## Cheryl Owen

Cheryl is an innovative and experienced crafter. Having originally trained and worked in the fashion industry, Cheryl went on to apply her design and creative skills to the fields of craft, especially sewing, paper crafts, and making jewelry. She is the author of many craft books, designs craft kits, and is a regular contributor of craft features to leading magazines and partworks.

Website: www.north-town.co.uk

Cheryl made the Simple squares tote (see pp.76–81), Triangle floor pillow (see pp.92–99), Bird toy (See pp.128–133), and Irish chain quilt (see pp.246–247).

## Beth Studley

Beth has been making quilts for over 20 years. She started sewing them by hand, but learned how to use a sewing machine at age 15 after going to an evening class with her mother. Originally from Devon, UK, she is now bringing up her two young children in Kent, UK.

Beth studied textiles at college in London, which gave her a valuable design perspective on her long-standing passion for quilting. She now works as a fabric designer and has collections selling around the world. She has also written more than 20 projects for UK magazines ranging from bags to quilts and children's projects.

Website: www.lovefrombeth.com

Beth made the Zigzag circus quilt (see pp.264–267) and Hive quilt (see pp.284–287).

## Sabi Westoby

Having been a traditional quilter for 10 years, retirement from full-time work in 2008 led to a change in direction and Sabi now makes art quilts and mixed media works. Combining paper and textile, paint and stitch, collage and appliqué, Sabi creates works inspired by both the natural and man-made worlds.

Sabi is excited by the challenge of embracing new techniques and exploring unknown materials, which can be dyed, printed, manipulated, burned, or sewn. She likes to create fabrics in vibrant colors and overprint them with her own designs.

Website: www.sabiwestoby.com

Sabi made the Garden fairies strip quilt (see pp.288–289), Fabric bowls (see pp.232–233), Chicken and egg quilt (See pp.234–237), Sweet as honey quilt (see pp.248–249), Courthouse steps quilt (see pp.250–251), Flying geese quilt (see pp.258–261), Tilted log cabin quilt (see pp.262–264), and Heirloom star quilt (see pp.288–291).

## Evelyn Wheeler

Evelyn has been a quilter for over 40 years, exhibiting and winning prizes at both Sandown and Malvern quilt shows in the UK. She has worked in adult education, teaching patchwork and quilting. She is currently a member of the Quilter's Guild of the British Isles and the Modern Quilter's Guild.

Evelyn made the Secret garden pin cushion (see pp.238–239).

## Michelle Zimmer

Michelle has a background in textile design and found her love for quilting after attending a class at Liberty department store in London seven years ago. Her blog, Makers Market, is for people who love to make and learn about other crafters. You'll find sewing tutorials, dressmaking projects, curated fabric finds, and a weekly dose of new crafter talent.

Website: www.makers-market.co.uk

Michelle made the Pear quilt (see pp.254–255).

# Consultant

## Michael Caputo

Michael Caputo was born and raised in New York City and moved to London, UK, four years ago. As a design graduate of the Fashion Institute of Technology in New York City, Michael has been using his skills to design and engineer children's pop-up books since he graduated from college.

Initially taught to quilt by his mother, Michael uses his background in color theory and layout to create one-of-a-kind quilts. Exploring different methods and techniques, Michael continues to quilt on a daily basis when he is not teaching quilting classes in and around London or making pop-ups.

Some of his work can be found on his blog: www.patchworkandpaper.com

Michael also runs the London Modern Quilt Guild: londonmqg.wordpress.com

Michael made the Pinwheel quilt (see pp.276–279).

# Acknowledgments

Dorling Kindersley would like to thank the following people and companies for their invaluable input, time, and dedication:

**Proofreaders** Angela Baynham and Jacqueline Hornberger
**Indexer** Marie Lorimer
**Photography assistant** Julie Stewart
**Additional photography** Andy Crawford
**Design assistance** Charlotte Johnson and Charlotte Bull
**Editorial assistance** Laura Palosuo
**Original project consultancy** Lucinda Ganderton

**Hearts and flowers quilt maker** Patricia Wildman
**Location for photography** 1st Option and jj Locations
**Prop hire** Backgrounds and China & Co
**Fabric swatches** The Eternal Maker
Website: www.eternalmaker.com
Ray Stitch
Website: www.raystitch.co.uk
**Models** Aleyah Ali, Eloise Fenton, Leo Flynn, Martha Jenkinson, Ella Kwan, Emily Nyamayaro, Luka Pavicevic, and Dylan Wightwick

All other projects were made by the team at DK.

Happy quilting!